Contemporary hermeneutics

Contemporary hermeneutics

Hermeneutics as method, philosophy and critique

Josef Bleicher
Glasgow College of Technology

Routledge & Kegan Paul

London and New York

First published in 1980
by Routledge & Kegan Paul Ltd
11 New Fetter Lane, London, EC4P 4EE
Published in the USA by
Routledge and Kegan Paul Inc.
in association with Methuen Inc.
29 West 35th St., New York NY10001
Set in 10/11pt Linocomp Plantin by
Rowland Phototypesetting Ltd, Bury St Edmunds, Suffolk
and printed in Great Britain by
St Edmundsbury Press Ltd, Bury St Edmunds, Suffolk
Reprinted in 1982, 1983 and 1987

British Library Cataloguing in Publication Data

Bleicher, Josef
Contemporary Hermeneutics.
1. Hermeneutics
I. Title
112   BD241   80 40019

ISBN 0 7100 0551 2
ISBN 0 7100 0552 0 Pbk

To my teachers

Contents

Preface

This book gives an overview of the main strands of contemporary hermeneutical thought. As such it is not mainly concerned with the relevance of hermeneutics for any particular field of study – even though some such aspects are discussed in relation mainly to sociology.

I have included a number of readings in order to give the reader a first-hand acquaintance with the subject-matter of hermeneutics and the debates within it. The glossary is hoped to assist in making sense of the sometimes difficult terminology employed.

Should this book lead to the further study of the theorists included and of the topic as such, as well as to the discussion of some of the issues raised, then it will have fulfilled its purpose as a stepping-stone.

My thanks go above all to Professor Z. Bauman for opening my mind and directing my attention to this area, in addition to which I received his initial support and continued encouragement in the course of writing this book; I hope he is not too dissatisfied with it. I would also like to express my appreciation of the way in which Dr Janet Wolff helped me to clarify my own ideas during my study at Leeds University. Mike Featherstone awakened my interest in Critical Theory during my undergraduate years at Teesside Polytechnic and has remained an interested partner in discussions ever since. I am also grateful to Pat Wilmott for typing the script so conscientiously and in such demanding circumstances. The library staff of a number of institutions, too, have done a remarkable and important job in coping with my unending requests for often obscure sources.

Professor J. Habermas was kind enough to arrange for me to translate and include his essay 'Der Universalitätsanspruch der Hermeneutik', last published in J. Habermas, *Kultur und*

Kritik, Suhrkamp, Frankfurt (1973). J. C. B. Mohr, Tübingen, have given me the right to translate and include E. Betti, 'Die Hermeneutik als allgemeine Methode der Geisteswissenschaften' (1962). Professor P. Ricoeur and Northwestern University Press have given permission to include the translation of 'Existence et Herméneutique' (1965) by Kathleen McLaughlin which appeared in *The Conflict of Interpretation* (1974). University of California Press have given me permission to include the essay by Professor H.-G. Gadamer, 'Die Universalität des hermeneutischen Problems' (1967), in the translation by David E. Linge which appeared in *Philosophical Hermeneutics* (1976).

Introduction

Hermeneutics can loosely be defined as the theory or philosophy of the interpretation of meaning. It has recently emerged as a central topic in the philosophy of the social sciences, the philosophy of art and language and in literary criticism – even though its modern origin points back to the early nineteenth century.

The realization that human expressions contain a meaningful component, which has to be recognized as such by a subject and transposed into his own system of values and meanings, has given rise to the 'problem of hermeneutics': how this process is possible and how to render accounts of subjectively intended meaning objective in the face of the fact that they are mediated by the interpreter's own subjectivity.

Contemporary hermeneutics is characterized by conflicting views concerning this problem; it is possible to distinguish three clearly separable strands:

- hermeneutical theory
- hermeneutic philosophy
- critical hermeneutics.

Hermeneutical theory focuses on the problematic of a general theory of interpretation as the methodology for the human sciences (or *Geisteswissenschaften*, which include the social sciences). Through the analysis of *verstehen* as the method appropriate to the re-experiencing or re-thinking of what an author had originally felt or thought, Betti hoped to gain an insight into the process of understanding in general, i.e. how we are able to transpose a meaning-complex created by someone else into our own understanding of ourselves and our world.

The methodologically developed use of our intuitive capacity serves the acquisition of 'relatively objective' knowledge. It approaches 'meaning-full forms' with a set of 'canons' which have been formulated in order to facilitate the correct interpretation of objectivations of human activity or consciousness, that is, of human expressions. The use of canons links Betti's hermeneutical theory with that of the Protestant theologian Schleiermacher, in whose work the art of interpretation achieved its highest point since its origin in ancient Greek thought. It is here that we find the first discussion of linguisticality as the universal medium of humanity which enters the 'hermeneutical circle' as that whole in relation to which individual parts acquire their meaning. The understanding of past sources is impeded by the *historicity* of the subject, so that the task of hermeneutics can be expressed as the avoidance of misunderstanding.

Hermeneutical theory as epistemology and methodology of understanding was further developed by Dilthey at the turn of this century. He dealt with the former in the context of a 'Critique of Historical Reason' which attempted a transcendental inquiry into the conditions of the possibility of historical knowledge by following the example set by Kant in his *Critique of Pure Reason*; the methodological aspect was narrowed down to the interpretation of linguistically fixed documents which represented a specific case of the use of the *verstehen* method as the mode of cognition appropriate in instances where the subject–object relationship is one where 'life meets life'.

Dilthey initially attempted to solve the problem of hermeneutics, which constituted the 'historical consciousness', by recurring to the Romanticist concern with 'lived experience'. Turning later to Hegel's theory of objective spirit and adopting the distinction between meaning and expression suggested by Husserl's *Logical Investigations* Dilthey came close to the mediation Betti recently achieved between the *historical consciousness* and the striving for theoretical truth.

It is precisely the hope to find a basis for the scientific investigation of meaning which *hermeneutic philosophy* rejects as 'objectivism'. A central insight of hermeneutic philosophy asserts that social scientist or interpreter and object are linked by a context of tradition – which implies that he already has a pre-understanding of his object as he approaches it, thereby being unable to start with a neutral mind. The conception of what is involved in understanding consequently shifts from the reproduction of a pre-given object to the participation in on-going communication between past and present. Hermeneutic philosophy does not aim at objective knowledge through the use of methodical procedures but at the explication and phenomenological description of human *Dasein* in its temporality and historicality. Heidegger could find a starting-point for his fundamental–ontological hermeneutic in Dilthey's category of *Leben*, which even underlay the 'transcendental consciousness' of Kantian a priorism. It, too, asks after the possibility of understanding in general but answers that any acquisition of knowledge can take place only by following the dictates of the 'hermeneutic circle' which commences with the projective anticipation of meaning and proceeds through the dialogical–dialectical mediation of subject and object. The aim of understanding, for example, a text can consequently no longer be the objective re-cognition of the author's intended meaning, but the emergence of practically relevant knowledge in which the subject himself is changed by being made aware of new possibilities of existence and his responsibility for his own future.

In Gadamer's work, the problem of hermeneutics is given a language-philosophical turn: as the 'hermeneutic problem' it is concerned with achieving an agreement with somebody else about our shared 'world'. This communication takes the form of a dialogue that results in the 'fusion of horizons'.

At this point it is necessary to insert a comment about the terminology used so far. I have chosen the terms 'hermeneutical' and 'hermeneutic'[1] in order to signify contrasting conceptions of hermeneutics itself; this choice is not an arbitrary one in that I hope that the former conveys a methodological orientation whereas the latter should indicate a more fundamental, philosophical concern. A similar distinction applies to their respective relationships to history: 'historical' approaches strive for objective knowledge of past events in contrast to their 'historic' significance for an interpreting subject *hic et nunc*.

These differences have found their explicit expression in what I would like to refer to as the 'hermeneutical dispute'[2] between Betti and Gadamer which centres around the possibility of objective interpretation and the question of whether Gadamer's analysis of the 'fore-structure' of understanding represents a danger to it in its emphasis on the esssential role of 'prejudices' in the process of cognition.

Within hermeneutics there exists yet another debate which brings together Gadamer and Habermas. The latter, as a representative of *critical hermeneutics* challenges the idealist assumptions underlying both hermeneutical theory and hermeneutic philosophy: the neglect to consider extra-linguistic factors which also help to constitute the context of thought and action, i.e. work and domination. Hermeneutic philosophy, furthermore, puts forward an unjustifiable claim to universality by regarding tradition embedded in language as forming a supportive consensus that cannot itself be questioned since it provides the conditions of its possibility. As this dispute touches upon the philosophical underpinning of the hermeneutic approach it would seem appropriate to term it the 'hermeneutic dispute'.[3]

It is in its course that both Apel and Habermas arrive at their critical hermeneutics which combines a methodical and objective approach with the striving for practically relevant knowledge. 'Critical' should here be taken to mean mainly the appraisal of existing states of affairs in view of standards that derive from the knowledge of something better that already exists as a potential or a tendency in the present; it is guided by the principle of Reason as the demand for unrestricted communication and self-determination. More specifically, this epithet should indicate an affinity with both the 'critical theory' of the Frankfurt School and with Marx's work. Their legacy is the exhortation to change reality rather than merely interpret it.

Marx's method of counterposing concrete reality to its mystifications, be they the idealist account of the self-realization of man or the empiricistic analysis of political economy, provides the paradigm for the critique of ideology through evidencing the material conditions that gave rise to them.

The question of whether all intellectual manifestations have to be regarded as ideological, and the problem of what the term 'ideology' itself should mean, is answered differently within critical hermeneutics, giving rise to formulations of the hermeneutic(al) problems that differ from the critical hermeneutics developed by Apel and Habermas. The 'materialistic hermeneutics' of Sandkühler conceives of critique as a reconstruction of the genesis of intellectual phenomena and regards any interpretation of meaning as 'idealistic'. In this respect it also differs from Lorenzer's 'materialist' hermeneutics.[4] He, like Apel and Habermas, considers critique as essentially self-reflexive and liberating, even though he places greater stress on the concrete socio-historical constellation under which meaning is acquired. These theorists draw on psychoanalysis as the model for an emancipatory science that dialectically relates both interpretative and explanatory approaches.

This conflicting array of possible forms of hermeneutics leads me to Ricoeur's phenomenological hermeneutics which, while not representing a clearly separable strand, brings into sharp relief the other three and also attempts to integrate them into a larger framework. Not only does he discuss the place of Freud in relation to the other 'critics' of modern society, Marx and

Nietzsche, but he also acts as a mediator in both the hermeneutical and the hermeneutic disputes – in the course of which he also provides a highly necessary appreciation of the role of the structuralist analysis of a system of signs in relation to the hermeneutic(al) interpretation of a text. Ricoeur's theory of the text as a formation of signs semantically related not to reality as such but to a 'quasi-world' which itself, however, stands in a semantic relation to reality in addition provides the basis for the transcendence of the *verstehen*–explanation dichotomy at the level of textual criticism.

Part I

Hermeneutical theory

Introduction

The necessary as well as autotelic function of understanding one's contemporaries or, in fact, any human expression, for individual and social existence Dilthey successfully established in his outline of 'The Rise of Hermeneutics'. The awareness of one's own history and of that of mankind as a whole is an indispensable condition for a rich and fulfilled life. Through it, the limits of one's time are transcended and new sources of strength are opened up. Knowledge of past civilizations enriches our lives and their study itself affords us great pleasure; understanding the emotional states of other human beings not only accounts for a large amount of happy moments in our lives but also constitutes a precondition for action on our part. We recognize ourselves as individuals only through intercourse with others and so become aware of characteristics which are specific to ourselves.

Access to other human beings is possible, however, only by indirect means: what we experience initially are gestures, sounds, and actions and only in the process of understanding do we take the step from external signs to the underlying inner life, the psychological existence of the Other. Since the inner life is not given in the experiencing of sign we have to reconstruct it; our lives provide the materials for the completion of the picture of the inner life of Others. The act of understanding provides the bridge for reaching the spiritual self of the Other and the degree of enthusiasm with which we embark on this adventure depends on the importance the Other has for us.

Understanding, then, is motivated by our interest in partaking in the inner life of somebody else and is both necessary and rewarding. It establishes a communion of the human spirit dwelling in all of us and addressing us in multifarious forms from all directions.

As the title of the essay suggests, it is mainly concerned with outlining the emergence of a discipline that regulates, and thereby improves, the 'art of understanding permanently fixed expressions of life' (Dilthey, V, p. 319). The methodology of this activity which Dilthey refers to as 'exegesis or interpretation' has come to be known as 'hermeneutics'. The exposition of the rules that guide successful interpretation not only leads to more efficient interpretation but also safeguards the general validity of its results from the intrusion of arbitrariness and subjective elements. It represents a *Kunstlehre*, i.e. the systematization of formal procedures to assist the art of understanding in its endeavour to arrive at certainty of knowledge.

Chapter 1

The rise of classical hermeneutics

1. The origin of hermeneutics

Hermes transmitted the messages of the gods to the mortals, that is to say, he not only announced them verbatim but acted as an 'interpreter' who renders their words intelligible – and meaningful – which may require some point of clarification or other, additional, commentary. Hermeneutics is consequently engaged in two tasks: one, the ascertaining of the exact meaning-content of a word, sentence, text, etc.; two, the discovery of the instructions contained in symbolic forms.

In the course of its history hermeneutics sporadically emerged and advanced in its development as the theory of interpretation whenever it became necessary to translate authoritative literature under conditions that did not allow direct access to it, owing either to distance in space and time or to differences in language. In both cases, the original meaning of a text was either disputed or remained hidden, necessitating interpretative explication in order to render it transparent. As a technology for correct understanding, hermeneutics has therefore been employed at an early stage in three capacities: one, to assist discussions about the language of the text (i.e. the vocabulary and grammar), giving rise, eventually, to philology; two, to facilitate the exegesis of biblical literature; three, to guide jurisdiction. I shall turn to Dilthey[1] for an exposition of the first two, and to Betti (1954) for the third use of hermeneutics.

Literary interpretation has its origin in the Greek educational system where it assisted in the interpretation and criticism of Homer and other poets. Its subdivision into rhetoric and poetics eventually merged into the art of textual verification. A second stage was reached in the formulation of a methodology for the interpretation of profane texts in the Renaissance and Humanism, where classical literary monuments were once again scrutinized. These philological investigations sprang from a practical interest – since Greek culture not only represented a model for artistic and scientific education, but for life in general.

This ethical–pedagogic interest was, however, even more pronounced in biblical exegesis. It is here that we find the main impetus for the development of hermeneutics: practically all religions relying on a sacred text have developed systems of rules of interpretation. The Rabbis had established rules for the interpretation of the Talmud and the Midraschim. Dilthey himself refers to Philo, an Alexandrian, to indicate the origin of canons and laws for the interpretation of allegories (*Kanones* and *nomoi tes allegorias*) and the distinction between pneumatic and literal meaning.

Biblical hermeneutics reached its first major formulation in the course and the after-effects of the Reformation with Matthias Flacius. As a Lutheran, he regarded the Bible as containing the word of God (*revelatio sacrio literis comprehensa*). In opposition to the dogmatic position of the Tridentine Church that re-affirmed the Catholic emphasis on tradition in the interpretation of allegedly obscure parts of the Scriptures, Flacius insisted on the possibility of universally valid interpretation through hermeneutics. Allegorical interpretation was restricted to the case of simile and is not required for the understanding of the Old Testament at all. Any passages, the sense of which was not immediately clear, could be understood if one employed the following procedures: grammatical interpretation, reference to the context provided by the actual lived experience of Christianity and, above all, the consideration of a passage in the light of the intent and form of the whole.

The insight that individual parts have to be dealt with in relation to the whole and to the other parts marks a significant step in the development of hermeneutics which, in its early, pre-Schleiermacher, form progressed yet further. The anti-dogmatic self-understanding of early Protestant hermeneutics did not escape a hidden dogmatic of its own: the presupposition of the unity of the Bible apparent in the hermeneutic principle of considering parts within their 'whole'. Dilthey regards this as a 'formal deficiency' that was overcome by the work of Semler, Michaelis and Ernesti, who were able to completely liberate exegesis from dogma by introducing grammatico-historical procedures to complement the existing aesthetico-rhetorical ones. After the rejection of any dogma that might be brought to bear on exegesis, it was only a small step to the attempt to incorporate the 'specific hermeneutics' of Biblical exegesis into a 'general hermeneutics' which was to provide the rules for any interpretation of signs,[2] be they of profane origin or not.

We associate the names of Ast and Wolf – both were philologists – with this development which leads immediately to Schleiermacher, whose genius resided in giving their 'hints' a systematic foundation. Before considering his general theory of hermeneutics, I would like to at least give a mention to the contribution made by juridical interpretation to the development of hermeneutics.

The task of mediating a particular case with the generality of the law proceeds under presuppositions which are, by necessity, dogmatic. Its normative character is, for example, quite apparent in cases where an existing law requires some form of supplementation. Betti has developed one canon of interpretation from this practice of civil law in which the public good, i.e. a social interest, is introduced into the juridical process. The canon of the 'actuality of understanding' stresses the need for the interpreter to reconstruct the genesis of a thought, law, etc., and to adapt its formulation to changed circumstances. Juridical hermeneutics displays, consequently, a dual character in that the problems arising from its interpretative task are intimately connected with the application of its results. Apart from drawing our attention to the practical dimension of interpretation, juridical hermeneutics has provided us, through Betti's important work, with three more canons which help to form the core of a general hermeneutical theory and among which 'the canon of totality and meaningful coherence', frequently referred to as the 'hermeneutical circle', figures again prominently.

Reference to the practice of hermeneutics alone cannot suffice for the formulation of a theoretical framework in terms of which the limits and validity of hermeneutical procedures can be evidenced – itself a precondition for the development of a general hermeneutics. The first approach in the history of hermeneutics that attempted to inject epistemological considerations into methodological discussion is that of Schleiermacher.

2. Romanticist hermeneutics

Some of the main themes that still characterize hermeneutics can already be found in Schleiermacher's precursors. I have referred to the importance that was attached to the canon of totality and the associated employment of the hermeneutical circle. Ast (in 1808) had regarded the process of understanding as a repetition of the process of creation – a principle that was echoed by another philologist, Wolf, when he demanded that the thoughts of an Other had to be understood as he had understood them himself.

The limitation of the pre-Schleiermacher effort consisted, conversely, in the lack of reflection that transcended merely methodological considerations – which themselves did not reach any systematic formulation and remained on the level of ad hoc insights that were forthcoming from interpretative practice.

Schleiermacher

The two traditions Schleiermacher brings to bear on his developmental hermeneutics are those of transcendental philosophy and romanticism. From these he derived a form of questioning – the conditions of the possibility of valid interpretation – and a new conception of the process of Understanding. Understanding is now seen as a creative reformulation and reconstruction. Fichte's emphasis on the productivity of the active I (Ego) led Schleiermacher to the discovery of the hermeneutical law that every thought of the author has to be related to the unity of an active and organically developing subject: the relationship between individuality and totality become the focal point of romanticist hermeneutics.

Individuals are able to understand without having to problematize their activity – until they find themselves unable to come to grips with the meaning expressed in speech or writing. The experience of mis-understanding, and the consequential attempt to avoid it happening again, lies at the heart of the search for certainty which culminates in Schleiermacher's formulation of a systematic hermeneutics.

His systematic contains two parts: grammatical and psychological interpretation. For the former he develops forty-four 'canons' (*Kanones*). The two first are most important and certainly shed some light on Schleiermacher's overall approach: one, 'Everything that needs a fuller determination in a given text may only be determined in reference to the field of language shared by the author and his original public'; and, two, 'The meaning of every word in a given passage has to be determined in reference to its coexistence with the words surrounding it'.[3] The stress on the linguisticality of understanding, apart from evidencing Schleiermacher's debt to Herder's concern with language, certainly distinguished Schleiermacher's hermeneutics from that of his predecessors and points into the future as a recurrent theme in hermeneutical discussions.

The canons developed for psychological interpretation centre around the investigation of the emergence of thought from within the totality of an author's life. The use of these hermeneutical rules allows for the understanding of the meaning of a given text. But this is not all: given adequate historical and linguistic knowledge, the interpreter is in a position to understand the author better than he had understood himself. Dilthey, to whom we owe a great debt for his important work on Schleiermacher, traces this possibility to Fichte's conception of the soul as containing conscious and unconscious intuition and finds that 'the interpreter who follows conscientiously the train of thought of the author will have to bring many elements to consciousness which could remain unconscious[4] in the latter – he will thereby understand him better than he had understood himself' (Dilthey, XIV/I, p. 707).

Schleiermacher's formulation of a system of interpretative rules brings to fruition a development within hermeneutical practice that sprang from the gradual move away from a dogmatic starting-point. The unity of procedure enabled the interpreter to disregard the specific content of the work under consideration. General hermeneutics does not allow the use of a specific methodology for a – supposedly – privileged text such as the Bible. The only allowance made for specific content consists in the variegated use made of the methods approved by the science of hermeneutics.

Apart from continuing the tradition of hermeneutics by systematizing and generalizing the methods of interpretation that had already been in use, Schleiermacher ranks as a central figure for two more reasons: one, he complemented grammatical exegesis with psychological interpretation, which he referred to as 'divinatory'. Hermeneutics is as much art as it is science; it endeavours to reconstruct the original creative act – 'how it really was'. Two, it is with Schleiermacher that we encounter the first attempt to analyse the process of understanding and inquire into the possibilities and limits of it. Adumbrating Dilthey's conception, Schleiermacher refers to the substratum of general human nature that underlies potentially successful communication. Individual differences are acknowledged, which leads to the requirement of congeniality: the interpreter ought to approximate the intellectual – 'spiritual' – stature of the author as closely as possible. The existence of qualitative gradations among people who may be separated in space and time, on the other hand, provides the incentive and rationale for the hermeneutical task: understanding the Other, being able to see things from his perspective, strengthens and emphasizes the spiritual processes within oneself. As the poet – Hugo von Hoffmansthal – stated: the shortest way to yourself is around the world.

3. Historical hermeneutics

In retrospect, Schleiermacher's stature in the history of hermeneutics rests mainly on the impetus with which it had provided Dilthey's thinking. Within the span of fifty years hermeneutics developed from a system of interpretation relevant for theology and philology only into the methodology of a new science: *Geisteswissenschaften*. Its claim to provide the precondition for all understanding shifted to the securing of 'objectivity' in the methodical reconstructions of historical events – and to provide the foundation on which the positivist incursion into the territory of the mind and its manifestations could be repelled.

Vico

The Cartesian dualism which restricted valid knowledge to the *res extensa* that could be expressed in mathematical terms had provided the scheme for the development of scientism. It is to Giambattista Vico and his *New Science* (1725) that we have to look for the first – and still highly respected – formulation of a philosophy of history that established the possibility of true knowledge gained from the study of history. It is here not necessary to examine in depth Vico's pioneering work; suffice it to mention only its seminal insight which provided the impetus for the establishing of a science of history one hundred and fifty years later. His statement, that '*verum et factum convertuntur*', that truth and fact are convertible, lies at the root of his view, which was to be echoed by Marx and Dilthey, that man can understand history because he made it himself. The principle Bacon had applied to the experimental investigation of nature was taken to hold equally in the case of human creation. In fact, the primacy of knowledge switches to the latter since here subject and object are of the same kind.

I shall later show how closely Vico's conception is still tied to the ideal of knowledge characteristic of natural science. As I am at this stage only concerned with tracing the development of the *Geisteswissenschaften*, there is only one other point I should refer to: Vico's recognition of historical development presented him with the task of showing (1) how it was that correct understanding could take place across time and space, and (2) whether different positions within the stream of history made for differences in knowledge about earlier periods and events. I am here, of course, referring to the 'historicity' of meaning and the emergence of an historical awareness which set the stage for debates about the scientific status of historical understanding that continue to flare up today.

Proceeding – with what may seem like undue haste – towards the central figure in nineteenth-century hermeneutical theory, I shall only give a fleeting mention to Dilthey's immediate precursor. Droysen can be credited with having synthesized romanticist conceptions stemming from Herder and Humboldt which centre around the importance of the study of history for individual and national identity and self-fulfilment, with the Schleiermacher–Boeckh formulation of theological–philological hermeneutics into a theory of historical science that saw itself as the indefatigible opponent of positivism.

Droysen

As Gadamer[5] has shown, the 'historical school' emerged as a rejection of Hegelian *a priori* construction of teleological history and insisted on a restriction to historical research in opposition to speculation. The necessary theoretical underpinning of this development was provided by Herder's formulation of an historical point of view: to attribute to each historical epoch its own value and perfection; before the eye of God, Dilthey argued later, all epochs are equal.

The transference of the *Kunstlehre* of interpretation, developed by Schleiermacher for theological, and by his follower Boeckh for philological, purposes, from within the framework of romanticist conceptions and its emphasis on individuality, to the study of history required further philosophical reflection. The schema of part and whole applicable to the interpretation of a text had to be made possible by reference to universal history which formed the totality in reference to which the meaning of 'individual' events could be ascertained. 'Only through a conception of the totality of history as the development of mankind, can singular formations, people, cultures, states, individuals be given their full meaning.'[6]

Droysen's conception of the object of history is characterized by the duality of nature and mind. The phenomena of 'nature' have no individual existence – we do not regard them as individualities but as members of a species. Phenomena created by mind, on the other hand, allow us privileged access since they are 'flesh of our flesh'. We can understand them.

Droysen's hermeneutical theory contains two central points: the theory of experience and that of reconstruction. The former, which indicates some Hegelian influence, refers to a human need for expressing 'inner' processes. In the perception of such expressions, they are projected into the inner life of the perceiver where they give rise to the same processes. The correspondence of re-experienced and original process is guaranteed by an 'absolute totality' which we only have a faint conception of, but in which the originator and perceiver participate on account of their shared humanness.

How the perception of an expression leads to inner reproduction is more properly dealt with in the second theory. In the study of history we are, initially, confronted with something unfamiliar and it is our task to assimilate it so that we can grasp it adequately and use it.

Droysen's *Historik* emerged in the course of a debate with Hegelian speculation and newly emerged positivism. He emphasized the importance of a factual basis – without, however, going so far as Ranke and his school who advocated the 'self-effacement' of the historian in order to arrive at a correct knowledge of the facts; the historian has to 'see values and set them', he has to inspire and therefore approach his work with enthusiasm.[7] And so he reserves his real venom for positivists such as Buckley who try to raise history to the status of science by introducing quantitative methods which would reduce historical change to the law-like effect of external factors. The introduction of physicalist methods which have proved successful in their appropriate field brings in its train not only methodological but also ethical dangers. 'History brings to consciousness what we are and what we possess': our existence is not mere 'metabolic change' but we participate in a 'second creation' – that of an 'ethical world'.[8] Accordingly, Droysen refuses to concern himself solely with methodological questions at the cost of substantive considerations. His theory of the study of history is motivated, furthermore, by a three-fold impulse: the immanent reflection of historical research, the political constellation and the situation in intellectual history (i.e. positivism).[9]

The method appropriate to an object that is already structured meaningfully is that of *forschend zu verstehen* (inquiring understanding). For the working-out of its theoretical underpinning Droysen called for a 'Kant' – that is to say, the founding of the historical method along the model of Kant's *Critique of Pure Reason* that had already evidenced the conditions for the possibility of natural science. That 'Kant' was to be Dilthey.

4. Dilthey and the *Critique of Historical Reason*

Hermeneutical theory is, in principle, unable to provide the theoretical foundation of the *Geisteswissenschaften*. What is required is nothing less than the contribution Kant made to the foundation and justification of natural science and mathematics.

Dilthey's *Critique of Historical Reason* represents the counterpart to that of pure reason and at the same time a critique of the latter: 'Historical' as overarching 'pure' reason. Historically oriented understanding of everything human was hoped to lead to the same depths that Kant had explored – and which for Dilthey lay in the 'metaphysical consciousness' of man – while at the same time allowing him to go beyond Kant in showing that pure reason is itself based on Life. That is to say, Kant sees the factors of mental life merely in isolation, neglecting two other vital components of man's existence: feeling and the desire for action. As a result of the failure to take regard of the whole self, Life, as the unity of these activities which require their own particular categories, became more pronounced in the work of post-Kantian philosophers. As Hodges (1944, p. 89) observed, they perceived the activity of mind in terms of one or other faculty: Reason (Hegel, Schelling) or Will (Fichte, Schopenhauer).

Kant's a-historical approach, furthermore, led him to conceive of an historically specific science, Newton's mechanics, as a model of knowledge, thereby making apparent his rootedness in the Enlightenment. By contrast, it was one of Hegel's most significant achievements to have stressed the historicity of thought. Like action, it has to be considered within the coordinates of time and space which influence even the principles upon which thought is based.

Dilthey's approach owes a great deal to both Kant and Hegel, uniting as it does the former's antipathy to metaphysical reasoning and the latter's concern with history, albeit rejecting his teleo-theological assumptions about the world-spirit coming to itself. It can be summarized (Hodges, 1944, p. 97–8) by stating that for Kant's transcendental argumentation he substituted the psychological–historical study of the conditions under which we act and think, and the totality of the empirical self for the transcendental self.[10]

Dilthey and the philosophical foundation of hermeneutics
Dilthey draws on the insights derived in the course of his outline of the object and method of the *Geisteswissenschaften* for providing them with their epistemological foundation. This he attempted through the synthesis of the tenets of science with those of the philosophy of life.

The need to attempt a critique of 'historical reason' to complement Kant's *Critique of Pure Reason* arose out of tensions inherent in modern philosophy which, in the event, gave rise to a dualism variously depicted as one between philosophy and science, metaphysics and epistemology, belief and knowledge, logos and ethos, pure and practical reason, systematic philosophy and philosophy of life, logic and history.

Misch (1947) has traced this dualism to the two sources of modern philosophy: the theoretical spirit of Greek philosophy and science and the religious–ethical position of Christianity, expressing itself in the opposition of ontology and logic to the 'logic of the heart' (Pascal's *ordre du coeur*). Galileo's stance, as a Platonist, for Reason – the ideal of Greek metaphysics seen as residing in mathematical science and thereby representing the *vinculum rationis* – led him into conflict with the Church's stress on the life-forces and the *vinculum fidei et amoris*.

The tension between logic and ethics bears witness to the continuance of the dualism between Reason and Life in modern philosophy which eventually leads to their deliberate separation. Their unity, which has characterized Greek philosophy, proved unattainable, if not undesirable, to the philosophers of the Enlightenment in their zeal for pure knowledge cleansed of all claims to authority that could not be legitimized by reference to the guiding light of Reason.

Kant's *Critique of Pure Reason* constitute a decisive attempt at resolving the issue within the limits of the Enlightenment. Recognizing the multi-dimensionality of philosophy, he nevertheless proceeded to separate ethics and logic – the latter representing a reflection upon the work of active scientists and their findings, especially, of course, Newton's physics.

A number of lacunae in Kant's efforts become immediately apparent: his 'critical' approach is limited to establishing the logical basis for science while relinquishing the area of ethics to the individual's subordination to the demands of religion; his epistemology draws on an historically specific, thinned-out and intellectualized conception of 'science' which restricts the area from which valid knowledge can be gained to relations between phenomena, thereby finalizing the split between theoretical knowledge and the conduct of life – severing knowledge from its motivating force and limiting its use potential.

From this position it was only a small step to the proclamation of philosophy as the handmaiden of science whose sole task was to facilitate the progress of the latter in the accumulation of '*Herrschaftswissen*' (Scheler).

Seen from a Kantian angle, Dilthey's *Critique of Historical Reason* represents merely the, legitimate, extension of the *Critique of Pure Reason* into a new field of knowledge which had emerged with the historical–philological sciences and providing their epistemological foundation. But it is also a significant step beyond Kant. Kant's negative verdict for the scientific investigation of those realities which decide upon the meaning of human existence, the knowledge man has of himself, was meant to provide room for belief by restricting the realm of science. It is, however, precisely this area that Dilthey intends to render positive through the combination of philosophy and *Geisteswissenschaften*; the latter are concerned with evidencing the knowledge which men have of themselves and which becomes apparent in history.

Theory and praxis
Dilthey's *Critique of Historical Reason* was to fulfil the dual purpose, of overcoming the dualism which he depicted as one between logic and Life through connecting systematic philosophy with the *Geisteswissenschaften*, and of reclaiming, for rigorous investigation, that area which had been banished as 'metaphysical', thereby bringing into fruitful communion once again what had artificially been torn asunder: science and Life, theory and praxis.

The corollary of the restriction of knowledge to the instrumentally utilizable is the abandoning of other fields to irrationalism. Through his *Critique of Historical Reason* Dilthey hoped to bring the area of the conduct of life within the orbit of science by providing a foundation for the possibility of generally valid standards of moral action. Plato regarded the task of philosophy to be the guidance of the conduct of life through knowledge and, like Socrates, could regard logic and ethics as inseparable: the contemplation of the *kosmos*, which embodied divine reason, provided insights into the order of things which could be transposed onto the conduct of everyday life. This naive unity of *theoria* and *praxis* had been superseded in modern philosophy by the split between logic, which remained cosmic, and ethics, which became subjective, itself a product of the tension that characterizes its development, epitomized by the figures of Galileo and Pascal (cf. Misch, 1947, p. 41), and the role reason and faith respectively play in establishing the link between man and the transcendental source of meaning as experienced in the science of mathematics and the mystic's submersion into the self.

Dilthey's attempt at re-uniting theory and praxis after the Kantian schism takes the form of widening the concept of science (and providing it with a new epistemological basis), so that generally valid knowledge can be derived both from appearances and inner experience, now conceptualized as the sphere of Life.

Misch seems to have allowed for this revolutionary development in the field of meta-science when he defines *Lebensphilosophie* as 'the science of the mental contents which give meaning to life'; and he has pinpointed the crucial innovation with great acumen when he states that Dilthey replaced the Greek '*to on*' with the German '*Leben*', as the name for '*das Seiende*'. This is the central concept in Dilthey's foundation of the *Geisteswissenschaften*.

Dilthey refers the task of establishing the categories employed in the acquisition of knowledge in the sphere of history – which speaks to us through philosophy, religion, and art – to the historical *Geisteswissenschaften* and here, of course, to hermeneutics. The categories of Life are employed in this field when one refers back from the objectivations of Life to that which is objectivated in them. The number of categories cannot be delimited – as Aristotle, Kant and Husserl had thought – owing to the dynamics of Life. The 'categories of Life' are not 'mere conceptual forms through which the understanding of every context of existence takes place', i.e. they are not mere tools of thought, or a resource, but 'the structural forms of Life itself, which, in its temporal process, finds expression in them' (VII, p. 232).

Such a structural analysis would proceed from the context of Life and centre on the basic category of 'meaning'; other categories emerging in the investigation of expressions of Life include those of sense, value and purpose.

It is clear that the categories of Life are specifically different from those employed in natural science; this point is apparent when one refers to the difference between the concept of 'cause' and that of a 'structure of interactive forces' where a singular event is not subsumed under a general law for its explication but is understood by reference to that of which it is a part so as to be able to define its meaning, purpose, etc. Secondly, these categories are constitutive; they are part of human, historical existence and only 'emerge' with it. It is apparent from the above outline of Dilthey's metascience that he applied hermeneutical insights to epistemology by determining the possibility of hermeneutical knowledge through reference to the actual process of understanding.

The influence of the philosophy of life on Dilthey's thought not only accounts for the criteria he develops for distinguishing natural and human science, but also leads to insights about the possibility of valid knowledge in the latter.

Dilthey refers to Life, that productive force all humanity shares in, in order to explain the possibility of an interpreter being able to reconstruct its objectivations. He states that 'the first condition for the possibility of a science of history consists in the fact that I myself am an historical being, that he who researches into history is the same as he who makes it' (VII, p. 278).

It is the next question, how the individual's knowledge of objectivations of Life or mind can claim general validity, that evidences the extent to which Dilthey still remained within a scientistic conception of interpretative, or communicative, knowledge.

5. Conclusions: objectivist remnants in classical hermeneutical theory

Dilthey considered himself to be a 'stubborn empiricist'[11] and it is in this light that his quest for objectivity in the *Geisteswissenschaften* had best be considered. The stipulation that the *Geisteswissenschaften* be of use for social–political activity necessitates that, in Dilthey's thinking, their results aspire to the degree of certainty and generality normally attributed to the natural sciences. Gadamer (1975, pp. 61–2) and Habermas (1968a, pp. 226–8) have retraced the line of argument that leads Dilthey on to scientistic territory. Empiricistically he focuses on something 'given': the ultimate unit of experience which in the sphere of hermeneutics is the 'lived experience'. Equally, 'reliving' – a concept Dilthey never seemed able to free himself from – functions as the equivalent to observation: 'both fulfil on the empirical level the criterion for a copy theory of truth; they guarantee, it seems, the reproduction of something immediate within an isolated consciousnes that is free of any subjective elements' (Habermas, 1969, p. 226).

By dealing with the problem of objectivity in such terms Dilthey seems to have fallen behind his own intentions – to establish the *Geisteswissenschaften* as a non-scientistic study of man – and high standard of reflection.

By regarding historical objectivations as 'givens' that could be deciphered with the help of hermeneutical techniques, Dilthey failed to do justice to his characterization of the relationship of interpreter and text as one of subject/subject and stylized it into the familiar subject/object one. The price for securing a degree of objectivity in the study of expressions of an other mind is the inability to take the step from 'historical consciousness' to 'historical experience' or 'hermeneutic consciousness'; that is to say, Dilthey was too concerned with emphasizing the need and value of taking a critical stance towards the past and also with trying to secure an objective status for this undertaking. This posture shows Dilthey as a child of the Enlightenment and as following in the Cartesian tradition; but it leads him to overlook the challenge an historical 'object' may make on the interpreter's conceptions and values, and to remain blind to the need for self-reflection in which the subject realizes his indebtedness to tradition and language as the bases and media of his thinking: the 'hermeneutic experience', to which Gadamer and Ricoeur refer as *Zugehörigkeit* or *appartenance* (belonging-to) respectively.

Accounts of Dilthey's backsliding into an objectivist stance differ. Gadamer refers to a conflict between the philosophy of life and a scientistic conception of knowledge in which Dilthey ultimately took the side of the latter. Habermas considers his objective to be already inherent in the philosophy of life: its tenets seem to 'allow for the transposition of the ideal of objectivity of the natural sciences onto the *Geisteswissenschaften*' (1968a, p. 230).

In any case, it is obvious that Dilthey's metascience failed to escape from its Cartesian pre-suppositions and thereby remained unable to do justice to its interest in guiding hermeneutical cognition. But even though his metascience forcibly remained within scientistic limits it is, nevertheless, apparent that, in methodological terms, Dilthey's insights are of great value – and proved singularly fruitful.

Dilthey and sociology

Dilthey's metascience did not succeed in bringing into harmonious union his twin concerns with the philosophy of life and scientific objectivity. This should not, however, distract from the valuable insights he arrived at on this level, especially that of the historicality of man and society, and the historicity of knowledge; there are also his more methodology-oriented discussions which centre around his critique of idealist, biological and positivist formulations of social theory and his theory of *verstehen*.

Dilthey's central objection to idealist philosophies of history (Hegel) and to 'naturalistic metaphysics of history' (Comte) is directed against their aggrandizement: to provide an explanatory framework for the whole of socio-historical reality. 'My rejection of Sociology concerns a discipline that attempts to comprehend under one science all that which happens *de facto* in human society' (I, p. 241). Sociology then either represents the collection of all the *Geisteswissenschaften* concerned with social reality without any unifying principle – 'a new label but no new knowledge' (I, p. 422), or it claims the status of the philosophy of the *Geisteswissenschaften*. Sociology, in the Comtean and Spencerian mould, is 'metaphysical' in that 'it explains religiosity, ethics, art, law, from the point of view of society, the differentiation and integration effective within it, the solidarity of interests, the progress towards an order that is of communal usefulness as its principle' (I, p. 422). Sociology itself does not provide any specific knowledge about a definite area but merely represents a method that arose in the nineteenth century in response to the French tradition, and which subjects as many facts as possible to its adopted explanatory scheme.

Dilthey's alternative assigns the various segments of socio-historical reality, which have artificially been segregated from their totality, to different *Geisteswissenschaften*, and it is here[12] that he makes a number of interesting observations – even though some passages, ironically, exhibit strong positivistic trains of thought.

Simmel's 'formal sociology' focuses on the constant forms of societal existence such as competition, hierarchical organization, division of labour, etc. Knowledge about society and history is reduced to the tension between life-processes and objectivations – the latter restricting the former which are, nevertheless, required to take form in order to continue in existence. This approach had been anticipated by Dilthey's conception of the 'systematic *Geisteswissenschaften*' of the 'external organization of society' which would correspond to a sociology of the morphology of social formations.

The distinction made by Dilthey within the sphere of objective spirit between systems of culture and systems of organization foreshadows Parsons's theory of socio-cultural spheres. Dilthey could be regarded as a forerunner of Parsons, furthermore, on account of his conception of social systems which was later characterized by concepts such as 'balance', 'function', 'adaptation'. Another strand of Dilthey's adumbrates structuralist theories when he stresses the importance of 'structures' which can be examined synchronically and which contain their 'meaning' within themselves.

Dilthey's main contribution to social scientific thought consists, of course, in his exposition of the method of *verstehen* in the 'historical *Geisteswissenschaften*' which occupied Max Weber's methodological reflections and which provided the models for all subsequent approaches concerned with the understanding of 'action'. The *verstehen* approach opens up a dimension within the object of social science that would otherwise remain submerged – or, put more correctly, it is guided by the category of meaning which constitutes parts of the object which would either slip through the conceptual net of scientistic approaches or be reduced to them. Historical objectivations are interpreted by reference to that which objectifies itself in them. This understanding cannot take the form of a search for causes and effects, but can succeed only through the consideration of contexts and through forming a relationship between inner and outer, part and whole.

A consideration of the further development of hermeneutical theory should make apparent the usefulness and limits of the *verstehen* method.

Chapter 2

Betti's hermeneutical theory

Betti consciously set himself the task of harvesting the wealth of hermeneutical thought that has by now accumulated. He remains within the idealist–romanticist tradition that has so far characterized this sphere of activity. He hopes to overcome the psychologistic residue in Dilthey's work, which even in his later work provided a basis to his theorizing, by recurring to Hegelian themes but also by drawing on Husserl and neo-Kantian thought, especially N. Hartmann.

As a result of his objective-idealist approach to the comprehension of expressions of mind, Betti's hermeneutical theory promises the added bonus of supplying us with arguments in favour of the possibility of *verstehen*[13] as a methodically disciplined form of understanding. The question of how the 'operation called *verstehen*' can be justified as a valid form of knowledge-acquisition *vis-à-vis* neo-positivist reservations will form the conclusion to this chapter in which I first consider Betti's epistemology before outlining his methodological insights. I shall herein follow his voluminous work *Allgemeine Auslegungslehre als Methodik der Geisteswissenschaften* (Betti, 1967) of which the paper following this introduction is a very condensed summary.

The question underlying my outline can be formulated as follows: does Betti succeed in capturing the process of understanding as a dialectical process between two subjects – i.e. does his focus on objective interpretation preclude the recognition of the practical dimension of acquisition of theoretical truth?

1. The metascience of hermeneutics

Objective interpretation
Betti introduces his general theory of interpretation by considering the problematic relationship between perceiving mind and

object. The case of the interpretation of 'meaning-full[14] forms' is hoped to provide insights into the possibility of – objective – understanding in general.

Like Dilthey before him, Betti recurs to Kant and accepts, without reservation, his 'Copernican Revolution'. Knowledge is not a passive mirror of reality; its objects are determined by the way we comprehend them. The origin of the categories employed in judgment, i.e. the autonomy of Reason, has always been under attack from two sides: one, the psychologism and sensualism originating with Hume; two, the 'subjectivism' and 'relativism' concerning intellectual and ethical values of the 'existentialists' who collapse the distinction between phenomenal and ideal objectivity. Betti notes, furthermore, that the spheres of 'ethical and aesthetic values belong to a second dimension of objectivity which is neither phenomenal nor any less different from the subjectivity of consciousness than the others [i.e. logical categories, J.B.] . . . Spiritual values represent an ideal objectivity that unerringly follows its own lawfulness' (Betti, 1967, p. 9).

Having referred to the autonomous character of values, Betti is confronted with the task of indicating how consciousness can discover these values. He solves it by stating that 'the ability to recognize the values presupposes within the subject, and postulates as an a priori condition of its own possibility, an open-mindedness and receptivity appropriate to them' (p. 21), 'a value is something absolute that has an ideal existence-in-itself as its essence; something that contains the basis for its own validity; an entity that remains removed from any change and any reduction through subjective arbitrariness – and which nevertheless remains an entity that can be reached by consciousness with the help of a mental structure that transcends the empirical self and incorporates it into a higher cosmos which is shared by those who have acquired the necessary spiritual maturity' (p. 23).

Since the subject is involved in a continuous process of learning and self-recognition through his communication with meaning-full forms, it can be assumed that his capacity for understanding and his axiological judgment are themselves subject to change. For this reason Betti follows Dilthey in emphasizing the need for 'historical categories which guide and elucidate the inner coherence and style of various meaning-full constructs and which have the character of changeable elements in accordance with given historically conditioned situations – even though they are a priori insofar as they exist on the epistemological level prior to these constructs and provide their transcendental justification' (p. 24).

Looking ahead to his methodological formulations, Betti states that 'such changeability has to be considered within the standards of interpretation wherever the process of understanding has to be adjusted to the given historical character of the object' (p. 24). The ideal objectivity of spiritual values can, however, only be comprehended through the 'real objectivity' of sensible objects. In a line of argument that strongly rejects the early Dilthey's introspective psychologizing centring on the notions of 'empathy' and 'reliving', Betti reserves the possibility of *verstehen* for the interpretation of objectivations of mind. Here, individual creativity has given form to valuable and meaningful ideas which can, therefore, be transmitted to a general public. This formative process which underlies the creation of a work of art, literature, etc., represents the precondition for the hermeneutical exercise: 'here we are concerned with re-translating these [the meaning-full forms, J.B.] into the ideal objectivity of the values which have been realized in them' (p. 36).

Interpretation is, consequently, confronted with a kind of objectivity which is neither purely ideal nor purely real, but always includes both. Betti draws on W. Humboldt's philosophy of language to illustrate this point: 'human nature possesses the idea of an ideal cosmos of values that goes beyond language, and even beyond any meaning-full form, and which is actually limited by language, or rather by this specific form; at the same time, language and meaning-full forms are the only means given to us for investigating this ideal world' (p. 40).

After these 'prolegomena' Betti enters the area of epistemology proper with the consideration of the object and the process of *verstehen*. He begins by reiterating his central point that 'we commence our interpretative activity whenever we come across perceivable forms through which an other mind, that has objectivated itself in them, addresses our Understanding; it is the purpose of interpretation to understand the meaning of these forms, to find out the message they wish to transmit to us' (pp. 42–3). Interpretation is an activity the aim of which consists in arriving at Understanding.

These manifestations of mind take the form of anything from texts to mimic expression and unite mental and physical moments. As givens, meaning-full forms provide the precondition for intersubjective communication and for the objectivity of the results of interpretation. The process of interpretation remains controllable and has a triadic form comprising, in addition, the existence of an other mind and its expressions. As long as hermeneutics is concerned with objectivations of mind it is possible to distinguish it from metaphysics. The acceptance of the 'objective' existence of manifestations of mind allows Betti to draw a fundamental distinction between two forms of interpretation. Hermeneutical understanding, *verstehen*, follows the maxim of exegesis that '*sensus non est inferendus sed efferendus*'.

This conception of interpretation draws on a recognized procedure, and its results can be tested intersubjectively as to their correctness: Betti considers *Auslegung* (objective interpretation) as the only valid form of interpretation and the best rendering of the term may simply be 'interpretation'. Diametrically opposed to (objective) interpretation we find another form of understanding which Betti refers to as '*Deutung*' and '*spekulative Deutung*'; to mark it off from (objective) interpretation I shall refer to it as 'speculative interpretation'. It is characterized by Betti as 'remaining dependent on intuition and the internal coherence of an a priori established system' (p. 66).

Despite his focus on (objective) interpretation Betti still remains largely on a non-objectivist basis. Complete objectivity has to be abandoned in favour of 'relative objectivity'. This limitation Betti traces to the dialectical relationship between the 'actuality' of understanding and the objectivations of mind. The subject, be it an individual or collective entity – Betti refers to the Hegelian terms of subjective and objective spirit – and the object – objectivations of mind – of the process of interpretation are locked together in an antinomous relationship: mind has congealed into permanent forms and confronts the subject as an 'other'; but both are dependent on one another 'because the given, interested subjective mind requires objectivations as a support in order to free himself by gaining in consciousness; and the objectivations contained in what is handed down are themselves completely dependent on an interested mind in order to be brought to the understanding, i.e. to be reintroduced into the sphere of understanding via the process of interpretation' (p. 93).

Betti's vitriolic attack on the position of Croce and his follower Antoni, and their 'atomistic and adialectical historism' (p. 98), brings his own views into sharp relief. Objectivity is a being-in-itself and represents an 'other' which is comprehended through conceptual frames which are appropriate to the living concreteness and the originality of the creation of its content. Croce denies the legitimacy of the use of technical aids for the recreation of the spontaneity of a work of art, whereas Betti firmly believes that 'in historical reconstruction, the procedure of typification . . . is totally justified' (p. 98). This use of typifications is, of course, closely related to Max Weber's ideal-typical approach; that is, as 'conceptual schemes with an heuristic and hermeneutical function' (p. 95). Betti notes that Antoni would approve of sociological typification for pragmatic reasons, but he makes it clear that types are to be employed for the investigation of all states of affairs 'in which the general becomes individuality and value objectivates itself in a concrete existence' (p. 99). Type is to be distinguished from species since the former captures a series of phenomena with a common characteristic which is more or less typically represented in a created form, whereas the latter is comprised of instances.

Verstehen can, in this way, be marked off from explanation since it is concerned with the 'meaning', 'relevance' and 'value' contained in phenomena, i.e. something fundamentally different from merely representing a case of something general. Recognizing the need for flexible concepts to take account of a changing subject-matter, Betti sounds a caveat: the types envisaged merely have an ordering function and must not be allowed to congeal into hardened forms without any adaptability.

Language and speech
Re-entering the field of epistemology Betti is able to develop a number of highly relevant insights. He again refers to Humboldt's philosophy of language and finds prefigured there a distinction made later by de Saussure's structural linguistics between *langue* and *parole* which Humboldt names *Sprache* (language) and *Rede* (speech, discourse). De Saussure considered language as a system of forms of meanings that follow their own law and which imply and support one another quite independently of the speaker's linguistic skills. The phenomenon of language would, in this conception, be regarded as a fixed system with speech being reduced to a merely accidental appearance. It is here that Humboldt's distinction between language as an *ergon* that objectivates itself in *energeia* (living speech) acquires its relevance. Their relationship can, with the help of Husserl's distinction between actuality and objectivity, be conceived of dialectically as one obtaining between the activity of the subject that is guided by meaning-intentions and the meaning inherent in the object, or form: 'if one considers the speech-act as a mediating activity, then the totality of

language appears as the living actuality of the linguistic formulation of inner experiences. Language is, therefore, actualized in speech as thought and position-taking, and speech transforms language into a living presence' (p. 111).

By establishing the relative autonomy of speech, Betti correspondingly established the need for, and specificity of, the activity of *verstehen* – in fact, the relationship between language and speech is reflected in the one existing between interpretation and understanding. Elementary understanding of spoken or written speech takes place in everyday life and consists of the correct comprehension of the sense of it. Understanding is always more than knowing the meaning or signification of the words used in speech – the listener, or reader, has to participate, ideally, in the same 'form of life' as the speaker or writer so as to be able to understand not only the words used but to 'share into the communion of thought offered to him' (p. 115). Understanding is directed at a whole and presupposes a total engagement – intellectual, emotional, moral – on the part of the subject.

Misunderstanding, from this perspective, is an occurrence that requires rectification. This is the sphere of hermeneutical activity: 'Interpreting, in view of its task, is to render understandable' (Betti, 1962, p. 11). The likelihood of misunderstanding – from *perverse interpretari*, i.e. inaccurate understanding, to *non intellegere*, i.e. the missing of the sense altogether – increases with the distance in space and time between speaker and listener. Whether this gap can be bridged with the help of hermeneutical rules, as Betti proposes, is a question that will be considered later on.

At this stage it is worth confirming the importance of a speech community and a universe of discourse for correct understanding. Speech and understanding are only possible within a communicative context in which two subjects participate on equal terms so that intended and perceived meaning can most nearly coincide. This requirement is, for example, obvious if one considers the case of homonymous words or locally coloured meanings of words, or by referring to the essentially elliptical character of language. Betti stresses the need to distinguish between phenomenological and axiological, 'normative', analyses. Within the latter he makes the interesting observation concerning criteria for the truth of expressions or meaning-full forms that 'such a standard does not always consist of empirical verifiabilities but rather in the investigation of its authenticity which can be recognized as a value through the immediate or mediate intuition of the inner consequences of speech; this value depends for its acceptance on the members partaking in the process of communication' (p. 146). There is no meaning outside a speech community.

This systematic stress on language-ability and the community of speakers indicates a theme that never recognized explicit enough formulation in Dilthey's work, which did not seem to have recognized the parallel strands his hermeneutical theory shares with pragmatism. Betti meanwhile uses this notion, which he attributes to an idealistic conception, to refute the materialistic view that centres on the external similarities of individualizations of mind. This view cannot escape a vicious circle, since it has to explain the process of communication with the help of categories that already presuppose its existence and effectiveness. The community of speakers represents a supra-individual entity with a transcendental character.

Understanding is, consequently, directed at a meaningful totality which itself is always present as its precondition, and of which the subject is already a part.

Understanding as reconstruction of intention
The existence of a supra-individual entity is, then, the precondition for the possibility of the process of interpretation; the latter Betti considers – in line with Schleiermacher and Dilthey – as the inversion of the process of creation. The creative mind expresses, through meaning-full forms, a content which is then transferred onto the subject of interpretation – following Betti's triadic scheme. In this 'dialectical' process, the meaning derived from expressions is that which the author had originally intended: 'it is the task of interpretation to find out the sense of an uncompleted creation, i.e. to reconstruct the train of thought underlying it' (p. 158). The necessity to inquire into the author's full intentions, made possible via his creations, leads Betti to endorse another maxim proposed by his precursors: that author and interpreter should be of a similar intellectual and moral stature in order that full justice be done to the worth of the creation.

Just as creative activity does not take place out of nothing (*creatio ex nihilo*) but draws on an immense range of past achievements and present influences,[15] so understanding too has to be envisaged as total perception that goes beyond abstractive consideration or atomistic observation. Given sufficient inner affinity such an act can take place; in it interpretative activity only plays an ancillary role.

The existence of a relationship of some sort between author

and interpreter not only provides the basis on which communication across time and place can occur, it also constitutes an
obvious problem for the objectivity of the results of interpretation. It is to this problem of how to reconcile 'subjective
conditions' and the 'objectivity of understanding' that Betti
addresses himself in the final part of his epistemological considerations.

Preconditions for correct understanding
Betti stresses the requirement on the part of the interpreter to
engage his whole sensibility. Under the rubric 'metatheoretical
conditions for the process of interpretation' he lists interest in
understanding, attentiveness, open-mindedness and self-
effacement: a specific noetic interest in understanding determines the degree to which one engages in understanding; it is at
its highest point when the desire to understand arises from an
actual need. The existence of a gap between the interpreter and
his object – which originally led to the application of interpretative procedures – necessitates a reflective approach which
recognizes the 'otherness' of objectivations of mind and, at the
same time, stimulates and trains the receptive apparatus of the
investigator; in negative terms, this reflectivity appears as self-
effacement and humility, as *pietas vis-à-vis* the magnificence of
an other *humanitas*.

At the same time, Betti demands that a number of obstacles be
removed in order that the 'other' be received in the right spirit.
By indicating the major barriers to correct understanding, it
should become apparent why Betti can attribute educational
value to hermeneutical understanding, viz. the development of
an attitude of tolerance, which is helped by the recognition of
one's own prejudices and shortcomings which only become
apparent in the sincere attempt to understand an Other and
which have to be overcome before successful understanding can
take place. Among these obstacles are Bacon's 'idols', but in the
main they are: (a) the conscious or unconscious resentment of
ideas and positions which differ from the more common ones,
and especially from those held by the observer; which leads (b)
to their denigration and distortion; (c) the attitude of 'self-
righteousness' which sees issues in terms of black and white and
is unaware of the dialectic between good and bad; (d) the
conformism towards dominant conceptions and the pharisaic
acceptance of 'conventional bias' in judging others; (e) the lack
of interest in other cultures, as well as intellectual and moral
narrowness or laziness – which shows itself in the growing

tendency to shirk sincere theoretical discussions and an open exchange of opinion in general. Betti here makes the interesting remark that 'the intolerance of political and cultural propaganda tries everything to suppress and suffocate the critical spirit' (p. 202, and note 18).

All these barriers to correct understanding 'stem from the totality of prepossessions and selfish concerns which can be traced back to a shared form of preconceived intellectual attitudes: the complex that has recently been termed "syntagma" and which finds its most advanced pathological stage in the "contorted thought" of the fanatic and the party-member who is possessed by an ideology; here, this perversion appears as "psychom"' (p. 203).

But the fact that the highest subjectivity of the interpreter, i.e. his receptivity, sensitivity, sensibility and openness, represents a precondition for successful interpretation should not lead to the confusion of interpretation with speculation in general, and the problem of 'self-understanding' in particular. Betti traces this, the confusion characteristic of existentialism, back to Dilthey, who had conceived of a necessary relationship between *verstehen* and *erleben*. In a 'lived experience' which engages the whole of our intellectual, emotional and moral capacity, we reconstruct objectivations of mind which form the object of the *Geisteswissenschaften*. Dilthey goes wrong in his view that the process of creation, e.g. that of a lyrical work by a poet, can equally be regarded as a personal interpretation of existence. The result: 'Dilthey is finally led to confuse the process of *verstehen* with the "inner lived experience" itself; he thereby loses the clear distinction between *verstehen* and causal explanation, and also regards *verstehen* as the elementary position of experiencing any kind of objectivity, thereby moving it closely towards the status of a pre-understanding' (p. 166).

It is, of course, Heidegger who attributes central significance to the role of a pre-understanding which has always already taken place when we make a conscious attempt at *verstehen*. In the formulation of the 'hermeneutic circle', this conception will be more extensively dealt with in the next chapter. At this stage I shall only indicate the bone of contention between Betti and the Protestant theologian, Bultmann, whose 'demythologization' is greatly indebted to Heidegger's existential interpretation of existence.

Two implications of this conception attract Betti's great displeasure. The first one is expressed by Jaspers' view of *verstehen* as 'mere understanding of what is already understood': it is only concerned with correct results; it is the hallmark of this kind of cognition that it becomes less effective the more neutral, 'value-free', it is. Only 'fundamental understanding' can distinguish between good and bad, true and false, beautiful and ugly.

The second implication not only relegates methodical understanding to the 'antiquarian' reproduction of the past, but even denies the *possibility* of objective historical knowledge. The work of Bultmann provides Betti with an exposition of this 'subjectivist and relativist conception'. The postulation of pre-understanding as the condition for understanding eliminates the distinction between interpretative understanding and 'lived experience' and insists on the necessity of an existential relationship between interpreter and object (text) in which the latter addresses the former and discloses new possible ways of existence. The underlying relationship determines not only the questions that will be put to the object but also the whole position of the interpreter *vis-à-vis* his object and the standards applicable for evaluating the result of this encounter. Interpretation, in the narrow sense, only plays the ancillary role, in the interpretation of Being-there (Dasein), of testing and developing the pre-understanding. Betti regards this topic as closed by referring back to his distinction between objective and speculative interpretation; since existential interpretation fails to follow the maxim that 'meaning has to be derived from the text and not imputed to it', it has excluded itself from the prospectus of valid interpretation.

2. Methodological implications

In his rejection of the subjectivism and relativism introduced into hermeneutics by existentialist philosophers Betti reaffirmed the possibility of, at least, relative objectivity of the results of interpretation. Objectivity is possible in principle owing to the autonomy, the existence-in-themselves, of objectivations of mind; but their objectivity can never be absolute owing to the distance between written or spoken speech and its addressee – a factor that pertains even to communication here and now. A more important factor intruding into the objective reconstruction of human artefact is, in fact, apparent in any process of cognition: the antinomy between the objectivity of the meaning under investigation and the subjectivity of any understanding, i.e. the spontaneity and 'actuality' of the knower.

In hermeneutical activity we have to be aware of its 'axiological moment': the interpreter has to participate in the values he finds in his object, it is 'the recognition of noetic value, an appropriation and adaptation' (p. 210).

But, as Betti stresses, following Husserl, 'meaning' as the recognition of something that is valuable, important, i.e. meaning as an act, need not be confused with meaning-in-itself, as unchangeable, i.e. 'meaning as the ideal unity of the manifold of possible acts'. The former, the meaning-activity, is a prerequisite for the understanding of the meaning-content of an object, and is, therefore, axiological since it guides the recognition of something as something. But this form of participation with the object, while making for subjective fluctuations, does not lead to a collapsing of the difference between subject and object since 'the evaluative position-taking is directed at objectivity insofar as the subject negates himself' (p. 210). The 'anthropocentrism' of the existentialists would, from this perspective, appear as self-indulgent 'intellectual egotism'.

It is this dialectic between subjectivity and objectivity, the actuality of the subject and the otherness of the object, that has, in the course of hermeneutical practice, given rise to the formulation of a methodology which, it is hoped, will guarantee correct results. Since Betti has given ample treatment to the 'hermeneutical canons' in the paper included here, I shall only give a brief mention of them:

The four canons are subdivided into two groups of two which pertain (a) to the object, and (b) to the subject of interpretation:

a_1: the canon of the hermeneutical autonomy of the object and immanence of the hermeneutical standard;

a_2: the canon of totality and coherence of hermeneutical evaluation;

b_1: the canon of the actuality of understanding;

b_2: the canon of the harmonization of understanding – hermeneutical correspondence and agreement.

Among these canons the same difficulty is reproduced that initially led to their formulation, i.e. that of reconciling unavoidable subjectivity and required objectivity, and which here emerges as the 'intersection of the canon of autonomy (a_1) with that of the actuality of understanding (b_1).

Betti is able to put the apparent dichotomy to good methodological use. The tension between objectivity and subjectivity is a precondition for the perception of a personal or cultural 'style' in which continued 'tendencies' and an 'inner coherence' are apparent. But it is the epistemological solution to the problem of objective understanding of meaning that provides the crux of the entire argument.

Referring to Schleiermacher's emphasis on the need for a total commitment of the interpreter's inner experiences and intellectual and aesthetic capabilities, Betti re-affirms the importance of the actuality of understanding. When it comes to evidencing the precise, necessary and justifiable subjective moment in interpretation Betti follows, among others, Simmel, who had argued against the possibility of a 'direct' contact between subject and object in which the former could suppress any categories that are not appropriate to the object; the interpreter can commence his activity only on the basis of the use of categories of thought – or rather, these categories have already been 'put to work' when he approaches anything.

It is already apparent that the 'dialectic of the process of interpretation' is asymmetrical. The subject anticipates the meaning of the object, the interpretation of which is characterized by semantic intersubjectivity; the subject's spontaneity is functional in this context in that he brings to bear his concrete experiences on the process of interpretation – without, necessarily, impinging on the autonomy of the meaning-full forms under consideration. The only apparent consequence of the subjective moment accounts for the fact that, owing to variations in individual and social circumstances, interpretation can never be complete and final.

Existential self-understanding, by the same token, turns upside down the relationship between these two moments; but as a form of practical knowledge, it provides a foil to Betti's sole concern with theoretical truth. The Cartesian–Kantian background to his conception is not only apparent in his emphasis on method and demonstrable knowledge, or the setting of the whole problematic of hermeneutics within the subject–object scheme, but also underlies his, ultimate, failure to provide a consistent account of the role of the subject. 'Subjectivity' is subdivided by Betti into subjective and intersubjective moments which he equates with normative and theoretical approaches to the subject-matter. Betti follows neo-Kantianism in general and Max Weber in particular when he affirms the primacy of the theoretical and exemplifies this point by referring to the investigation of values. These represent the ideal being-in-itself for value-oriented interpretation; in opposition to mere feeling or empathy it is that which is able to become the content of an articulated and conscious 'judgment', i.e. something that claims 'validity'. Value-orientation, as a form of anticipation, allows for intersubjectivity – it is, at all times, open to scrutiny.

It should have become apparent from these remarks that Betti's metascience cannot escape a form of scientism. Despite his affirmations and copious quotations, which indicate his close affinity to idealist thought and his roots in the humanist tradition, he remains within the orbit of the mode of knowledge acquisition characteristic of the natural sciences. It is only from this perspective that he is able to reduce the interpreter's historic situatedness, which fuses understanding-of-others and self-understanding into a dialectical unity, to a factor making only for subjectivism and relativism. Betti's methodology is thus trapped by the same constraints that had already been limiting Dilthey's systematic contribution to the epistemology of the *Geistes-wissenschaften*. But it is with the latter that we find some sign-posts pointing in the direction in which an answer to the questions so far left unanswered may be found; as Betti himself has remarked, Dilthey fuses 'understanding' and 'lived experience'; both take place on the basis of a shared experience. Betti strongly disapproved of this conception, sensing that it implied the transformation of the subject–object relationship in which the former questions the latter, into one pertaining between two subjects of a communicative interaction. It is not that Betti has failed to recognize the moment of self-development in the process of understanding; in his epistemological 'pro-legomena' he provides a cogent defence of it: 'by discovering the cosmos of values a thinking being develops in the course of a process of communication that takes place among various subjects . . . . The axiological judgment is, just as is cognition, in a continuous state of development . . . so that the continuous development of one point necessarily brings to light new aspects in the other' (pp. 20–1).

It is just that I cannot find any evidence that Betti made use of this insight on the level of methodology where he seems to deny the 'freedom of the subject [which] . . . is nothing else than the inner form of a mysterious, continuous self-realization as the self which one has only potentially been' (p. 21).

3. The practice of interpretation

Betti never intended to explore the ontological dimension of understanding. The task he set himself was (1) to clarify the problem of understanding by investigating, in caring detail, the process of interpretation; (2) the formulation of a methodology that barred subjectivist intrusions into the objective interpretation of objectivations of mind. I shall now outline the various forms of interpretation considered by Betti.

Types of interpretation

Betti notices four 'theoretical moments' within the process of interpretation which each represent different forms of receptivity and intellectual approach and which alternate in the course of this process:

(a) the philological moment is effective in the general effort to understand permanently fixed symbols (text, score, etc.), i.e. the reconstruction of the grammatical and logical coherence of spoken or written speech;

(b) the critical moment is called upon in cases requiring a questioning attitude, such as the emergence of incongruences, illogical statements or gaps in a line of argument; this approach, furthermore, allows us to distinguish between, for example, original, authentic and such elements that have been added at a later stage;

(c) the psychological moment is active when we follow the task of putting ourselves in the author's place and re-cognize and re-create his personal, intellectual position;

(d) the technical–morphological moment, finally, 'aims at understanding the meaning-content of the objective-mental world in relation to its particular logic and formative principle; it is a meaning that can be sensed in these creations and can be reconstructed' (p. 209); here the object is considered in its own right without reference to contingent, external factors.

After this outline of the moments constituting the process of interpretation it is possible to consider the 'types of interpretation' to which Betti has dedicated the bulk of his work and which exhibits outstanding erudition and scholarship of the highest calibre.

The three types to be considered are: 'recognitive' and 'reproductive' interpretation and 'normative' application. They can be distinguished in terms of the interest guiding them: re-cognition is autotelic, i.e. Understanding for its own sake; reproduction aims at communicating some experience; and normative application is intended to provide a guidance for action.

Philology

Philology is concerned with pure reconstruction, or restoration, of factual and intended meaning – it tries to show 'how it really was'. In this endeavour, philology and history proceed along parallel lines.

Philological interpretation of written speech has to follow the fundamental character of any text: it tries to understand the two moments of (1) the totality of language used, which necessitates fluency in it, and which is the domain of the grammatical perspective, and (2) the continued process of development in which the author was engaged, which requires a psychological perspective in order to capture speech as the outcome of the interaction of a host of influences; this kind of 'divinatory' procedure later refers to the whole life-content which the work is part of and which formed it. Attention is here focused on the *style* of the author as the relationship between speech (text) and its intellectual and moral content.

One aspect of philological interpretation Betti deals with in detail concerns instances where either a lack or an excess of meaning is apparent. In both these cases there exists a discrepancy between meaning-full forms and the meaning-content that seeks expression in them. The former requires a 'supplementary interpretation' whereas the latter can take the form of an 'allegorical interpretation'. Here the form of expression is allusive and contains an excess of meaning. In 'allegorical interpretation' one, therefore, searches for a meaning 'next to or behind, that is beyond, literal or actual meaning' (p. 282).

Symbol and myth

The problem of dealing with excess meaning is even more pronounced in the interpretation of symbols and myth. A symbol, in contradistinction to a sign, represents another entity and refers to something outside itself. Its interpretation aims at deriving the meaning-value that transcends the literal meaning, i.e. it expresses, with linguistic means, a meaning that can only be hinted at and which would otherwise have to remain silent. This endeavour consequently 'replaces the metaphoric judgment that has been grafted on to the symbol by a non-metaphoric judgment, i.e. it reiterates, now from the opposite direction, the translation that had occurred in it from a graphic metaphoric context to another non-metaphoric, i.e. abstract-discursive, one' (p. 291).

The interpretation of symbols does, however, 'not aim at replacing a symbolic meaning by a literal one, but at a deepening and enriching of the meaning of the symbol . . . a symbol remains such only as long as it keeps its graphic basis' (p. 291).

Is is the hallmark of a 'naturalistic' approach that it should place symbols within a causal context and regard them as 'deceptions masking an underlying intention which the author is himself not aware of'. Betti counterposes to this view his idealist conception of the triadic process of Understanding which implies that the author 'very well knows – maybe not always completely – the meaning of a symbol, and he is aware that the sign of actuality is charged with an excess of value or meaning that transcends its existence in the appearance' (p. 291).

The reductionist approach to excess meaning – which, according to Betti, both Bultmann and Croce are guilty of – is rejected even more strongly in the case of legends and myths; he chastizes Croce's rationalistic historism and Bultmann's 'demythologization of the Bible' with the 'intellectualistic denigration' of their object. There can be no bridge between *mythos* and *logos* since the former deals with meaning-full images and comparisons and appeals to the imagination, whereas the latter, focusing on methodical research, hopes to arrive at demonstrable truths.

I mention this view in order to draw attention to Betti's conception of myth as something completely outside the sphere of theoretical knowledge since it is a point of argument that will recur in later discussions.

Historical interpretation

Reconstructive interpretation is also employed in the investigation of historical phenomena. Here the task is not to bring to life again whole historical epochs but to 'enlarge, complement and correct our limited, fragmentary, questionable conception of these epochs' (p. 299).

The materials the historian comes into contact with should be used to 'try and re-cognize what the people who produced them were thinking, what they used them for, what motivated them' (p. 299). Betti differentiates between two kinds of sources, (a) traces, remnants, and (b) representative material (written, pictorial documents), when it comes to understanding an event. The criteria for separating and using various sources are formulated in accordance with the four hermeneutical canons. The 'immanence of standards', for example, has to be preserved by the prior consideration of whether a source emerged with the intention of portraying an event – which therefore already represents an interpretation of it – or whether it can be considered as merely a fragment of life that survived. In both cases it is not sufficient to merely reconstruct a past event in analogy to philological interpretation: historians have to consider the context in which a document was produced. This move is all the more necessary in tracing how a certain event came to be represented, say, in writing, because one always has to be aware of a possible discrepancy between the intention underlying a given creation and its eventual form. History is the *locus classicus* for the possibility of the interpreter understanding the author better than he had understood himself. By considering the situatedness of a source, and by attending to diachronic and synchronic developments which have had a bearing on the event or the motives of the author under consideration, historians, in fact, comply with the canon of the 'totality and coherence of hermeneutical evaluation'.

It is a consequence of the problem of the reliability of sources – which arises from the two-fold problem of whether an historical witness was in the position to know and was willing to truthfully report an event – that historians prefer to deal with original material rather than rely on contemporary or even later accounts; they thereby express the underlying assumption that they are in a better position to know.

The subject's spontaneity is called upon when the historian is required 'to reconstruct within himself another mentality' (p. 307) and when he employs his ability to empathize with a past actor; in both instances it enables the historian to understand historical data in terms of one underlying intellectual and moral constitution. This psychological moment echoes the need for a 'congeniality' between author and interpreter. Schleiermacher, who first emphasized the desirability of such a mental affinity, also included a technical moment in his methodology, and Betti stresses this aspect of historical interpretation, too. It does not suffice to know only the personality of the author, it is also necessary to refer to the epoch and cultural climate in which he lived.

I cannot, of course, do justice here to the comprehensive grasp and suggestiveness of Betti's views about historical interpretation and shall now turn to the sphere of 'technical interpretations with an historical task'.

Technical–morphological interpretation
Betti referred to the technical moment of interpretation throughout his outline of philology and, especially, history, where its use prevented the study of history from sliding into mere *Geistesgeschichte* (history of thought). While recognizing the

superlative work of people like Dilthey and Max Weber in this field, Betti nevertheless advises caution when dealing with creations of mind. It is possible here to lose sight of the totality of the work, which can only be preserved by locating it within the context of its emergence. To redress the balance Betti does not confront intellectual history with a 'naturalist' (by which he presumably means a materialist) conception, but with the methodological device of a complementary technical–morpho-logical interpretation. Here intellectual and cultural history give way to *Problemgeschichte*, the investigation of the genesis, continuance and solution of problems arising out of the form that has been given to issues of meaning and value. The sphere in which these problems, which require a technical–morpho-logical interpretation, arise extends from religion to social structures.

Centring on the notion of an 'unconscious teleology' (p. 448) Betti overcomes the complementary limitations of both psy-chologistic and naturalistic approaches to social phenomena. Sociology cannot be reduced to a *verstehen* psychology since only a limited part of human actions are consciously undertaken. It is equally impossible to rely on a naturalistic, generalizing approach since that would lead to the neglect of the historical specificity of these phenomena.

Betti rejects Rickert's 'either–or' scheme of individualizing and nomothetic science and moves towards an historically-oriented, general framework. Sociology is characterized by the duality of its conceptualization which integrates the consider-ation of individuality with a general, structural approach. It may be possible to refer to socio-morphology as the object of technical–morphological interpretation since it contains both anthropomorphic and materialistic moments without ever being reducible to either. The possibility of the socio-morphous character of social phenomena can be attributed to the dialectical mode of societal co-existence. The intentions of social actors and the 'objectivity' of social structures intersect but have to be considered in relation to their own standards. This does not preclude the possibility of observable trends and regularities occurring within that on-going process of formation and in-vestigation, which leads Betti to the postulation of an 'inner form' (p. 462) of objectivations of mind which has arisen by following a certain developmental law and which yields insights into the technique of construction. 'Inner forms' are apparent in other spheres of objective mind, and, through the organic–genetic constitution, alert us to the need to regard meaning-full forms as 'traces, indications and the means of cognition of inner forms' which have to be interpreted by reference to an overarching context. The technical–morphological interpretation of social phenomena is, of course, significantly different from that of other objectivations of mind, e.g. works of art, since the subject-matter consists here not of fixed objects but of rules of action which are objectivated in norms and, mostly, transmitted orally. Research here has to concern itself with linguistic symbols or communal activities, such as rites. Social co-existence gives rise to structures which require continuous, active affirmation by the participants if they are to remain in existence: the relationship of individual and structure, as meaning-context, is one of mutual influence, a give and take. The meaning-full forms that emerge from social processes now acquire the objectivity of other objectivations of mind; here one 'has to take account of the renewable agreement of the members existing under it in a living and thinking agreement' (p. 467).

Betti's idealist standpoint leads him to neglect the contingent factors of relationships of power and economic development, and thereby to over-stress the self-transparency of human actors; he can, consequently, only visualize the mechanism operative in social development as a linear one that is propelled by its own lawfulness which he refers to as 'noo-nomie', as 'logic of mind' (p. 469).

Betti also refers to Dilthey's concepts of *Strukturzusammenhang* and *Wirkungszusammenhang* ('structural coherence' and 'structural efficacy') and it is here that we gain important insights for the investigation of social phenomena. Structures are apparent on the psychological as well as social level and provide the context within which individual events have to be located and referred back to in order to acquire their meaning. Understanding a social phenomenon as a 'generality in particularist garb' (p. 456) is, therefore, always directed at its over-arching totality. Unfortunately, we are not given sufficient indications by Betti as to the way in which individualizing and generalizing approaches are to be synthesized within a conceptual framework that allows us to translate one into the language of the other.

The above aspects Betti mentions only as illustrations, and in a contrapunctual way, while outlining his main concern with the teleological rationality of action as it relates to technical–morphological interpretation. Here he gives support to Weber's ideal-type approach which he regards as 'the technical analysis of the objective situation and economy of action'. The 'lawfulness' of action referred to above enters into an interpretative scheme, which possesses only heuristic status, as 'tendency' or 'normality'. The use of 'types' derives its legitimacy and usefulness from the existence of permanent expressions of communal life, from which one can extract significant aspects.

The establishing of types of sociological structures in no way represents a preliminary move in the direction of social laws: their control and structure is historical and their validity is tied to their heuristic efficacy; their task is to help understand the uniqueness of literal situations. Technical–morphological interpretation supplements this activity by considering the inner coherence and meaning-context of social structures.

Betti's exposition of philological, historical and technical interpretation with an historical task – the latter is at times tantalizingly elliptical – is followed by that of 'reproductive' and 'normative' interpretations. Here things are less complicated, and I shall be content to give a cursory overview.

Reproductive interpretation

Understanding is, by its nature, reproductive in that it internalizes, or translates into its own language, objectivations of mind by means of an actuality that is analogous to the one that brought forth a meaning-full form. Hermeneutically trained understanding of linguistic, dramatic or musical creations adds, however, another dimension – and with it a specific responsibility to what is, in fact, a process of 'rendering understandable': it is directed at an audience, potential or actual, and requires complete self-surrender on the part of the interpreter in order to remain 'faithful' to the work and author in question. The characteristic difficulty encountered in this sphere is located in the need to bring to full expression what the author may have, intentionally or not, left vague. Reconstructive interpretation, therefore, can come perilously close to the line separating objective from speculative interpretation. In the translation of a text, the dramatization of a play and the performance of a piece of music, the 'interpreter' is engaged in the activity of transposing one context of meaning into another and in this sense re-creates the work in question. The principal guideline in this process, which can so easily fall prey to subjectivism and arbitrariness, is the demand to try and fulfil the intention of the author, and all energy has to be put into the task of making it apparent.

Normative interpretation

Normative interpretation, 'application', occurs in the fields of jurisdiction and theology which are both characterized by the endeavour to derive from a meaning-context (e.g. legal code, Bible) guidelines for present activity. In the former, action has to take place within the framework of given directions and becomes acute in cases which are not directly covered by written laws; interpretation with a normative intention is thus called upon here and takes the form of, for example, an analogy judgment.

The interpretation of the Bible has to meet an additional condition: it has to commence from a 'dogmatic' position, i.e. belief, which itself becomes apparent in correct interpretation. Even in this area Betti regards it as important to follow hermeneutical canons in opposition to Bultmann's Protestantism, which favoured an historical–critical exegesis (demythologization) of the Christian message.

4. Conclusions: *Verstehen* as a method of the social sciences?

When summarizing Betti's general theory of interpretation it is worth keeping in mind that he regards interpretation as a means towards Understanding. Objective interpretation is to help overcome barriers to understanding and facilitate the re-appropriation of objective mind by another subject; the need for 'relatively objective' knowledge requires the subject of interpretation to enter into a subject–object relationship with, for example, a text even though the object represents the expression of another subject.

How, then, does the process of interpretation outlined so far help towards solving the problem of Understanding?

Any interpretative act is a triadic process in which meaningfull forms mediate between the mind objectivated in them and the mind of the interpreter. These forms confront the interpreter as something 'other'. The crucial difference between the process of interpretation and that of any other process of cognition, in which subject and object are confronted, lies in the fact that here the object consists of objectivations of mind and it is the task of the interpreter to re-cognize or re-construct the ideas, message, intentions manifested in them; it is a process of internalization, in which the content of these forms is transposed into an 'other', different subjectivity.

In this way, elementary understanding occurs through the

mediation of language: the speech of an other subject represents an appeal, a call on us to understand, which we follow by reconstructing its meaning with the help of our categories of thought and by fitting together the various pieces of evidence in order to reconstruct an author's intended meaning.

Adequate understanding can, however, only develop on the basis of correct knowledge. Betti has remained sufficiently close to the neo-Kantian tradition of the *Kulturwissenschaften* to insist on a firmly conducted analysis of the phenomena under consideration – without allowing it to become an end in itself: the ultimate aim of hermeneutical investigation is the explication of their meaning, leading to a better Understanding.

It may be helpful to consider the remarks Abel (1974) made concerning an 'operation called "verstehen"' which has gained wide currency and which neatly summarizes the misconceptions rampant about *verstehen*.

According to Abel, this 'operation' involves three steps: '(1) internalizing the stimulus, (2) internalizing the response, (3) applying behaviour maxims' (p. 49). In all of these, *verstehen* consists of the 'application of personal experience to observed behaviour' (p. 51). He provides three cases in which *verstehen* is operative, and the conclusion he arrives at is the following: *verstehen* can at best provide us with 'hunches'; it serves as an heuristic for properly scientific investigations which rely on objective, experimental, and statistical tests. *Verstehen* adds nothing 'to our store of knowledge, because it consists of the application of knowledge already validated by personal experience; nor does it serve as a means of verification' (p. 54).

A further important argument appears in a note. Here he follows Lundberg in stating that 'understanding is the end at which all methods aim, rather than a method in itself' (p. 54).

So far, 'understanding' has been used to (a) indicate comprehension in general, as the result of an acquisition of knowledge in any sphere; and (b) to indicate a methodical procedure, here referred to as *'verstehen'*.

The method of *verstehen* or 'motivational understanding' is 'viewed by its proponents as a method by means of which we can explain human behaviour' (pp. 54–5). This view is, however, somewhat misleading. *Verstehen* has, to my knowledge, never been considered by any hermeneutician as a form of causal explanation or even a substitute therefor.[16] In fact, it is, if anything, the reverse: causal explanation has often been regarded as necessary only where *verstehen* proved impossible owing to the impenetrability of the object.[17] A closer look also reveals that, what Abel refers to as a characteristic of *verstehen*, viz. the application of what is already known from personal experience, only captures a borderline situation where only 'very little evidence' is available; Jaspers terms this approach *'deuten'* (speculative interpretation). In addition, Abel here manages to stand Hegel on his head in his own way by inverting the relationship between understanding and explanation; for Hegel it is the latter, and not the former, which represents a 'tautological movement of thought'.[18]

How does the *verstehen* of motives, 'subjective interpretation of meaning' (Abel), compare with Betti's attempt at 'objective interpretation'?

By focusing on the former, Abel, of course, depicted Weber's view concerning motivational understanding which could fulfil all the heuristic functions Abel attributes to it. But as Betti's work shows (relatively), objective knowledge of expressions of meaning is possible, not only in the sphere of value-interpretation but also in all areas where we are confronted by meaning-full forms. Hirsch (1967) would equally subscribe to this view, albeit after having arrived at it from a somewhat different route which takes in a logic of guessing and validation based on Popper's falsificationism.

In any case, to deny the status of valid knowledge to the results forthcoming from the hermeneutical sciences would represent, in addition to the misunderstanding of what *verstehen* is about, the erection of barriers to scientific progress in the name of an outdated conception of science.

The critique of Abel's conception of *verstehen* also leads directly to the consideration of an aspect of the hermeneutical understanding of meaning so far not sufficiently dealt with: the historic situatedness of the access to any objectivation of meaning.

One example Abel gives in order to evidence the limited use of an interpretative access to the facts of social science draws upon the relationship between harvest yield and the number of marriages within a rural community over a certain time. According to Abel we 'understand' a drop in the marriage rate once we realize that bad harvests give rise to feelings of insecurity and a reluctance to enter into any new obligations.

As Habermas (1973, p. 142) shows, the application of trivial behavioural maxims, along the lines of the stimulus–response model, rests on certain basic, unquestioned assumptions which one takes for granted – for example, the importance of material factors in deciding on marriage in Western culture.

In any case, the understanding of human behaviour has to recur to the traditioned values and institutionalized roles in terms of which it becomes meaningful.

This form of understanding is always presupposed in the gathering of social data and, therefore, equally applies to objective interpretation. It can remain a residual, if important, element in social research only because the 'object' is so close to the subject's 'world'. Only when the taken-for-granted identity of interpretations of meaning breaks down do we become aware of the hermeneutic situatedness of our intellectual activities.

In a later paper (1975) Abel takes account of these criticisms and refers to *verstehen* I and II whereby he includes motivational understanding among the former; the latter consists of the 'hermeneutical analysis of culture and history as not only a relevant but as an indispensable task of the social sciences' (1975, p. 99). This widening of his position does, however, not encompass my main reservations since he (1) still adheres to his original conception of *verstehen* as a subjective 'motivational understanding' and (2) does not draw any consequences from the kind of Understanding 'achieved in the process of enculturation' (p. 101) for the process of *verstehen and* explanation.

In the next chapter I shall consider a philosophical approach to hermeneutics that focuses precisely on the latter point and tries to explicate the systematic role of what is, variously, termed 'pre-understanding', 'pre-judices' (Gadamer), 'horizon of expectation' (Popper), 'fundamental patterns of expectation', 'set of pre-suppositions', etc., and which I have referred to so far as 'hermeneutic situatedness'.

Recognition of this sphere, which is responsible for the constitution of the objects of social science, not only evidences the basis of explanatory approaches to the social world, but also undermines the autonomy of *verstehen* as the method of the *Geisteswissenschaften*.

Reading I
Emilio Betti

Hermeneutics as the general methodology of the *Geisteswissenschaften*

Contents of Reading I

The place of the hermeneutical problematic in contemporary consciousness

Hermeneutics, as the general problematic of interpretation which blossomed so richly during that glorious epoch of the unfolding of the European spirit we now call the romanticist period and which formed the common concern of those dedicated to all the humanist disciplines – a concern shared by linguists such as Wilhelm von Humboldt; theologians such as Ast, August Wilhelm Schlegel and Boeckh; jurists such as Savigny; political historians such as Niebuhr, after him Ranke, then Droysen – this time-honoured hermeneutics (as the theory of interpretation) is today in Germany no longer a living heritage within the *Geisteswissenschaften*: it appears to have become outmoded. It would appear that, with some notable exceptions, the rich hermeneutical heritage has in many cases been forgotten in present-day Germany and that the continuity with the great romanticist tradition has nearly been broken (it is difficult to gauge the extent to which this has already happened).

This cultural situation of our time appears in a particular light through a talk given on 28 January 1959 by Professor Coing in Düsseldorf in the context of the Study-Group Nordrhein–Westfalen, on 'the juristic methods of interpretation and the theories of general hermeneutics' to a circle of colleagues, only half of whom were jurists. He expressed regret at the decreasing awareness among his fellow-countrymen of the hermeneutical problematic, especially so since it had been advanced considerably in recent times by German thinkers such as Wilhelm Dilthey and Georg Simmel – as is shown by the high praise their contributions attracted from the philosopher Collingwood, the sociologist Aron and the historian Marrou. Characteristic in all this was the reserved attitude of the speaker whose references to existing literature remained too vague, and who refrained from presenting his audience with an accurate account.

Objectivations of Mind

Nothing is of greater importance to man than living in mutual understanding with his fellow-men. Nothing appeals as much to his understanding as the lost traces of man that come to light again and address him. Wherever we come into contact with meaning-full forms (*sinnhaltige Formen*) through which an other mind addresses us, we find our interpretative powers stirring to get to know the meaning contained within these forms. From fleeting speech to fixed documents and mute remainders, from writing to *chiffres* and to artistic symbol, from articulated language to figurative or musical representation, from explanation to active behaviour, from facial expression to ways of bearing and types of character – in short, whenever something from the mind of an Other★ approaches us there is a call on our ability to understand, issued in the hope of being unfolded. The different levels on which these various objectivations present themselves to us must not, of course, be confounded with one another. Statements, above all, have to be clearly distinguished from the sounds that embody them, and they have to be separated from the signs in which they are expressed. In general, we have to beware of confusing the perceptible bearer which belongs to the physical level – on a permanent basis or through being objectified only fleetingly – with the meaning-content it has been entrusted with; it is a vehicle that, as it were, carries that meaning with it as a content which belongs to a level fundamentally different from the physical.

★*Fremd* is rendered as 'Other' in order to avoid the strongly negative connotations of 'alien' which already imply a distance that cannot be bridged in understanding; 'foreign' suffers from similar restrictions.

Meaning-full forms

On the other hand, it is equally important that we insist that an interpretation is possible only in view of meaning-full forms. 'Form' is here to be understood in a wide sense as an homogenous structure in which a number of perceptible elements are related to one another and which is suitable for preserving the character of the mind that created it or that is embodied in it. The representational function of a meaning-full form which transmits a piece of knowledge need not, by the way, be a conscious one: the meaning-content it carries can be known through its meaning-representational function in such a way that, owing to its mediation, another mind, which is nevertheless closely related to ours, can 'speak' to us by addressing our ability to understand with an 'appeal'. It is possible to enter into a spiritual relationship with one's fellow-men only on the basis of such meaning-full forms which are either given in actual perception or can be evoked as an image in one's memory.

It would, however, be a grave materialist prejudice to envisage these forms, and, in particular, explanations, as a kind of shell or wrapping, the transmission of which would effect a transference of the thought contained within it. In truth, people do not establish mutual understanding by exchanging the material signs of objects or by the mutual production of the same thought with the help of an automatic transference, but rather through the reciprocal mobilization of corresponding elements in the chain of their conceptual universe and the striking of the same chord on their mental instrument to bring forth thoughts that correspond to those of the speaker. This is because the gates of the mind open only from the inside and on account of a spontaneous impulse; the outside contributes only the invitation to resonate in harmony.

Representational function and meaning of expression

Interpretation, by the way, does not presuppose that the thought-content has been expressed with an intent towards conscious representation or towards communicating something about social life. It is nevertheless possible that thought without such an intent, or any activity which is not directed at expressing thought, can at any time become the object of interpretation, given that one is wishing to elicit the meaning expressed in that activity, or to gather its style of production or life-style. Every practical activity possesses internal meaning which may be of an unconscious but nevertheless symptomatic kind, and which becomes important if one wishes to use it as a basis for further consideration. Viewed as a symptom, it could be used for arriving at a person's fundamental conceptions and his characteristic way of perceiving and judging things around him. Without any knowledge about the circumstances of an action and the events preceding or following it, which locate it within a chain of events, it would be difficult to attempt such an inference on the basis of one single action alone; if such knowledge is, however, available then it becomes possible to refer to the whole personality.

Both jurists and historians are interested in such practical activity. Because of the absence of any conscious intent at representation, it provides the most genuine and reliable indication of the attitude of their author by allowing safe inferences as to the underlying mentality. In the case of the historian, such an interest is due to his task of having to provide an assessment of the relative worth of competing interests on the basis of maxims of behaviour adopted by the person in question; this is because the truthful presentation of this assessment may either suffer from possible moralizing tendencies, which may elevate it to the sublime, or from an interest in leaving in the dark the motives underlying a course of action. One should be aware that the object of interpretation in the above-mentioned case is always an objective activity of thought which is recognizable in practical behaviour. Since this activity is to be regarded as a mediate, or implicit manifestation of a certain way of seeing and thinking, that behaviour, if considered from the point of view of its symptomatic value, can by all means be viewed as a meaning-full form in the wider sense of an objectivation of mind. Here we come to a distinction in the field of hermeneutics which is directed at the fundamental characteristics of the representational function inherent in meaning-full forms and which is concerned with finding out whether the mode of existence of this function is mediate or immediate, intentional and consciously developed or only implicit and undeveloped. This is why one differentiates within historical material between sources of information which have been transmitted in writing, by word of mouth, or in the form of an object and remnants, traces, or findings which, as fragments of the past, point beyond it; the latter is characterized by the absence of both a conscious representational function as well as a context that would connect the fragment with the whole of a past epoch.

Interpretation and Understanding

The process of interpretation is, in my opinion, destined to solve the epistemological problem of Understanding. Drawing on the familiar distinction between action and outcome, procedure and its result, we may tentatively characterize interpretation as the procedure that aims for, and results in, Understanding. Interpreting, in view of its task, is to bring something to the Understanding. To comprehend the unity of the process of interpretation we need to refer to the elementary phenomenon of understanding as it is actualized through the mediation of language. This phenomenon has been unravelled with unsurpassable clarity by Wilhelm von Humboldt. It shows us that speech produced by our fellow-men cannot be regarded as a ready-made physical object simply to be received by us; it is instead the material source of a stimulation directed at our insight to re-translate what has been perceived and to reconstruct its meaning from within so that the line of argument, as it is apparent in the spoken word, can, with the help of our categories of thought, be brought to expression anew in a creative, form-giving process.

Interpretation as a triadic process

It is now clear that we can generalize von Humboldt's observation. To the extent that the process of interpretation is designed to solve the problem of understanding, it remains, in its essential elements, unified and homogeneous despite the differentiations required in its application. Each time there is a demand made on the mental spontaneity of the one called upon to understand, an appeal that cannot be successful without his active participation: a challenge and an appeal emanating from meaning-full forms in which mind has objectivated itself and which is directed at a subject, an active and thinking mind, whose interest in understanding has been stimulated by the variegated concerns of everyday life. The phenomenon of understanding is therefore a triadic process at the opposite ends of which we find the interpreter as an active, thinking mind, and the mind objectivated in meaning-full forms. They do not come into contact, into touch, immediately but only through the mediation of these meaning-full forms in which an objectivated mind confronts the interpreter as an unalterably other being. Subject and object of the process of interpretation, i.e. interpreter and meaning-full forms, are the same that can be found in every process of cognition; only here they are characterized by specific traits which derive from the fact that we are not dealing with just any object but with objectivations of mind, so that the task of the cognizing subject consists in recognizing the inspiring, creative thought within these objectivations, to rethink the conception or recapture the intuition revealed in them. It follows that understanding is here the re-cognition and re-construction of a meaning – and with it of the mind that is known through the forms of its objectivations – that addresses a thinking mind congenial with it on the basis of a shared humanity: it is a bridging through a kind of arc, a bringing together and reuniting of these forms with the inner totality that generated them and from which they separated; it is, of course, an internalization of these forms in which their content is transposed into the differing subjectivity of an Other.

Inversion of the creative and transposition into the subjectivity of an Other

What occurs here, then, is an inversion of the creative process: in the hermeneutical process the interpreter retraces the steps from the opposite direction by re-thinking them in his inner self.

The difficulty involved in such an inversion rests in the mentioned transposition into another subjectivity that differs from the original one. This is also the basis of the antinomy of two contradictory requirements which an interpretation has to satisfy equally well. On the one side is the demand for objectivity: the interpreter's reconstruction of the meaning contained in meaning-full forms has to correspond to their meaning-content as closely as possible; for this reason, the requirement mentioned is one of honest subordination. On the other side, the requirement for objectivity can only be met thanks to the subjectivity of the interpreter and his awareness of the preconditions of his ability to understand in a manner adequate to the subject-matter. That is to say, the interpreter is called upon to reconstruct a thought and recreate it from within himself, making it his own, while at the same time having to objectify it. We therefore have here a conflict between, on the one hand, the subjective element that cannot be separated from the spontaneity of understanding, and, on the other, objectivity as the otherness of the meaning to be arrived at. It will soon become apparent how this antinomy gives rise to the whole dialectic of the process of interpretation and that it provides the starting-point for a general theory of interpretation just as the antinomy between the being-for-itself of the subject and the otherness of the object leads the dialectic emerging in any process of cognition.

Guidelines for interpretation: the canon of the hermeneutical autonomy of the object

We find that some of the criteria and guidelines, which I would like to call hermeneutical canons, relate to the object of interpretation while others relate more to the subject.

As far as the canons relating to the object are concerned, the first and basic canon is immediately apparent. Since meaning-full forms, as the object of interpretation, are essentially objectivations of mind and, in particular, manifestations of some thought-content, it is clear that they have to be understood with reference to that other mind that has been objectivated in them, and not in relation to any meaning the form itself may acquire if abstracted from the representational function it had for that mind or thought. Not so long ago, theoreticians in the field of hermeneutics formulated this canon of the *'mens dicentis'* emphatically as *'sensus non est inferendus sed efferendus'*, the meaning to be determined may not be inferred into meaning-full forms in an arbitrary act, and in something of an underhand manner; rather it ought to be derived from it.

May I suggest that we call this first canon the canon of the hermeneutical autonomy of the object, or the canon of the immanence of the standards of hermeneutics. By this we mean that meaning-full forms have to be regarded as autonomous, and have to be understood in accordance with their own logic of development, their intended connections, and in their necessity, coherence and conclusiveness; they should be judged in relation to the standards immanent in the original intention: the intention, that is, which the created forms should correspond to from the point of view of the author and his formative impulse in the course of the creative process; it follows that they must not be judged in terms of their suitability for any other external purpose that may seem relevant to the interpreter.

The canon of the coherence of meaning (principle of totality)

A second fundamental canon relating to the object of interpretation was emphasized by the Roman jurist Celsus with exemplary accuracy in a famous text that contains a polemical attack against the hair-splitting activities engaged in by pleading rhetoricians. We may call the hermeneutic canon referred to in this text the canon of totality and of the coherence of meaning of hermeneutical investigations. This canon sheds some light upon the interrelations and coherence existing among the individual elements of speech, as is the case with any manifestation of thought – and upon their mutual relationship to the whole of which they are a part. It is that relationship of elements between themselves and to their common whole which allows for the reciprocal illumination and elucidation of meaning-full forms in the relationship between the whole and its parts, and vice versa.

One can assume that even plain common sense would accept that this interrelation between the whole and its parts, i.e. their coherence and synthesis, answers to an intellectual need shared by author and interpreter. A glance at romanticist hermeneutics would, furthermore, show us that the demand for totality was established by Schleiermacher in a particularly emphatic and insistent way. He stressed the hermeneutical interrelation existing between the unity of the whole and the individual elements of a work which allows it to be interpreted in such a way that clarification is achieved by reference either to the unity arising out of the ensemble of individual parts or to the meaning which each part acquires in respect of the whole. One proceeds thereby to the pre-supposition that the totality of speech, just as that of any manifestation of thought, issues from a unitary mind and gravitates towards a unitary mind and meaning. From this, and on the basis of the correspondence of the processes of creation and interpretation already referred to, we arrive at this guideline: the meaning of the whole has to be derived from its individual elements, and an individual element has to be understood by reference to the comprehensive, penetrating whole of which it is a part. Just as the signification, intensity, nuances of a word can only be comprehended in relation to the meaning-context in which it was uttered, so the signification and sense of a sentence, and sentences connected with it, can only be understood in relation to the reciprocal coherence of meaning-context, the organic composition and conclusiveness, of speech.

The principle of the reciprocal illumination of parts and whole can further be developed so that, in turn, every speech and every written work can equally be regarded as a link in a chain which can only be fully understood by reference to its place within a larger meaning-context. The comprehensive totality into which the part has to be integrated can be conceived of, if we follow Schleiermacher, as the whole life of a person. In a subjective, personal reference to the life of an author each of his actions can be understood in relation to their totality, according to their mutual effects and clarification, as one moment interconnected with all the others of the life of a whole person. A comprehensive totality can, in an objective reference, be conceived of as a cultural system which the work to be interpreted belongs to, inasmuch as it forms a link in the chain of existing continuities of meaning between works with a related meaning-content and expressive impulse. It follows that, on this higher level, too, understanding retains its tentative character at the outset and is corroborated and widened only in the further course of the interpretative procedure.

The hermeneutical canon of totality is nowadays applied in the legal sphere in the interpretation of explanations and modes of conduct as well as legal norms and other legal directives and maxims of judgment. Its field of application is, however, much wider than that. For example, there is the case concerning a criminal which is conducted in accordance with the postulate of the positive school of criminal law. This postulate requires that one concludes from the criminal act under consideration to its symptomatic value for the personality of the culprit as it reveals itself in that act. It is clear that this procedure follows the demand to refer to the whole of the matter. In the same way, one appeals to the canon of totality, more or less consciously, in the interpretation of legal norms and laws. This is especially so in cases where interpretations have to be excluded which would conflict with the consistency of a system that has been established with the aids provided by legal dogmatics, and that contains the norm in question; this is the case, for example, when the application of particular norms derivable from other legal systems – in accordance with the directives of international private law – has to be excluded in so far as it would conflict with the spirit of one's own legal order. Disregarding the peculiarly defensive attitude apparent in the introduction of extraneous norms, a look at the concept of legal order, as formed in modern legal dogmatics, leads one to the directive that each norm, or maxim for decision-making, which is to become an integral part of it will necessarily have to be related to the whole.

This whole forms, in the words of Dilthey, a *Wirkungszusammenhang* (effective-structure) which generates an organic interrelationship, mutual dependency, coherence, and conclusiveness, even between norms, and groups of norms, from different areas of the law.

Analogy and further development

We now move from the object to the subject of interpretation, where we find a further guideline in the application of the law by a jurist. As the theologian's task of application would confirm, it applies whenever either an amendment to an incomplete ruling or a restriction is judged to be necessary in instances where there are either legalistic reasons for it, or when it is disputed that a provision allows additional conclusions in cases where it has been established or adopted in opposition to the consequence of the law. In these situations, the task is not only to relate one part to an overarching whole – be it the whole of a legal order or universe of belief – but to either supplement the purposive rationality of an established evaluation by having recourse to the excess meaning evident in it, which allows for further interrelated conclusions with regard to the social coexistence of the members of a legal or religious community, or by restricting its applicability in view of the limitation of its basis. It is immediately apparent that the required integration or restriction, nowadays known as analogy, extensive and restrictive interpretation, introduces an element into the process of interpretation that goes beyond the simple task of the purely recognitive investigation of meaning, and which adds to it the further task of adaptation and assimilation, that is, one of improvement and application aimed at the systematic further development of legal norms and religious demands within their existing life structures, and of bringing them closer to the actuality of contemporary life.

Reflective consideration, then, uncovers further guidelines that have to be followed in interpretation. Apart from the categories of the autonomy of the object and of hermeneutical totality which respond to the need for standards immanent in the internal coherence and totality of the object of interpretation – which together correspond to the moment of objectivity of the meaning arrived at – there exist guidelines which fulfil the demand for an active involvement of the subject in this process; they consequently correspond to the moment of subjectivity

referred to which is inseparable from the spontaneity of understanding.

The canon of the actuality of understanding

There is, accordingly, a third canon to be followed in every
interpretation which I would like to call the canon of the
actuality of understanding, and which Rudolf Bultmann[1] has
drawn attention to recently. It states that an interpreter's task is
to retrace the creative process, to reconstruct it within himself,
to retranslate the extraneous thought of an Other, a part of the
past, a remembered event, into the actuality of one's own life;
that is, to adapt and integrate it into one's intellectual horizon
within the framework of one's own experiences by means of a
kind of transformation on the basis of the same kind of synthesis
which enabled the recognition and reconstruction of that
thought. It follows that the attempt of some historians to rid
themselves of their subjectivity is completely nonsensical. It
would be naive to assume, especially in the context of historical
interpretation, that the task of the historian would be exhausted
by a mere reporting of what is contained by his sources and to
assume that the only true history is that contained in these
sources. What one forgets here is that everything our mind
gains possession of enters the whole structure of our representations and concepts which we already carry within ourselves. In
this way, each new experience becomes an integral part of our
mental universe through a process of adaptation and remains
subject to its changes in relation to the interpretation of new
experiences.

Affinity with the subject-matter and the 'upon-which' of inquiry

It is, of course, correct that the interpreter's task is merely to find
out the intended meaning of a manifestation of someone's
thought and to understand the style of thinking and imagining
apparent in it. The meaning and way of imagining is, however,
not something that is simply offered to a passive interpreter by
meaning-full forms and only needs to be gathered in a mechanical procedure. On the contrary, it is something that the
interpreter has to re-cognize and reconstruct within himself
with the help of his subtle intuition and on the strength of his

own insight and of the categories of thought located in his own creative, practical knowledge.

One is, today, generally aware and agreed that the interpreter's attitude cannot be merely passively receptive but has to be actively reconstructive. But then, there are cases where this has, in my opinion, been taken too far. I do not mean the postulation of a so-called '*Vorverständnis*' (pre-understanding) on the part of the interpreter – a somewhat equivocal formula that could easily be made unequivocal, for all it states is that an interpreter should have an expertise in the area concerned, i.e. a living relationship with the subject-matter. This formula is, in itself, really quite harmless – until the possibility of objective knowledge in interpretation is itself being questioned. In order to avoid any misunderstanding, it should be admitted that objectivity means something quite different in the *Geisteswissenschaften* compared with the natural sciences where we are dealing with objects that are essentially different from ourselves. But it is necessary to reject the unwarranted conclusion that it is impossible to maintain a clear distinction between the knowing subject and his object, or that the 'in-itself' of an historical phenomenon is nothing more than 'the illusion of objectifying thought which may be legitimate in natural science but never in study of history'.[2]

In this context it would be appropriate to refer to Bultmann's argument which amounts to the thesis that 'objectivity in historical knowledge can never be achieved, not even in the sense that phenomena can be known as they are "in-themselves"';[3] this 'in-self' would be the illusion of objectifying thought. Such arguments are presented by B.[4] in the following way: interpreting is possible only on the basis of a preceding involvement with a subject-matter directly or indirectly expressed in a text which itself determines the *Woraufhin* (upon-which) of the inquiry (this is what B. means by '*Vorverständnis*' – an equivocal word that had best be avoided because of its ambiguity). According to B., the interest in a subject-matter gives rise to the kind of the questions asked, i.e. the upon-which of inquiry. The upon-which may coincide with the intention of the text; in this case, the subject-matter under investigation is provided directly by the text. It may, however, also emerge from an interest in states of affairs contained in all kinds of texts; here, the subject-matter is provided by the text, only indirectly. (1) The upon-which of the inquiry may, for example, be given by an interest in the reconstruction of past history that can take the form of a psychological interest, which leads to the examination of a text in relation to the psychology of the individual, group or religion, and inquires into the psychological aspects of language, poetry, art, law, etc. (2) The upon-which may be given in an aesthetic interest which subjects the text to a structural analysis and studies the inner form of a work of art (it may do so in conjunction with a religious interest or remaining within the sphere of stylistic considerations). (3) The upon-which may finally be given in an interest in history 'as the living sphere in. which human existence takes place'.[5] This would revolve around 'the question of human existence as the mode of Being of the Self'. Such an inquiry which would initially involve philosophical, religious and poetic texts would always be guided by a tentative understanding of human existence (existential understanding) 'from which alone the categories necessary for any such inquiry would be able to emerge' – for answering questions concerning, for example, 'salvation', the 'meaning' of individual existence, ethical norms of action, the community of man, etc. One would only have to critically examine this '*Vorverständnis*' and to stake it in understanding: in the course of inquiring into a text one should submit to the questions of the text and listen to its claim.

The question whether objectivity of historical phenomena is attainable

B. bases his answer to the question 'whether we can attain objectivity in our knowledge of phenomena, i.e. objectivity in (historical) interpretation' on the above-mentioned insight; it is certainly unattainable in the sense of the natural sciences. B.'s reasoning seems to indicate, in my opinion, a slight confusion; in any case, it does not stand up to critical examination. Historical phenomena have no existence, in Bultmann's view, without an historical subject called upon to comprehend them, 'since past events can turn into historical phenomena only if they become meaningful for a subject that is itself part of, and participating in, history; i.e. if they acquire significance for someone who is connected with them in his historical existence' (!). According to B., then, 'an historical phenomenon contains its own future, where it will reveal itself as that which it is'. It would be acceptable if this referred to historically distant and consequential effects; but then something quite different would be meant than the historical conditioning of a phenomenon by the existence of an observing subject.

B., though, considers a phenomenon to be unequivocal in terms of scientific understanding and not open to the arbitrariness of speculative interpretation; but every historical phenomenon is seen as many-sided in that it is subject to different kinds of inquiry: intellectual history, psychological, sociological or any other kind, as long as it emerges from an historical affinity between interpreter and phenomenon. B. accepts that any such kind of inquiry leads to clear, unequivocal understanding and objective knowledge – i.e. knowledge that is adequate to an object considered from a certain perspective – given that it is the result of a methodically correct interpretation.

To call an inquiry 'subjective' because it has to be chosen by a subject would, however, be pointless. One has only to consider that every phenomenon presents a number of aspects, i.e. it is meaningful from various perspectives and every interpreter chooses the kind of inquiry that will yield the information he is interested in.

It follows that it is plainly absurd to require the interpreter to efface his subjectivity; all he, in fact, has to do is to exclude any personal preference concerning the result. In this respect it is, of course, necessary that interpretation, just as any scientific research, should proceed presuppositionless. Apart from this, understanding pre-necessitates the subject's vividness and the highest possible development of his individuality. B. maintains that, just as the interpretation of poetry and art can succeed only if it is undertaken by someone who is stirred by them, so it is only an interpretation that questions texts about the possibility of our existence as a truly human one 'that can be regarded as the understanding of historical phenomena in its ultimate and highest sense'. He concludes, therefore, 'that the most "subjective" is here the most "objective" interpretation, i.e. only he who is moved by the question about his own existence can hear the message of the text'. This he follows with a remark from Fritz Kaufmann,[6] that the monuments of history 'speak to us from the depth of the reality that created them only if we know, through our openness towards new experiences, of the problematic, of the finally insurmountable destitute and insecurity which form the basis and the abyss of our being-in-the-world'.

The role of the historian's values: value-oriented interpretation

After this exposition of Bultmann's theory I would like to provide a critique of it. It is possible, in my opinion, to evidence in it a slight and inconspicuous shift of meaning; if this were the case, then his arguments would lose their logical conclusiveness. One can accept both an affinity with the object and the vividness of a subject who allows himself to be gripped by it and who inquires into a text in terms of the possibility of human and personal existence as the condition for the possibility of historical interpretation. It is, however, important to know more about that historical 'reproduction' of emotional and psychological contents wherever they become historically relevant. The recourse to 'feelings' makes nonsense of the principle of scientific verification as long as they cannot be transformed into a matter for precise and demonstrable judgments, i.e. into conceptually formed experiences. All it does is to bear witness to the psychological genesis of an hypothesis in the mind of the historian. As long as it remains in the state of personally felt values there can not be the slightest guarantee that these feelings correspond to the ones held by the historical person with whom the historian empathizes. A subjective and emotionally derived speculative interpretation (*Deutung*) of this kind does not constitute historical knowledge about actual complexities; nor is it something else which it, in fact, could be: a value-oriented interpretation.

I shall now refer to Max Weber's[7] theory. A value-oriented interpretation is, for Weber, directed at an object that can be considered from an aesthetic, ethical, intellectual, or any other cultural viewpoint. It is not part of a purely historical representation but is, from an historical standpoint, the 'formation' of an historical individual, i.e. the investigation of values which are realized in that object, and of the individual form in which they are apparent. This effort falls within the philosophy of history and is, indeed, 'subjectivizing' in the sense that we do not regard the validity of these values to be the same as the validity of empirically derived facts. A value-oriented interpretation does not aim at finding out what the people who created the object felt at the time, but what values can and should be found in the object. In the case of the latter, a value-oriented interpretation has the same aims as a normative, i.e. dogmatically oriented, approach such as aesthetics, ethics, or jurisprudence and is itself evaluative. In case of the former, it is based on a dialectical value-analysis which is only concerned with 'possible' value-orientations of the object. Because of this orientation, it fulfils the important function of going beyond the indeterminateness of mere 'empathy' and of moving towards that kind of determinacy which knowledge about the content of individual consciousness is capable of. In contrast to mere 'feeling' and empathy, in which the vividness of the understanding subject becomes apparent, we restrict the term 'value' to something that is able to become an issue, the content of a conscious and articulated 'judgment': i.e. it is something that seeks 'validity' and that requires us to give a value-answer; something the validity of which is recognized by us as a value for us; or that is rejected as such, or is judged in intricately varied ways in an evaluative manner. The attribution of an ethical, aesthetic or juridical value always implies a 'value judgment'. It is of decisive importance for our critical considerations to state that it is the determinacy of its content that lifts the object of our value judgment out of the sphere of mere 'empathy' and on to that of knowledge. The suggestion of shared value judgments concerning a state of affairs would be nonsensical if the central points of a content of a judgment were not understood in an identical way: in some way one always goes beyond mere intuitive feelings when relating something individual to a possible value. It is because an historical individual can only be an artificial unity constructed by value-orientations that 'evaluation' is the normal psychological stage of transition for intellectual understanding: it serves noetic understanding as a means and as a midwife, however much this stage in the genesis of knowledge ought to be striven for by the historian. This way I have – following Weber's hint[8] – indicated the limitations of value-oriented interpretations within the historian's process of cognition, where this subjectivizing element occupies a justifiable place.

Answer to the historical question posed

The questionable character of the grounds on which the subjectivist doctrine of Bultmann seems to be resting becomes indeed apparent upon examination; one then finds them to be either inconclusive or the result of slight shifts of meaning. Firstly, it can be agreed that any view of history depends on the historian's perspective and that each historical phenomenon can be looked at from different points of view; but it is impossible to derive a conclusive objection to the objectivity of historical interpretation from the historicity of the standpoint of the historian. An historical judgment, conditioned as it is by various interests, is merely an answer which the historian is able to give to an intellectual situation and to the 'historical question'

(Droysen) arising out of it. Objective truth can now be glimpsed from any standpoint and point of view within the limits of their perspective; the picture that is arrived at would only be misleading if that particular perspective was claimed to represent the only admissible and legitimate one. The second objection against the objectivity of historical interpretation concerns the so-called 'existential encounter with history'. Here it is possible to evidence a slight shift of meaning which occurs when a condition for the possibility of historical knowledge, viz. the necessary noetic interest and the responsible participation of the historian in history entailed by it,[9] is confused with the object of knowledge itself, and when the question concerning the meaning of an historical phenomenon, in respect of its distant and consequential effects, is confused with a completely different question: that concerning its present *Beutsamkeit* (significance) and relevance in changing historical epochs, and changing historical conceptions about the same phenomenon in view of self-knowledge and self-education.

The meaning of an historical phenomenon and present significance

The shift of meaning referred to in the first case is obvious when it is asserted[10] that 'objectivity of historical knowledge in the sense of absolute and final knowledge is unattainable' – this contention can be accepted as justified owing to the impossibility of ever completing the hermeneutical task; but then it is added that 'neither is it attainable in the sense of getting to know the phenomena as they are authentically in-themselves'. The second assertion that follows on is directed at something quite different in that it negates the being-in-itself of historical phenomena – and this is obviously going too far. The task of interpretation, which depends at all times on the actuality of understanding, can, as a matter of fact, never be regarded as finished and completed because no interpretation, however convincing it may seem at first, can force itself upon mankind as the definitive one. The fact that the hermeneutical task can never be completed entails that the meaning contained within texts, monuments and fragments is constantly reborn through life and is for ever transformed in a chain of rebirths; but this does not exclude the fact that the objectivated meaning-content still remains an objectivation of the creative force of an Other, to which the interpreter should seek access, not in an arbitrary way, but with the help of controllable guidelines. Here, the mind of an Other speaks to us not directly but across space and time through transformed matter that is charged with mental energy – which makes it possible for us to approach the meaning of this product, since it is part of the human spirit and is, to speak with Husserl, born of the same transcendental subjectivity; but it nevertheless remains a steadfast, self-contained existence that can confront us owing to the fact that here the mind of an Other has objectivated itself in meaning-full forms.

Next, the second case of a shift in meaning, viz. the failure to distinguish between the meaning of historical phenomena on the one hand, and the significance of these phenomena for the present and for our responsibility for the future on the other, is no less apparent when it is asserted[11] that 'historical phenomena are what they are, not in isolation but only in relation to the future'; 'a future (it is said) in which the phenomenon will emerge as it really is' (an assertion that would make sense in view of the consequential effects of this phenomenon). But then it is added that the question is about the 'meaning (more accurately: significance) of historical events of our past in relation to our present: a present which is responsible for the future'. As it is stated, 'only the historian, who is open towards historical phenomena on account of his responsibility for the future, is in a position to understand history'[12] (in this sense the 'most subjective interpretation would also be the most objective'). This, of course, is a paradox which we are familiar with from earlier discussions and which is irresolvable.

Dialogue and monologue

In contrast to these views I would make the following remarks: historical phenomena do not acquire meaning if they are considered in isolation but (in accordance with the hermeneutical canon of the totality of interpretation already referred to) only within the meaning-context of its distant and consequential effects, as far as they can be assessed; this kind of meaning can be found by the historian in a completed form if sufficient time has passed since the phenomenon occurred. If, in contrast, it is asserted that the true essence of a phenomenon 'will be visible only at the end of history',[13] one then falls victim of a confusion between the point of view of an historical interpretation and the standpoint of an eschatological meaning-inference. It is, indeed, only from the standpoint of such a meaning-inference that the significance of a phenomenon for the present is situationally determined; this is because it only makes sense for a present, 'which is responsible for the future', to ask after any present-day significance and to regard it as the product of a value-positing meaning-inference that is conditioned by the position of the observer. If one identifies the definitive meaning of an historical phenomenon (how it really was) that is given and only needs to be found, with its significance for the present and the future of an observer, which is conditioned by meaning-inference, then it can easily be discerned what, in fact, lies at the heart of this 'existential encounter with history'. The dialogue that should occur between the historian and the mind objectivated in his sources would fail completely and turn into a mere monologue because one partner would be missing altogether: the partner that should be represented by the text as the unchangeable mind of an Other, without whom any interpretative procedure cannot be envisaged at all. Dialogue therefore turns into monologue: the interpreter who should inquire into the meaning of phenomena (meaning-full forms) allows himself indeed to be questioned by the text. Is it still possible to regard such a procedure as an interpretation? I shall leave this question open for the moment.

Historical interpretation and eschatological meaning-inference

Since we have distinguished between interpretation and meaning-inference, and have used this distinction as a lever for the above critique, it is now necessary to elucidate the concept of meaning-inference and consider the difference between eschatology, where it comes into effect, and the study of history. The comprehending potential of mind is actualized in both procedures – even though they fulfil different requirements. Meaning-inference takes place in relation to the whole of existence – which is not the case with interpretation – but mind engages in this activity in a higher and more exact way in relation to objects of its own kind. In relation to the world, the meaning is inferred randomly; but where man is concerned it is no longer accidental. In the case of the world, man is not aware of the meaning he infers, nor does he fulfil any moral obligation placed upon him by it. In the case of his fellow-man, however, he is obliged to do justice to their esteem of values, not so much in his actions nor even in his way of thinking, but merely through looking, participating, appreciating or in any other way of attending. Man can either respond to the demand for inner justice in the answer he gives to values or he can fail to do so. He has not merely the power to infer meaning, but he can do so by following his own free decision. He perceives the call, which he receives as an obligation that concerns him personally and which requires his effort in doing justice, as a moral claim which he can fulfil dutifully or sin against. Man cannot sin against wordly goods as he passes them by inattentively, but he can do so against his fellow-man. To fail here is not merely the missing of an opportunity (a loss that is obvious when one follows Nietzsche in thinking that 'the whole world is full of beautiful things but nevertheless very poor in beautiful moments and the opening-up of these things');[14] it is rather a case of man wronging his fellow-man, who then feels ignored, pushed aside and excluded from real existence, the living community of minds.

What, then, can be said about eschatological meaning-inference? What is meant by it? Here, meaning-inference concerns the '*Verbum Dei* as *viva vox*', the living word of God. Since the eschaton is positioned beyond historical time, it could appear that the historical passage of time is immaterial to eschatological meaning-inference; but this is not so.

I am not in a position to give a judgment on eschatological problems; but the point of issue here is the demarcation of competence between two intellectual activities, one of which I am familiar with but not the other; the latter, however, lays claim on the former and thereby endangers its independence and questions the objectivity of its results. How, then, can one draw a line of demarcation between eschatology and history? Since eschatology does not wish to be a doctrine about an atemporal, other-worldly state of affairs but has as its object precisely the activity of God on human existence, and because man does exist within progressing time, eschatology has to incorporate the temporal course of human existence; time, as chronological progression, consequently enters the field of vision of eschatology. But how is Bultmann's postulated polarity of presence and transcendence to be understood in this context? Upon a closer look, historical progression seems to be of only secondary importance to Bultmann's eschatology. History can never provide the framework around which eschatological events can crystallize; these events occur, in fact, within existence, which cannot be determined by reference to history alone. The presence of Christ, the Parousia, is not limited by history according to Bultmann's Protestant viewpoint; this, however, does not make it something that is pregiven in the essence of man, but rather a continuing and specific encounter. The eschatological situation is characterized by the question whether one's existence is open towards the 'On-coming', or whether it remains tied to itself; through its factual openness (towards the future), existence is no longer 'transitory' but responsible and able to decide. Faith has to prove itself in the course of time: it is a venturing, meaning-inferring anticipation of the future; the trusting belief that what has already become real in respect of Christ still remains for faith beyond the struggle.[15]

Bultmann would consider this meaning-inferring approach of eschatology as completely identical with the quest for knowledge in the study of history; only the historian, who is moved by his participation in history – i.e. who is open to historical phenomena on the basis of his responsibility for the future – would be in a position to understand history. In Bultmann's view, knowledge of history and self-knowledge would correspond to one another in a characteristic way.[16] Bultmann establishes this peculiar correspondence and assimilation in the following way: self-knowledge is awareness of one's responsibility towards the future, and the act of self-knowing is by no means a contemplative and merely theoretical attitude but at the same time an act of decision-making – just as the venturing anticipation of the future lies at the heart of eschatology. If this is accepted, then the historicality of human existence would be completely understood only when human existence is seen as a life of responsibility for the future – and as a life within decision.

If that was the case, it would follow that historicality is not just a natural attribute of human individuals: it should be seized and realized as an opportunity that is offered to them. Any human being who lives without self-knowledge and awareness of responsibility would, according to this view, not only be someone who has failed in his task to infer meaning, but he would have delivered himself into the hands of the relativity of the historical conditions of his environment, and thereby represent 'an historical Being to a far lower degree'. As Bultmann concludes, following Collingwood, 'true historicality means "to live a life of responsibility", and history is a call towards historicality'. The consequence that necessarily follows from these considerations can be found in a statement that could be considered the theme of the whole issue under discussion:[17]

'In this kind of understanding the traditional opposition between the understanding subject and the object understood vanishes. Only as a participant and as, himself, an historical Being can the historian understand history. In such understanding of history, man understands himself. Human nature cannot be grasped through introspection; instead, what man is can only be seen in history which reveals the possibilities of human existence through the wealth of historical creations.'

The threat to objectivity

This contention which raises a completely new problematic and which would lead to the negation of objectivity we, as historians, have to oppose with all firmness. Our outline has shown that the subjectivist position rests on a shift of meaning which identifies the hermeneutical process of historical interpretation with a situationally determined meaning-inference (as it is the case in eschatological meaning-inference) and which has the effect of confounding a condition for the possibility with the object of that process; as a result, the fundamental canon of the hermeneutical autonomy of the object is altogether removed from the work of the historian.

In this hermeneutical approach, the danger of confusion increases with the possibility of deriving only what is meaningful and reasonable to oneself and of missing what is different and specific in the Other or, as the case may be, bracketing it as a presumed myth. The objection to this is obvious: the texts which are approached with a meaning-inferring 'pre-understanding' (*Vorverständnis*) are not to be used to confirm already held opinions; we have to suppose, instead, that they have something to say that we could not know by ourselves and which exists independently of our meaning-inference.[18] It is here that the questionable character of the subjectivist position comes to full light; it is obviously influenced by contemporary existentialist philosophy and tends towards the confounding of interpretation and meaning-inference and the removing of the canon of the autonomy of the object, with the consequence of putting into doubt the objectivity of the results of interpretative procedures in all the human sciences (*Geisteswissenschaften*). It is my opinion that it is our duty as guardians and practitioners of the study of history to protect this kind of objectivity and to provide evidence of the epistemological condition of its possibility.

On theological hermeneutics and the 'demythologization' of the *Kerygma*

The misunderstanding mentioned has been brought to light and partially resolved by some corrections Professor Ebeling[19] has made recently to the current views about hermeneutics. In order to distinguish between general and specific-theological hermeneutics he proceeds from Bultmann's point that the different 'upon-which' of the inquiry necessitates a specifically theological form of questioning that leads, owing to its particular structures and criteria, to an exegetic and dogmatic understanding of the text. This postulates, however, a demonstrable connection with a general theory of understanding; the question is, therefore, how such a connection is to be conceived. One could formulate the problem in a different way: how are the Word and Understanding related to one another; and further: what is it that is finally constitutive of hermeneutics? The answer Ebeling gives is the opposite of what is usually thought: the primary phenomenon of understanding is not the understanding of language but the understanding through language. The word is, therefore, not the 'object of understanding' but that which enables and mediates understanding; the word itself has, according to Ebeling, a 'hermeneutic function'[20] – not as the mere expression of an individual but as a message which requires two human beings (as in the case of love), as a communication that appeals to experience and leads to experience through its 'upon-which' and 'into-what'.

In this way, it is the word event itself that is the object of hermeneutics because understanding becomes possible whenever communication takes place 'upon' and 'into' something. As a mediation of understanding, hermeneutics has to reflect upon the conditions of the possibility of understanding, i.e. the essence of the word. As a theory of understanding, hermeneutics has to be a theory of the word: a theory that regards the word, which enables understanding to take place, as constitutive when it comes to orienting oneself on states of affairs. Drawing on the Greek language Ebeling regards hermeneutics as the theory of Logos since 'the Logos that dwells within object and knower provides the condition for the possibility of understanding'.[21] He accordingly defines theological hermeneutics as the 'theory of the Word of God'.[22] Since this word is to be hermeneutically relevant, the essential structure of the Word of God should lead to the structure of understanding characteristic of theology. The question now arises as to what kind of understanding it is that emerges here. Ebeling asks himself the question:[23] should one apply the same strict criteria to the concept of the Word of God as in the case of an inter-human word event (this is the view favoured by Ebeling), or is the Word of God a mythical concept and therefore only of symbolic character with its speech structure being that of mythical speech? In Ebeling's opinion, the mythical as such cannot be brought into connection with an idea of hermeneutics that is rooted in the Greek concept of Logos. In relation to the mythical, hermeneutics would, in his opinion, have to turn into 'demythologization'. The question now arises: if such demythologization were to be unavoidable in order to understand, would not the *kerygma* be translated in such a procedure from the language of God into human language and thereby be transformed? And would we not have to accept certain curtailments and distortions as is often the case in translations? It is a procedure that one would like to reject on account of its arbitrariness and unclear pre-suppositions.[24]

In any case, the point I am trying to make is that hermeneutics, as the mediation of understanding, does not imply a *reductio ad rationem*, i.e. an Enlightenment-inspired 'rationalization' of the text to be interpreted, since that would no longer be an interpretation but an evaluative meaning-inference! One could here cite two parallel procedures, both concerned to a high degree with practical issues: one, where the biblical text, expounded in a sermon, renders hermeneutical services for the understanding of contemporary experiences; two, juridical hermeneutics concretizes abstract legal norms for contemporary jurisdiction. These issues I cannot, however, deal with within the limits set for these hermeneutical considerations.

We shall now turn our attention to the above-mentioned epistemological conditions for the possibility of objectivity in the process of interpretation. The above comments about the canon of the actuality of understanding have by no means exhausted the examination of those hermeneutical guidelines (*canones*) that relate to the subject of interpretation – as Bultmann seems to think. Spontaneity is, certainly, indispensable on the part of the interpreter; but it must not be imposed upon the object from outside since that would lead to the curtailment of its autonomy and, ultimately, endanger the cognizance of the object which here takes the forms, essentially, of comprehension and re-cognition.

The recent turn towards the historicality of understanding

Such danger is posed not only from the side of those theologians who are intending to 'demythologize' the Christian *kerygma* but also from the side of some scholars who are under the influence of Heidegger's existentialism and who regard the 'existential foundation of the hermeneutic circle' as a new development of the greatest importance. The danger apparent here is even greater since the new turn towards the 'historicality of understanding' cannot be contained through a delimitation of competence between historical interpretation and eschatological meaning-inference.

A recently published book provides us with the possibility of evidencing the position of Heideggerian existentialism *vis-à-vis* historical hermeneutics; I am referring to Hans-Georg Gadamer's *Outline of a Philosophical Hermeneutic. Truth and Method.* The author's negative point of departure is a sharp criticism of romanticist hermeneutics and its application to history; I cannot here discuss these criticisms but they seem to be based on a biased view that leads to some misunderstanding about Schleiermacher's hermeneutics and to what is, in my view, an unjust assessment. At this point I am only dealing with the positive point of departure which the author derived from Heidegger's exposition of the so-called fore-structure of understanding and which he employs to elevate the historicality of understanding (i.e. the historical conditioning of the process of interpretation) to the principle of hermeneutics – which leads him to the paradox of having to regard prejudices as 'conditions of understanding'. In the author's view,[25] historical hermeneutics should commence with the dissolution of the abstract opposition between tradition and the study of history, between the historical process and the knowledge of it. The efficacy of continuing tradition and the efficacy of historical research constitute a unity, the analysis of which always arrives at a web of reciprocal action. What is required is to recognize the moment of tradition in historical activity and to determine its hermeneutic productivity. Understanding itself should not so much be regarded as a subjective activity but as an entering into the process of tradition in which past and present constantly mediated each other.[26] What, then, are the consequences of the hermeneutic condition of participating in tradition for understanding?[27]

Prejudice as the condition of understanding

The circular relationship that is in evidence here reminds Gadamer of the hermeneutical rule that one should understand the whole from its parts and the parts from the whole. In this way, the anticipation of meaning, by which is meant the whole of tradition, would be brought to explicit understanding in that the parts, which are determined by the whole, themselves determine that whole.[28] The author opines that 'understanding that proceeds in full methodical awareness should seek not just to follow its anticipations but to become aware of them in order to control them, and to be then able to gain a correct understanding from the things themselves'. This is what Heidegger means when he asks that the scientific theme be 'secured' from the things themselves in the working out of *Vorhabe* (something we have in advance), *Vorsicht* (something we see in advance), and *Vorgriff* (something we grasp in advance) – thereby distorting Husserl's famous formula.

In accordance with this train of thought, Gadamer[29] sees the hermeneutic significance of temporal distance in that it wards off any excess resonance pertaining to actuality and filters out the true meaning, whereby this distance is envisaged to be in a process of continuous 'extension'. This distance has a positive hermeneutic effect, according to Gadamer,[30] as it 'allows those prejudices to die off which are of a particularistic nature and allows those to come to the fore which enable veracious understanding' (the interpreter is always dealing with prejudices and it is the hermeneutic task to 'separate the true prejudices from the false ones'). A hermeneutically trained historical consciousness would 'raise to awareness those prejudices that guide and condition the process of understanding so that the content of tradition can mark itself off as "different opinion" and claim recognition of its validity'. What stimulates a prejudice that has so far remained unnoticed to come into the open? Gadamer answers:[31] 'the encounter with tradition'; he believes that 'anything that attracts our understanding (i.e. interpretation) will already have had to assert itself in its otherness'. Understanding (Gadamer always means interpretation) commences with 'something addressing us' which necessitates 'in principle, the suspension of our own prejudices'. Seen from a logical point, this would have 'the structure of a question'; a question the essence of which Gadamer[32] sees as 'the lying-open,* and

*Gadamer (1975, p. 283) refers to *Offenlegen* (opening-up, laying-open); in Betti (p. 41) here it is quoted as *Offenliegen* (lying-open).

keeping-open, of possibilities'. The author charges historism – which demands the 'disregarding of ourselves' in order to bring to bear the Other in place of ourselves – with 'naivety' because it 'evades dialectical reflection and forgets its own historicality by relying on its methodical procedures'. By contrast, better understanding would, according to Gadamer, 'include reflection upon its own historicality'. Only then would it 'not chase after the phantom of an historical object, which is the object of continuing research, but, instead, learn to recognize the object as another part of the self and thereby come to know both'.

One could now try to refute the dialectical procedure suggested by the author with the help of Hegel's dialectic. This is, however, not my intention. I merely wish to show how the loss of objectivity, which is the result of Gadamer's theory, cannot be offset by the subject becoming self-aware of his own historicality; in addition, the proposed yardstick for distinguishing between true and false prejudices – a yardstick and criterion of correctness which he would like to call 'fore-conception of perfection' – rests on self-deception, i.e. it does not provide a reliable criterion for the correctness of understanding.

The existential foundation of the hermeneutical circle

Let us now follow Gadamer's argument[33] more closely. The precurrent 'expectation of meaning' of the interpreter of a text has to be adjusted, should the text require it, in such a way 'that the text acquires its unity of meaning from another expectation of meaning'. This would lead[34] to 'the movement of understanding from the whole to the part and back to the whole'; the task here would be 'to extend the unity of the understood meaning in concentric circles'. 'Harmony of all details with the whole' would be 'the appropriate criterion of the correct understanding'. But now Gadamer thinks,[35] by giving hermeneutics the task of 'achieving an agreement that may be lacking or be disturbed', that it would be 'the aim of all communication and understanding to come to an agreement about something', i.e. a substantive agreement. Here he notices[36] a fundamental difference between Schleiermacher's ideal of objectivity, that fails to take account of the concretion of the historical consciousness of the interpreter in his hermeneutical theory, and Heidegger's existential foundation of the hermeneutic circle, which, in Gadamer's view, 'represents a decisive turning-point'. Schleiermacher's theory requires the interpreter to adopt completely the perspective of the author so that he can dissolve any unfamiliar and disturbing elements within the text. 'In contrast to this, Heidegger describes the circle of whole and part in such a way that the understanding of the text is permanently directed by the anticipatory movement of the pre-understanding.' The anticipation of meaning that is thought to be directing our understanding of the text is, according to Gadamer,[37] 'based on the commonality that unites us with tradition and that is constantly being developed'. According to this view, the circle 'describes an ontological moment of understanding'. It follows that all attempts at understanding are guided by the presupposition that 'only that is understandable which forms a perfect unity of meaning'. This presupposition, that guides all understanding, Gadamer refers to as the 'fore-conception of perfection'.

The question concerning the correctness of understanding

The obvious difficulty with the hermeneutical method proposed by Gadamer seems to lie, for me, in that it enables a substantive agreement between text and reader – i.e. between the apparently easily accessible meaning of a text and the subjective conception of the reader – to be formed without, however, guaranteeing the correctness of understanding; for that it would be necessary that the understanding arrived at corresponded fully to the meaning underlying the text as an objectivation of mind. Only then would the objectivity of the result be guaranteed on the basis of a reliable process of interpretation. It can easily be demonstrated that the proposed method cannot claim to achieve objectivity and that it is only concerned with the internal coherence and conclusiveness of the desired understanding – one only needs to follow the advice given by the author. When reading a text we proceed, in his opinion, from the presupposition of perfection; only when this presupposition is found to be irredeemable or inadequate, i.e. when the text is found to be incomprehensible, do we query it and 'maybe question tradition and try to find out how to remedy it'[38] in order to arrive at an understanding of the content. It follows that the adopted 'fore-conception of perfection' would itself always be one of content, too. Consequently, 'what is presupposed is not only an immanent unity of meaning which directs the reader, but his understanding is always guided by transcendent expectations of meaning which spring from the relation to the truth of what is being said'. By way of contrast, Gadamer thinks that 'it is only the failure of the attempt to accept what is being said as true that leads us to try and "understand" the text – historically, or psychologically – as the meaning of an Other'. The 'fore-conception of perfection would, therefore, not only include the formal demand that the text should express its content perfectly (i.e. clearly and coherently), but also that what is being said is the complete truth'. This, then, is Gadamer's view.

His exposition presupposes that the interpreter, who is called upon to understand, claims a monopoly of truth – if not as an actual possession then, at least, in the form of a checking device. In my view, however, the interpreter should be content to comprehend and accept the differing opinion of the text as something different – even if it should contain inaccurate conceptions. The author himself[39] is forced to concede that indubitable exceptions to the supposed 'grasping-in-advance' (*Vorgriff*) do exist; so, for example, in the case of a disarranged or codified piece of writing where the disarrangement can only be deciphered if the interpreter is in possession of some factual knowledge that can serve as a key. If one, furthermore, considers that human use of language generally contains excess meaning in that it is guided by unarticulated value suppositions and is, therefore, elliptical, then one has to abandon the presumed pre-supposition concerning the conciseness of speech and generalize the exception.

In addition, Gadamer's position,[40] where the case of historical interpretation is concerned, confounds the differing role of the historian of law with that of the lawyer whose task it is to apply the law, by failing to recognize the fundamental difference in interest that guides them; he is also led to regard juridical hermeneutics, because of its relatedness to the present, 'as the model for the relationship between past and present',[41] that should be emulated by the historical *Geisteswissenschaften*. Gadamer does admit that the historian who intends to find out the historical significance of a law is dealing with a legal creation that has to be understood in juridical terms. But he would like to regard the special case of an historian who considers a legal document that is still valid today as exemplary for the way in which we should view 'our relationship with any tradition'. He feels that 'the historian who tries to understand a law by reference to the situation of its historical origin cannot disregard its juridical development: it would provide him with the questions he might like to direct at historical tradition'. Very well, but these are only distant and consequential effects that do not necessarily remain effective into the present and that, in any case, should neither directly influence the historian's practical engagement with the present nor his stance. For this reason, all of Gadamer's questions[42] which he poses immediately after this statement have to be answered in the negative. He asks: is it not the case with any text that it has to be understood in terms of what it says, and does that not mean that a transposition is required every time? And does not this transformation always take the form of a mediation with the present? We answer with a decisive 'No'. It is true that the inversion of the process of creation in interpretation requires the transposition of meaning from the original perspective of the author into the subjectivity of the interpreter. That, however, does not imply a 'transformation' that has to be conceived of as a 'mediation with the present'. The present furthers and stimulates the interest in understanding, but it has no place in the transposition of the 'subjective stance'. The shift of meaning that intrudes into the conclusion referred to is, in my opinion, apparent in the following line of argument.[43] The object of historical understanding does not consist of events but of their significance (which is related to the present), i.e. their significance for today.[44] Such understanding would consequently not adequately be described if one talked about an object existing in-itself which is approached by a subject. More accurately, it would be the essence of historical understanding that on-coming tradition influences the present and has to be understood in this mediation of past and present – or even as this mediation of past and present.

Historical understanding as mediation of past and present

If that was the case, then juridical hermeneutics would not be an exception but would be in a position to hand back to historical hermeneutics its full range of issues and thereby reconstitute its former unity in which jurist and theologian come to meet the philologist. That this is not so, however, is apparent from the basically differing approach of the jurist which is required of us when we move from the application of the law to the contemplative consideration of the history of law. The hermeneutical demand to understand the content of a text from within the concrete circumstances of its origin[45] is regarded by the historian of law only as the teleological evaluation of the content of a law which is in no way directed at the present or is intending to exercise any immediate normative influence on present-day modes of behaviour. The relationship to the present does have, in fact, quite a different meaning for the historian.

Another questionable conclusion of Gadamer's[46] is that of the demand made upon the historian, in contrast to the philologist, to interpret tradition in a way different from what would be required by the sources themselves, i.e. to inquire into the reality evident behind the texts and their sense which they unintendedly and unconsciously reveal; he thereby fails to recognize that today philologists, too, are required to locate a text within a larger context, and that their encounter with a text is inspired by elements adopted from a model for their work which implies a following and putting-to-use.[47] Gadamer believes that the relationship between the historian and his texts – i.e. his historical sources – corresponds to that obtaining between an investigative judge in a trial and a witness; he treats his historical evidence in the way the former treats a legal witness. In both cases, evidence 'is an aid for arriving at a finding'; it is not itself the actual object but merely provides the material for the task at hand: for the judge, to come to a finding – for the historian, to determine the historical significance of an event within the totality of his historical self-awareness![48]

It follows that the difference between them would shrink to a question of degree! The use of historical methods would always be preceded by the really important things! Thanks to a characteristic shift in the meaning of the intention of a text, the author seems to regard, despite all appearance, the problem of 'application' to be crucial for the more complicated case of historical understanding, too.[49] In each and every reading[50] 'there occurs an application, so that he who reads a text will himself be included in the meaning he derives from it'. He, therefore, acknowledges an internal unity of history and philology, not in the historical critique of tradition as such, but in the fact that both accomplish the task of application which differs only relatively: in his opinion one would only have 'to recognize the awareness of effective-history in all the hermeneutical activity of philologist and historian'!

Call for an applicative use of interpretation

This means that historians and all guardians and practitioners of historical hermeneutics, who are concerned about the objectivity of interpretation, are called upon to oppose such a presumptuous self-assertion of subjectivity that would demote the process of historical interpretation to a mere mediation of past and present. The supposed analogy of historical and normative-juridical hermeneutics is indeed based on self-deception. That the application of the law demands a legal interpretation that is related to the present and to contemporary society follows by necessity out of the function of the law as the ordering of co-existence in a human community. It is part of its essence, therefore, that it should achieve a concretion of the law; it should be practically relevant in that it is called upon to provide a legally adequate direction and directive for communal existence and behaviour. The same consideration applies to the theologian and his interpretation of the Scriptures on account of their directive, i.e. normative, task: the practical activity of the community of believers requires this interpretation to be of applicative use for moral issues.[51]

Only justified in normatively oriented interpretation

All this is, however, quite different in the case of historical interpretation. Its task is purely contemplative. It is concerned with the investigation of the finalized meaning of a segment of the past. In accordance with the hermeneutical canon of totality one has to consider all distant and consequential effects of the historical events in question, given that sufficient time has elapsed – but a transposition of their meaning on to the present is out of the question. On the contrary, it is precisely phenomena relating to the dispute between past and present, such as transposition onto the present, appropriation, assimilation, re-interpretation and transformation of parts of traditional works which have not been understandable, that characterize an unhistorical position towards the past – however productive misunderstandings may be when they are motivated by the attempt to do justice to creations of the past by regarding them as 'tools of life'. Productive completion, transposition, development, are all efforts at applying knowledge that serve and enhance the life of a community. But their sphere of justified activity has to be restricted to the field of practical co-existence. Where, however, historical interpretation is concerned, which is the only dimension of relevance here, its accuracy and competence has to be categorically negated. Procedures of this kind are obviously not suited to lead us to historical truth; on the contrary, they open the door to subjective arbitrariness and threaten to cover up or misrepresent historical truth and to distort it, even if only unconsciously. The historian who has arrived at an awareness of the historicity of understanding will be more modest and refrain from any 'applicative effort'. Anyone who has undertaken historical research will realize that the critique of the sincerity, honesty, and reliability of historical documents belong to a completely different dimension.

The partner in a discussion should, as a point of honour, not end his critical remarks without extending his chivalrous thanks to his opponents for their stimulating contributions. Every conscientious scientific criticism brings the disputants closer together and leads to self-criticism and better self-knowledge. Even when we are successful in enlightening our opponent and lead him towards self-reflection, something else will have happened, maybe unnoticed: we have changed ourselves through his help and have been led to self-reflection. We should, accordingly, not engage in a direct fight but make sure that our influence on future events balances the one exerted by him.

It is in this unbiased attitude that I shall receive the further comments that Professor Gadamer has announced and which will soon appear in the *Philosophische Rundschau*.[52] I thank him and our mutual friend Walter Hellebrand for the written clarifications I have received from them. These friendly clarifications are very valuable as they make clear the intention and theme of the new philosophical hermeneutic. In order to pose the question correctly it has to be mentioned, however, that the epistemological question – formulated in an exemplary form by Kant's pioneering *Critique of Pure Reason* – is not a *quaestio facti* but a *quaestio iuris*:* it is concerned with the problem of justification which does not aim at ascertaining what actually happens in the activity of thought apparent in interpretation but which aims at finding out what one should do – i.e. what one should aim for in the task of interpretation, what methods to use and what guidelines to follow in the correct execution of this task. After our critical excursions we now return to our considerations of the canons of hermeneutics.

The canon of the hermeneutical correspondence of meaning (meaning-adequacy in understanding)

If it is the case that mind alone can address mind, then it follows that only a mind of equal stature and congenial disposition can

---

*The issues posed by this point will be more fully discussed in the context of the work of Gadamer and Apel's 'normative-methodologically relevant philosophic hermeneutic'. (JB)

gain access to, and understand, another mind in a meaningfully adequate way. An actual interest in understanding is by itself not enough, however lively it may be, to establish the required communication; what is needed, in addition, is an intellectual open-mindedness that enables the interpreter to adopt the most suitable position for his investigation and understanding. This involves a stance that is both ethically and theoretically reflective and which can be identified as unselfishness and humble self-effacement, as it is apparent in the honest and determined over-coming of one's own prejudices and certain attitudes that stand in the way of unbiased understanding; seen more positively, this stance could be characterized as a broad viewpoint and wide horizon, an ability that creates a congenial and closely related outlook in relation to the object of interpretation.

This requirement is apparent in the fourth hermeneutical canon which is connected with the above-mentioned third one and, like it, concerns the subject of interpretation. I propose to call it the canon of meaning-adequacy in understanding or the canon of the hermeneutical correspondence of meaning (or harmonization). According to this canon, the interpreter should strive to bring his own lively actuality into the closest harmony with the stimulation that he receives from the object in such a way that the one and the other resonate in a harmonious way.

This aspect of the correspondence of meaning is especially apparent in the field of historical interpretation where it initially led to self-reflection. It is here that individuality, as it is expressed in an historical personality, should resonate with the personality of the interpreter if it is to be re-cognized by the latter. If this personality exhibits a unity in regard of the kind and degree to which the content of given objectivations are joined together, then it is precisely the congenial affinity with such a kind and degree of synthesis that presents the historian with one of the conditions for the inner reconstruction of a personality.

The canon of the harmonization of understanding we are here referring to is itself of general import and is relevant for every type of interpretation. If we focus on historical interpretation we find two possible orientations: one, the interpretation of sources of historical knowledge or of historical remnants; two, the interpretation of modes of behaviour requiring an historical interest – which itself varies with the problems the historian sets out to solve – for the inquiry into the life of individuals or social communities. In our opinion it is here necessary to make a distinction according to whether the investigation into historical material, and the evaluation of the historical activity in question, is conducted solely in terms of psychological, practical, ethical and political categories – as it is the case in biography, political history and the history of custom and ethics – or whether the historical investigation and evaluation requires a problematic of a higher order, owing to the character as a *product* of the forms of life in question.

The character as a product of historical forms of life leads to a problematic of a higher order

This is the case when the historical analysis of structures is concerned with such objects as: works of art in their various forms, linguistic works of art in all their kinds and types, different branches of science, legal constructs, economic systems, social and religious forms of organizations of societies and communities. Whenever these cultural values, which are generated by people within their living community, become the object of an historical analysis of their structure, then the process of interpretation of a part of historical existence which, after all, is the life of culture, requires a higher order and more complex problematic. The latter takes different forms in the history of art, language, literature, science, law, social, economic and religious structures, but it provides interpretation in these various fields with a common trait owing to the character as a product of these forms of life which sharply distinguishes these interpretations from general historical interpretation.

The objects of this type of interpretation are meaning-full forms with their definite character as a product and they can be regarded as belonging to the history of culture and mind in all its many forms. In order to identify successfully the type of interpretation under consideration here, it is necessary, in our opinion, to refer back to a distinction made for the first time in hermeneutical theory by the great Schleiermacher which subsequently seems to have been forgotten. In the sphere of psychological interpretation in the wider sense, Schleiermacher differentiates between the psychological aspect in the narrower sense and technical interpretation. He, of course, uses the term 'technical' in its narrow sense in the context of hermeneutics as referring to the technique of expression characteristic of a work of art – a technique that guides the reflection (meditation) and construction (composition) of a linguistic work of art; he consequently does not use it in the wider sense of a semantic or representational technique which is part of meaning-full constructs different from the written word. At the same time, it is clear that the technical, i.e. morphological, moment plays a more important role in interpretation and should be applied in a wider sphere in comparison with this narrow conception. Once it is recognized that each act of understanding takes place in the form of an inversion of an act of speech or thought, in so far as one tries to trace retrospectively the train of thought that provided the basis for the linguistic act and to raise it to consciousness, then it becomes clear that one can derive from this process of inversion the general principle of the correspondence of meaning obtaining between the process of the creation of a mental product and the process of its interpretation. One then recognizes the deep truth of Vico's statement that 'the whole world of culture has, for certain, been produced by the physical and mental activity of man, and for this reason one can, and, in fact, has to, find its principles and regularities within the modes of existence of the spirit of these self-same people'. As a matter of fact, the variegated and typical forms which human culture brings forth in the course of its historical development in the various cultural spheres – art, language, literature, science, law, economic and social structure – have their own logos, their own law of formation and development which, at the same time, is the law of a structure and a meaning-context. In the light of this lawfulness, a form of interpretation becomes possible which aims to understand the meaning of these cultural formations in view of their respective structural problems as regards typical, recurring factors as well as individual ones, both of which are historically conditioned.

Technical–morphological interpretation in view of the problems of formation to be solved

One could call such an interpretation that regards the various cultural products as solutions to morphological problems of formation – even though the artist himself may not have been aware that there was such a problem – a technical interpretation with an historical task, if one wanted to use Schleiermacher's criterion and expression. It would be more appropriate, from the point of view of the contemporary use of language, to call this kind of interpretation 'morphological' (Fritz Wagner[53] has recently suggested this term).

When one refers to 'technical' in the context of the history of civilization, it is usually material progress that one thinks of without, at the same time, including the higher forms of objective spirit within this concept. But here we are confronted with an arbitrary restriction. It is indeed possible in interpretation to employ a technique that aims at discovering the specific laws of formation of various products of mental forms of life and systems of culture from which human civilization derives nourishment; this technique could be used in the kind of interpretation that would want to re-cognize and reconstruct from the inside such products in their generation and formation, in their style, in the inner coherence of their structure and in their conclusiveness, and which attempted to give an over-view of the historical development of styles. If the evaluations dominant in consecutive stylistic epochs form a mental horizon which is determined by an historically conditioned perspective, then one may assume that the activities of feeling, comprehending and visualizing are directed by hermeneutical guidelines, not only in linguistic expressions but also in all other mental spheres of life and systems of culture; even though these activities are not subjected to atemporal and unchangeable categories they are, nevertheless, directed by hermeneutical guidelines of the kind that are part of the relationship between man and his environment, and which change in line with their historically conditioned context. The problem confronting the historian therefore consists in finding out whether these manifold changes in conception, modes of representation, feeling and thinking, theories and doctrines, institutions and structures, are subject to a developmental law and to such developmental tendencies as can be investigated with phenomenological means, and especially whether there are tendencies that make apparent a succession of styles.

Indeed, on the level of objective spirit there are operative laws of development that cannot be comprehended through psychological interpretation alone. In the history of art, literature, science, jurisprudence, economic and social systems, historical facts are not limited merely to the individual experience of given personalities; they rather constitute an entity that embodies a value, i.e. it contains meaning, value and its character as a product. It is necessary, above all, to understand its inner unity of style and the close relationship of its meaning with other, connected, values and products from within itself, independently of the conditioning circumstance of its appearance in time and of the chronological relationship to earlier and later times. If one wishes to arrive at the historical context and line of development that exhibits the main sequence of style, then one is faced, from the beginning, with the task of having to understand the character of the product, its conception and structure in relation to the particular lawfulness that objectively underlies the product, and of having to reconstruct the spiritual web of meaning into which it is woven.

Technical–morphological interpretation, as it has been proposed, contributes to a correct disposition towards historical knowledge in so far as it considers the various creations of the imagination, of thought and of active life, as solutions to problems which, in a wider sense, could be referred to as morphological problems of formation. A technical–artistic interpretation of pictorial works of art, for example, serves in the preparation of a history of the various arts from the point of view of their respective problems of expression. Equally, a linguistic, i.e. technical–literary, interpretation of linguistic works of art contributes to the construction of a history of language and literature with reference to the various language-areas and types of literature. Despite the criticisms levelled against it, such a history possesses a justifiable orienting function to the extent to which it corresponds to the various types of linguistic communication as they are determined by the direction and purpose of the language used in communicating one's own thoughts to one's fellow-men. Similar considerations apply to technical–scientific interpretation in the history of law and of economics as well as to sociological interpretation. The interpretation of theories and systems can equally serve a history of the scientific problems dealt with in the various areas of knowledge. Technical–juridical interpretation, that concerns itself with concept-formation in dogmatics, is, similarly, interested in presenting the history of law in respect of the inner logic of legal constructs and principles. Technical–sociological, or technical–economic interpretation of social and economic systems, finally, serves the history of social and economic structures; the task here is to recognize tendentially constant relationships between historical facts, which may be chronologically separate, by trying to bring together morphological problems of social existence which emerge in given areas of investigation according to perspectives which correspond to a specific interest within historical or comparative research.

In this way, specialists in the various *Geisteswissenschaften* develop hermeneutical key-concepts and ideal-types in the course of technical–morphological interpretation which they then employ in order to understand the history of the multitudinous expressions of human civilization as the history of the problems of formation and the solutions to problems which govern the creation and development of products and structures. In this context I only have to refer to Heinrich Wölffin's seminal *Kunstgeschichtliche Grundbegriffe* and the highly fruitful *Grundbegriffe der Poetik* by Emil Staiger.

Meaning-structure and style as products of the autonomy of mental powers

It is obvious that only an interpreter who is familiar with the problems of artistic expression from his own experience and who possesses a cultivated artistic sensitivity and some expert knowledge is able to unfold problems that have not been consciously solved in a work of art, and to understand its meaning-content. By the same token, it is only because of his familiarity with the conceptual tools of legal dogmatics, which a legal expert has acquired in the course of his training and practice, that an historian of law is in a position to tackle the problem of the formation of legal constructs and legal opinion when he concerns himself with separating the function which these constructs have acquired over time from their structure. Only the mind of a sociologist who has considered the morphological problems of the organization of social life enables an historian of civilization to be in a position to become fully aware of constant, typically recurring factors and developmental tendencies which are operative in the historical change of social structures and which account for the fact that a community existing in a given environment will react in the same way to the same conditions of power and position. An analogous demand was made by philologists and historians of the classical age in their call for a contemporary hermeneutics of figurative (sculptured or painted) works; the aim here was to go beyond the immediate semantical content of these works and to recognize and reconstruct these meaning-full forms and their excess of representational content through the complementary interpretation of literary texts. It is equally the case that only a theologian who is able to do more than just perceive external or internal changes is in a position to understand the immanent development of religions. He who is able to retrace the rise of forms of meaning and of their bearers with the fine sense of an historian can gain an idea of the laws according to which the dialectic of becoming proceeds as it submits itself to a general regularity while at the same time following an individual law.

In all these cases we are concerned with a meaning-content of historical interest which cannot be explored and fully comprehended with normal psychological and ethical categories. In respect of such meaning-content, a technical–morphological interpretation satisfies the requirement of the adequacy of meaning of understanding, or that of the hermeneutical correspondence of meaning, which traces the surplus meaning of cultural products and which constitutes, as has already been indicated, a fundamental canon of interpretation. It is the task of the historian of art, language, literature, law, economy and religion as well as that of the sociologist to understand a work of art, a formation, a typical behaviour respectively in its inner coherence and validity, in its relationship with similar meaning-full forms and types, and to characterize it in its 'style' as the product of autonomous mental forces. In this way, a technical interpretation turns into the structural analysis of meaning-full forms; this analysis helps us to comprehend their character as a product and to explain how something that is sharply separated by value-criticism into valuable and worthless can appear, in the light of technical–morphological interpretation, as something that is united by a shared essence with equally justifiable elements. It is possible to consider in this way the products of individuals and of a communal spirit. The interpreter can derive from them only as much as his training and expertise enables him to register, and whatever becomes clear to him about linguistic works, works of art, law and religion in the course of his sincere encounter with them. Interpretations which differ from one another always indicate that a genuine, organically developed work of art has remained alive within its confines. We, in addition, may remind ourselves of the eternal truth expressed by Goethe when he stated that it is only the whole of mankind that is in a position to completely understand a human product.

The fact of the matter is, that the subjective mind of an individual human being is taken up to heights and down into depths by objectivations of mind which would remain inaccessible to his own experiencing since they are situated beyond his own resources for making experiences. The deepening and elevation, expansion and enrichment which the interpreter receives in the course of understanding are clearly different from those which a human being reaches in the course of his own immanent development. The crucial point remains that it is an objectivated meaning-content, matter charged with mind, that touches us in its purity and depth. The gain we derive for our own education and self-development from great works of art is one thing; another is the realization that within the cosmos of objectivations of mind we can find meaning-contents which we acknowledge to be superior to our subjectivity and which we approach through understanding – not so much out of our own strength, but through being raised by them. Just as primitive man carries magic powers around with him in his fetish, so civilized man is surrounded by products which are infinitely greater than he is.[54]

If we think of all meaning-full forms as together forming the unity of human civilizations, then we can take in, at a glance, the tension between familiarity and unfamiliarity existing within the dialectical relationship between subjective and objectivated mind. Any given human being may well try to reap the yield of the past, but he will have come to realize that the treasures of thought accumulated through the gigantic effort of past generations contain meaning-contents which, although they are of human origin, are also of overwhelming meaning and significance. If one can state that the knowledge of history and of oneself correspond to one another in a peculiar and characteristic way,[55] then it has to be part of the essence of acquiring self-knowledge that the human mind can complete this process only if he brings forth an objective meaning-content which can confront him and which arises out of human existence as something superior to and different from himself. The return of our mind towards self-knowledge is possible only through the impetus received during the journey through objective meaning-contents; historical knowledge is not only man's route to himself but also, and at the same time, the path to something superior which far transcends individual human beings, in accordance with Goethe's famous dictum.

A common hermeneutical problematic, which takes different forms in different areas, therefore comes into sight in the field of the *Geisteswissenschaften*. I shall remain content, here, with having given the thoughtful guardians and practitioners of these sciences an indication of its possibility.

Notes

1 In *Geschichte und Eschatologie* (1958).
2 Ibid., p. 130.
3 Ibid., p. 136.
4 In 'Das Problem der Hermeneutik', in *Glauben und Verstehen*, vol. II, p. 211, and see pp. 227–30.

5 Ibid., p. 228.
6 In *Geschichtsphilosophie der Gegenwart* (1931), p. 41.
7 'Über Knies und das sogennante Irrationalitätsproblem', in *Gesammelte Aufsätze zur Wissenschaftslehre*, pp. 119–22 and 245.
8 Ibid., pp. 122–5.
9 Similarly Gadamer, *Wahrheit und Methode*, p. 311; cf. Nietzsche, *Menschliches, Allzumenschliches*, vol. II, p. 223.
10 Bultmann, *Geschichte und Eschatologie*, p. 136.
11 Ibid., p. 135.
12 Ibid., p. 137.
13 Ibid., p. 135.
14 In *Die fröhliche Wissenschaft*, p. 339.
15 Cf. J. Körner, *Eschatologie und Geschichte* (1957), p. 52.
16 Bultmann, *Geschichte und Eschatologie*, p. 162.
17 Ibid., p. 139.
18 Cf. K. Löwith, *Heidegger, Denker in dürftiger Zeit* (1953), p. 83.
19 In 'Wort Gottes und Hermeneutik', *ZThk*, vol. 56, pp. 224–51.
20 Ibid., pp. 236–8.
21 Ibid., p. 239.
22 Ibid., p. 242.
23 Ibid., p. 242.
24 Ibid., p. 224.
25 Gadamer, *Wahrheit und Methode*, pp. 267, 279.
26 Ibid., p. 274.
27 Asks the author, ibid., p. 275.
28 Ibid., p. 254.
29 Gadamer, *Heidegger-Festschrift*, p. 32.
30 Ibid., p. 33.
31 Ibid., p. 33.
32 Ibid., p. 34.
33 *Wahrheit und Methode*, pp. 275–9.
34 Gadamer thinks, ibid., p. 275.
35 Ibid., p. 276.
36 Ibid., p. 277.
37 Ibid., p. 27.
38 Ibid., p. 278.
39 Ibid., p. 278, note 2.
40 Ibid., pp. 308–10.
41 Ibid., p. 411.
42 Ibid., p. 311.
43 Ibid., p. 311.
44 Gadamer's agreement with Bultmann's train of thought is symptomatic here.
45 Ibid., p. 317.
46 Ibid., pp. 319–21.
47 Ibid., p. 321.
48 Ibid., pp. 319–21.
49 Ibid., p. 322.
50 Ibid., p. 323.

51 This is where the concept of 'application' originates; cf. Wach, *Das Verstehen*, vol. II, p. 19; also Ebeling, 'Wort Gottes und Hermeneutik', *ZThk*, vol. 56, p. 249.

52 'Hermeneutik und Historismus', *Phil. Rundschau*, vol. 9 (1962), pp. 241–76; [also as Appendix in Gadamer (1975)].

53 In *Archiv für Kunstgeschichte*, vol. 38 (1956), p. 261.

54 Freyer, *Theorie des objectiven Giestes*, p. 87.

55 Bultmann has recently made this point, *Geschichte und Eschatologie*, p. 137.

Part II

Hermeneutic philosophy

Introduction

Betti's work represents the most sophisticated exposition of the theory of hermeneutics, i.e. the methodology of the interpretation of objective mind. Hermeneutic philosophy, in relation to this approach, can be characterized by reference to its fundamental theme: the interpretation of Dasein. The concern now shifts from objective interpretation to a transcendental analysis which, through the interpretation of Dasein, examines the existential constitution of possible understanding from the standpoint of active existence. This mode of existence cannot be illuminated through methodical and intersubjective endeavours, but only comes to light in the act of self-understanding.

The difference between this view and Betti's emphasis on self-knowledge rests mainly in the fact that with him it could never be more than a desirable outcome of objective interpretation; now it refers to the event in which the individual realizes his debt to tradition and responsibility for the future: it is no longer the result of knowing something that has congealed into an object but it indicates a new way of being.

In these few lines I have, of course, already given hermeneutic philosophy a particular slant by relying on Heidegger's conception of it. But since his *Being and Time* contains not only the first elaboration of the underlying theme of those various approaches that I, somewhat forcibly, group together under the umbrella term of 'hermeneutic philosophy', viz. the concern with fundamental, theoretical, 'transcendental', issues, but also provides a number of analyses that are still recognized as relevant today, I shall first of all provide a brief outline of what I envisage as Heidegger's central contribution to the debate under consideration.

Chapter 3

Heidegger's existential–ontological hermeneutic

I have already referred to the unresolved dilemma in Dilthey's work between his intention to put the *Geisteswissenschaften* on the secure path of science and establish them on a par with the natural sciences and their notion of objectivity on the one hand, and his insights into the structure of understanding which points to the context of Life on the other: expressions of life can be understood via a lived experience in which the self-understanding of the interpreter and his pre-understanding of the 'object' are brought to bear on the process of cognition. With the later Husserl, the 'life-world' similarly provides the basis, as the realm of the 'natural attitude', for experience in general and the 'world of science' in particular. Heidegger's hermeneutic phenomenology, while in a sense developing this theme which centred on Life as the ultimate fraud behind which one could not inquire, follows Yorck's hint at the 'correspondence between life and self-awareness'.[1] In this monumental achievement that appeared in 1926, *Sein and Zeit*,[2] Heidegger states that 'it is the "fundamental shortcoming" . . . of any serious and scientifically-minded "philosophy of life" . . . that here "life" itself as a kind of Being does not become ontologically a problem' (p. 46). That is to say, that Life essentially is accessible only in Dasein (p. 50). The ontology of Dasein leads into the science of the interpretation of that which is the 'hermeneutic' of Dasein. In this phenomenological analysis of Dasein as the Being-of-mankind, Heidegger not only deepens the epistemological analyses of Dilthey and Husserl, but also provides a critique of the body of underlying assumptions that they share with the whole of Western philosophical tradition and which Heidegger identifies as 'metaphysics'. Since my topic concerns Heidegger's existential hermeneutic I shall only focus on such central notions as 'the hermeneutic circle' and 'the historicality of understanding'; but even for the limited concern of an exposition of the hermeneutic theory developed by Heidegger it is

98

still necessary to indicate the line of argument underlying his whole approach to the question of the possibility and limit of understanding, and which I, initially, would like to consider in terms of a transcendental approach.

1. Hermeneutic philosophy as a transcendental inquiry

Like Dilthey, Heidegger was led to a metacritique of Kant's transcendental critiques but unlike him regarded it as a task of ontological rather than logical inquiries. Dilthey approached the task of answering the question about the conditions for the possibility of *verstehen* by extending the logical foundations of knowledge, i.e. the formulation of categories appropriate to the *Geisteswissenschaften*. Heidegger's fundamental–ontological conception provided a complete re-orientation and a far more radical solution by developing a number of *Existentialien* (existentiales) which, in conjunction with the 'categories–characteristics of Being for entities whose character is not that of Dasein', 'are the two basic possibilities for characters of Being' (pp. 44–5).

This distinction corresponds to one of Heidegger's central insights in *Being and Time*: the 'ontological difference' between *Sein* (Being) and *Seiendes* (entities), the realm of the ontological and that of the ontical. The investigation of entities proceeds in the form of an enumeration of what shows itself in the world (trees, houses, people). 'Such a description is always confined to entities. It is ontical. But what we are seeking is Being' (p. 63). Existential–ontological interpretation is concerned with the constitution of Being rather than its 'theoretical–critical' generalization. But 'neither the ontical depiction of entities within-the-world nor the ontological interpretation of their Being is such as to reach the phenomenon of the "world"' (p. 64).

Since the latter has been 'presupposed' in both approaches, the task is that of fundamental ontology which lies at the basis of these two as the analysis of Dasein and which seeks an answer to the question after the 'meaning' of Being. It is clear that for this task the use of categories – be they those of space, time and causality Kant considered or Dilthey's addition of *Leben* – meaning, etc., does not suffice. 'All *explicata* to which the analytic of Dasein gives rise are obtained by considering Dasein's existence-structure. Because Dasein's characters of Being are defined in terms of existentiality, we call them "existentiales"' (p. 44). The meaning of Being can only be arrived at through an interpretative effort: 'hermeneutic' is therefore a fundamental concept of ontology and provides the basis for a transcendental inquiry.

Since Dasein is characterized by its understanding of Being, the meaning of Being can only be interpreted from within this pre-current understanding. The Archimedean point, from which transcendental philosophy has so far been operating – e.g. *cogito, ergo sum* (Descartes) – is now located at the more fundamental one of 'Being-in-the-world'. The conditions for the possibility of knowledge, the synthesis *a priori*, is given in Dasein's understanding of Being. Only the understanding of the meaning of Being, which has always already occurred when we consciously attempt to understand, e.g. a text, allows for the possibility of making sense of the 'what is' of entities. Hermeneutical theory, on this basis, can be no more than a derivative of the fundamental 'hermeneutic of Dasein', in which we try to explicate and clarify an already existing (pre-)understanding that is a structure of our 'Being-in-the-world'.

The existential structures of Being-in-the-world include, in addition to understanding, those of *Befindlichkeit* (state-of-mind) and *Rede* (talk) and they provide the conditions for the possibility of any new knowledge; they also find their total expression in *Sorge* (care) as the Being of Dasein. The ontological meaning of care, in turn, is that of 'temporality'; knowledge-acquisition, as an existential phenomenon, consequently has its ontological meaning in this temporality; it is, therefore, necessary to accept time 'primordially as the horizon of the understanding of Being, and in terms of temporality as the Being of Dasein, which understands Being' (p. 17). The relationship of Dasein, care, and temporality Heidegger formulates this way: 'Dasein's totality of Being as care means: ahead-of-itself-already-being-in (a world) as Being-alongside (entity encountered within-the-world) . . . the primordial unity of the structure of care lies in its temporality . . . the essence of which is the temporality in the unity of the ecstases of temporality . . . i.e. the phenomena of the future, the character of having been, and the present' (pp. 327–9). Temporality as the condition for the possibility of original care and as the ultimate horizon of the interpretation of Being-in-the-world represents the aim of fundamental ontology.

Heidegger's development of a hermeneutic philosophy has so far been considered in its relation to the question after the meaning of Being and to Dasein as Understanding. The third phase of a hermeneutic interpretation is given with the 'ontological' or 'existential circle' which provides for the methodically relevant formulation of a hermeneutic circle.

Understanding has already been referred to as an existentiale of Dasein. As such it 'is not a "what", but Being as existing. The kind of Being which Dasein has, as potentiality-for-Being, lies existentially in Understanding . . . Dasein is in every case what it can be, and in the way in which it is its possibility' (p. 143). Heidegger can now characterize Understanding as 'the existential Being of Dasein's own potentiality-for-Being; and it is so in such a way that its Being discloses in itself what its Being is capable of' (p. 144). It can do this because 'the Understanding has in itself the existential structure which we call "projection" (*Entwurf*)' (p. 145).

How does this Understanding relate to interpretation? It has been shown how Betti considered Understanding as the product of (objective) interpretation, i.e. as the appropriation of a meaning intended by an Other. Heidegger considers this kind of methodical interpretation as 'inauthentic understanding' and states that 'in interpretation, understanding does not become something different. It becomes itself. Such interpretation is grounded existentially in Understanding; the latter does not arise from the former. Nor is interpretation the acquiring of information about what is understood; it is rather the working-out of possibilities projected in Understanding' (p. 148).

It is, therefore, not so much a case of acquiring new knowledge, but that 'the world', which has already been understood, comes to be interpreted. Understanding is a fundamental existentiale that constitutes the disclosedness of Being-in-the-world; it contains in itself the possibility of interpretation, i.e. the appropriation of what is already understood. Not only is interpretation a derivation of fundamental understanding – it is also directed by the latter in respect to the 'in-order-to' which has the structure of something as something. Pre-predicatively one 'sees' what is ready-to-hand (*zuhanden*) as something: 'that which is disclosed in Understanding – that which is understood – is already accessible in such a way that its "as which" can be made to stand out explicitly . . . . It constitutes the interpretation'. Any perception of what is around us is preformed by 'our understanding of the world and this involvement is one which gets laid out by the interpretation' (p. 150).

The interpretation of something as something, i.e. the 'as-structure of interpretation' is founded on the fore-structure of Understanding. The pre-understood 'totality of involvement' precedes our understanding and interpretation as is 'laid-out' in interpretation in such or such a way. Heidegger terms the context and the anticipation of meaning the *Vorhabe* (fore-having), i.e. something we have in advance. The explication of what remains implicit, the appropriation of understanding in interpretation 'is always done under the guidance of a point of view, which fixes that with regard to which what is understood is to be interpreted. In every case understanding is grounded in something we see in advance – in a foresight' (*Vorsicht*). The framework of interpretability and the intuition of interpretation leads to a third condition for the possibility of interpretative understanding; the fore-conception (*Vorgriff*) in which we grasp something in advance. That is to say, that anything we understand is interpreted by either deriving the concepts used from it, or by forcing it into pre-existing categories which do not correspond to its Being. The hermeneutic of Dasein is therefore equally dependent on the categories and concepts used, as is the cognition of entities, and has to strive for the adequacy of concept and 'object' in interpretation. *Vorhabe, Vorsicht* and *Vorgriff* provide the pre-suppositions for the constitution of an 'object'; there can be no object-in-itself, or any *factum brutum*. The mere recognition of a fact is theory-impregnated and guided by a number of anticipations: 'In the projecting of the Understanding, entities are disclosed in their possibility. The character of the possibility corresponds, on each occasion, with the kind of Being of the entity which is understood' (p. 151).

It is in the development of this insight that Heidegger arrives at meaning – not as a property of entities but as another existentiale: 'the concept of meaning embraces the formal existential framework of what necessarily belongs to that which an understanding interpretation articulates. Meaning is the "upon-which" of a projection in terms of which something becomes intelligible as something; it gets its structure from a fore-having, fore-sight, and a fore-conception' (p. 193).

The circularity of argument apparent in the conception of interpretation as moving within the fore-structure of understanding – so that it can only make explicit what is already understood – characterizes the hermeneutic or existential-ontological circle. Hermeneutical theory has always stressed the importance of considering the parts within a whole, which itself can only be understood in respect of its constituent parts. I have referred to this circle as the hermeneutical circle in order to contrast it with the hermeneutic circle, of which it is only a derivative. In this context, the situatedness of the interpreter has proved an embarrassment to those theorists who so persistently strove towards approximating the ideal of objectivity, as they saw it realized in natural science. When we regard the pre-understanding of an 'object' of interpretation as a blemish and conceive of the ensuing circularity as a vicious or logical circle, 'and look out for avoiding it, even if we just "sense" it as an inevitable imperfection, then the act of understanding has been misunderstood from the ground up' (p. 194).

This circle is the expression of the existential fore-structure of Dasein, an entity that is concerned with its own Being, in its Being-in-the-world. It is not a question of avoiding this circle but of getting into it properly since it contains the possibility of original insight – if one does not accept any dominant fore-structure unquestioningly but attempts to 'make the scientific scheme secure by working out these fore-structures in terms of the things themselves' (p. 153). Understanding is not the result of a correct procedure but, 'in accordance with its existential meaning, is Dasein's own potentiality-for-Being' (p. 153). 'Objectivity' in knowledge is the result of a 'subspecies of understanding which has strayed into the legitimate task of grasping the present-at-hand in its essential unintelligibility' (p. 153). It would not be too iconoclastic to suggest that the objectivity of strict science is indirectly proportionate to the existentially relevant basis of its approach.

Heidegger's exposition of the existential structure of understanding and interpretation – which is never merely the pre-suppositionless grasping of something pregiven but the interpretation of something as something – covers all cognition: 'Knowledge is a mode of Being of Dasein as Being-in-the-world' (p. 61). The co-existence in the world of subject and object disallows the possibility of their strict separation at the cost of objectivism and the negation of the foundation of cognition as mode of Dasein. Even the apophantic 'as' of the assertion in its three significations as 'finding out' (*Aufzeigen*), 'prediction' (*Prädikativa*), and 'communion' (*Mitteilung*), which form a 'judgment', is a derivative form of interpretation. It only affirms the existence of the 'primordial "as" of an interpretation which understands circumspectively' (p. 158), and which we call the existential–hermeneutical 'as'.

This completes the three hermeneutic phases in the exposition of time-meaning-Being.

Chapter 4

Bultmann's theological hermeneutic

Heidegger's analysis of the existential structure of Dasein has mainly been referred to in respect of the transcendental interpretation of understanding. Understanding, as an existentiale, projects possibilities of human existence. This insight informed the formulation of the hermeneutic circle and it is this seminal development that will provide the focus for the outline of Gadamer's hermeneutic philosophy, where the reflection upon scientific objectivity, the historicality of understanding and the role of language and tradition represent a further elaboration of Heidegger's insight. Gadamer's theory of hermeneutic experience is of particular relevance as it can be used as an (ontological) counterfoil to the methodological and espistemological concerns of traditional hermeneutics in its Diltheyan mould.

Before Gadamer published his *magnum opus, Wahrheit und Methode*, in 1960 the debate about existential understanding revolved largely around Bultmann's[3] theological hermeneutic. Since his exegesis is based upon methodological reflections which take their cue from Heidegger, it would be appropriate to refer briefly to his work.

Bultmann's significance rests with his attempt to carry out the deepening of Dasein's methodological analysis by means of Heidegger's hermeneutic philosophy – thereby following the lead of the latter.[4] The problem which concerned Bultmann was centred on the dialectic between the mythological language in which the *kerygma*, the message about the advent of God in Jesus Christ, found expression in the New Testament and the existential understanding of the interpreter. The hermeneutic circle apparent in exegesis here asserts itself with the interpreter having to be a believer in order to understand, while understanding the message is itself necessary for acquiring belief. But this formulation would still remain within the confines of a psychologistic conception of understanding which aimed at arriving at the author's intended meaning as the original hearer would have understood it. In this sense, the interpreter would still approach the Scriptures as an objectivation of mind and, in a way, interrogate the 'object' to obtain answers to his questions. The limitation of this conception of the hermeneutic task is nowhere more apparent than in the exegesis of the Bible. In Bultmann's achievement, the demythologization of the New Testament, historical and philological interpretation is instrumental in determining the message it contains – which may mean piercing through the mythical veil of cosmological-eschatological explanations which are no longer acceptable to modern man.

But if we accept a further definition of 'myth' as something that expresses another possibility of existing, then we are once again in the terrain of Heidegger's existential interpretation: the interpretation of mythical conceptions in relation to the self-understandings that underlie and are expressed in them. Man takes possession of his origin and his destiny through the language of myth. It is not the meaning intended by the author but that contained in the text, which does not refer to itself but to an event, that directs understanding. Existential understanding consists in the submission to the content of a text, and the interpretation of the Bible takes the circular form of: understanding a text which expresses a belief in Jesus Christ and which was formulated by the Old Church; in order to understand the text it is necessary to believe what the text expresses, which itself can only be known through understanding it.

There is, however, one further level of myth that Bultmann considers and which requires the demythologization of myth itself. At this stage the scientist and then the philosopher are superseded by the one who hears the call, responds to it, and begins to make his existence meaningful. Demythologization here takes the form of an interpretation of concepts such as 'sin' in the light of our hopes,[5] i.e. the knowledge that the future in Christ has already commenced. Taking responsibility for our own future is therefore the consequence of having made the decision to accept the faith offered to us.

What, then, are the methodological insights applicable to all areas of interpretation that may be derivable from Bultmann's work? Bultmann himself summarizes them in reference to his term *Vorverständnis* (pre-understanding) which represents the methodologically oriented reformulation of Heidegger's fore-structure of understanding. 'A preceding living relationship to the subject matter which finds expression in a text either directly or indirectly and which guides the "upon-which" of any

inquiry is the precondition of every understanding interpretation . . . . Such an inquiry is always guided by a pre-existing and
preliminary understanding of human existence, i.e. a definite
existential understanding' (Bultmann, 1950, pp. 62–3).

The concern with the objectivity of the results of interpretation, which rely so fundamentally on the subject's pre-
understanding, has led Betti to reject Bultmann's existential
interpretation. The latter pointedly formulates his position in
this way: 'The most "subjective" is always the most "objective"
interpretation; i.e. in which he who is moved by the questions
concerning his own existence is in a position to perceive the
claims of the text' (p. 65). It would be utterly inappropriate to
demand from the interpreter that he suppressed his individuality
in order to achieve objective knowledge – even though personal
preferences as to the outcome of interpretative work have to be
regarded as an outflow of a dogmatic position that has to be
eliminated. The difference under consideration Bultmann neatly
conceptualizes as one between being free from pre-suppositions
(*Voraussetzungslosigkeit*) and being free from prejudice (*Vorurteilsfreiheit*). The latter condition is a *sine qua non* of any
attempt to remain within the orbit of objective knowledge,
whereas the former is an illusory and ill-conceived idea that has
its origin in scientistic views concerning the nature of true
knowledge. Pre-understanding, as the central element of the
system of pre-suppositions, 'does not have to be eliminated but
has to be raised to consciousness to be critically examined in the
course of understanding a text, to be gambled with; in short,
this is required: to allow oneself to be questioned during one's
inquiry of the text and to listen to its claims' (p. 63).

The engagement of one's own existential understanding in
extracting the message contained in a text, which will modify
the preceding understanding, is, of course, assisted by the
skilful use of the methodological approaches developed by
hermeneutical theory. The use of formal analysis is not restricted
to profane literature but equally applies to biblical texts – only
that here a specific pre-understanding comes into play: 'In
human Dasein there is alive an existential knowledge about God
as the question after "happiness", after "salvation", after the
meaning of the world and of history, as the question after the
authenticity of every human existence' (p. 66). This pre-
understanding guides our interpretation of God's revelation –
otherwise we would not know what to 'make of' the promise of
'salvation'.

Possibly the most fundamental criticism levelled against

Bultmann's existential hermeneutic concerns his neglect of any reflection about language in general. It is, however, precisely the concern with language that characterizes the modern debates within hermeneutic philosophy. This is particularly the case with Gadamer, who, in this respect, parallels the work of two contemporary theologians, both students of Bultmann, which would therefore provide an apposite lead into Gadamer's thought.

Bultmann still remains within the confines of an approach that centres on 'objectivations' rather than on language; this leads him to overlook the fact that, in the course of demythologization, the language of myth is replaced by another language.[6] The last stage of this process is achieved in relating existential decision to the claims of the 'Word of God'. With Bultmann, the path led away from language to an understanding prior to and more authentic than language. The 'linguistic turn' in hermeneutic philosophy seeks to counter this view.

The theological hermeneutic of Fuchs and Ebeling refers to the *kerygma* as a 'language event' or a 'word event'. 'Hermeneutic' refers to a 'theory of words' which is intended to facilitate the proclamation of the Word of God in the present, and the use of the text for the understanding of present experience; it is itself a bringing of the News. It is a theory of the 'word' in that understanding proceeds from it: existence is 'existence through word and in word' (Ebeling). The primacy in the new theological hermeneutic now shifts from the text to the 'word'; it is no longer a case of the interpreter subordinating himself to the text. Whereas for Bultmann the text remains the ultimate objective of interpretation, Fuchs goes a step further and argues that the text in turn interprets *us*; it provides a critique of our self-understanding in terms of the self-understanding the text addresses to us. The pre-understanding is absorbed into a self-understanding which represents the goal of the process of interpretation: 'The text unfolds itself, speaks up, in what it says about us. Here we can see interpretation taking place less as "understanding" than as "language", in that the text interprets itself by what it has to say about us.'[7]

Chapter 5

Gadamer's philosophical hermeneutic

Gadamer's philosophy completes the existential–ontological theory of understanding and at the same time provides the foundation for its supercession through the emphasis on the linguisticality of understanding.

My outline of Gadamer's contribution to hermeneutic theory will follow this development by focusing, first, on his account of the historicality of understanding, before considering its linguisticality, especially in relation to the universality of the hermeneutic problem.

1. The historicality of understanding

This aspect is dealt with by Gadamer in terms of the hermeneutic circle with the aim of raising the philosophical awareness of the *Geisteswissenschaften*. Gadamer builds on both Heidegger's exposition of the fore-structure of understanding and Bultmann's stress on pre-understanding in that the former is concretized and the latter is widened into the conception of 'prejudices' which constitute a given 'horizon of understanding'. All understanding is 'prejudicial', says Gadamer, and invests a great deal of thought into the rehabilitation of a concept that acquired its negative connotation with the Enlightenment.

From its claim to autonomy, Reason could consider prejudices only as remnants of an unenlightened mentality which impedes rational self-determination. This view also entered into the thinking of some romanticists and, consequently, shaped the formulation of the doctrine of historism. In their rejection of prejudices both the Enlightenment, and the natural sciences which sprang from it, and the historistic *Geisteswissenschaften* of the nineteenth century enter into an unholy alliance which finds its common denominator in the quest for objective knowledge which they hope to achieve by following a system of rules and methodological principles, and in the 'conquest of myths by logos' (pp. 257, 242).[8]

Gadamer sees in this, however, the loss of the continuity of tradition which nevertheless underlies both approaches. In addition to prejudices and tradition, authority, too, has been rejected by the Enlightenment as anathema to the use of one's faculty of Reason. As the demand for blind obedience it certainly deserved this fate, but this does not capture the essence of true authority which can only be maintained through the consent of those affected by it: it has to be acquired and continually re-affirmed through their consent. In fact, 'authority has nothing to do with blind obedience, but rather with knowledge' (pp. 264, 248).

The idea of absolute Reason overlooks the fact that Reason can only actualize itself in historical conditions. Even the most neutral application of the methods of science is guided by an anticipation of moments of tradition in the selection of the topic of research, the suggestion of new questions and the wakening of interest in new knowledge. It is therefore the task of a philosophical hermeneutic to evidence the historic moment in the comprehension of the world and to determine its hermeneutic productivity. In this sense, the hermeneutic problem underlies all knowledge. The natural sciences derive the direction of their development from the laws of their object, but reference to the element of tradition that affects them is not sufficient for grasping the systematic influence of historic factors on the *Geisteswissenschaften*: their object does not remain the same but is constituted ever anew by different questions directed towards it. The *Geisteswissenschaften* can only be freed from their obsessive identification with the procedures exemplified by the natural sciences if the historic character of their object is acknowledged as a positive moment rather than as an impediment to objectivity.

Gadamer's radical reappraisal of the situation of the interpreter is apparent when he evaluates the existence of prejudices. Lest he be misunderstood from the outset Gadamer sounds a caveat:

> a person trying to understand a text is prepared for it to tell him something. That is why a hermeneutically trained mind must be, from the start, sensitive to the text's newness. But this kind of sensitivity involves neither 'neutrality' in the matter of the object nor the extinction of one's self, but the conscious assimilation of one's own fore-meanings and prejudices. The important thing is to be aware of one's own

bias, so that the text may present itself in all its newness and thus be able to assert its own truth against one's own fore-meanings. (pp. 253–4, 238)

And so Gadamer rehabilitates authority and tradition and negates their opposition to Reason by referring to 'legitimate prejudices'. How are we able to separate legitimate from arbitrary prejudices, and what are their foundation?

Heidegger's temporal interpretation of Dasein points at Time as the ground in which the present finds its roots. When historism insisted on a gap between the present and the past, which issued in the methodological postulate to re-cognize past events in the concepts employed at the time so as to arrive at objective results, hermeneutic philosophy regards this 'distance' as continuous, i.e. bridged by tradition – which provides the interpreter with cognitive potential. Hermeneutical theory, we remember, focused on understanding as an activity of the interpreter's subjectivity which was best conducted on the level of two congenial minds. Betti's methodology, for example, set great store by the spontaneity of the subject – without acknowledging the overarching integration of the act of understanding into historic processes. Gadamer therefore states that 'Understanding is not to be thought of so much as an action of one's subjectivity, but as the placing of oneself within a tradition, in which past and present are constantly fused' (pp. 274–5, 258). It is this insight that obsessive concern with method has obscured.

One prejudice Gadamer examines is that of 'perfection' in which formal and material elements fuse in the understanding of the content of a text – which we antecedently assume to be unified under one meaning and to be telling the truth. We are, evidently, concerned with the content of a text and not with the opinion of the author as such. Methodological hermeneutics objectified the original reader and replaced him with the interpreter. By placing himself within his tradition, however, the interpreter brings into play his own prejudices in the attempt to do justice to the text's claim to truth, thereby superseding his initial isolated standpoint and his concern with the author's individuality. The interpreter is always embedded in a context of tradition which can now be regarded as the sharing of basic and supportive prejudices. It would be presumptive to imagine that the whole range of prejudices which make possible and guide understanding can be brought to awareness and be employed at will; outside the process of understanding it remains impossible to even separate misleading from productive prejudices. The filtering out of the 'legitimate' prejudices occurs in the dialectic between otherness and familiarity, between object and tradition, that is initiated by the temporal distance: 'It not only lets those prejudices that are of a particular and limited nature die away, but causes those that bring about genuine understanding to emerge clearly as such' (pp. 282, 263–4).

By bringing his own conceptions to bear on the text the interpreter does not, of course, aim at reproducing it in its pristine state; not only does the text, at all times, represent more than the author intended, it is also read differently in different circumstances and understanding is, therefore, a productive endeavour. In this process our prejudices will have to either prove adequate to the subject-matter or have to be modified, and it is in this trial and error approach that the truth-claim of the text can come to the fore. The relevance historism places upon methodical certainty leads it to neglect its historic element in understanding and to chase after the phantom of this historical object that can progressively be comprehended. In opposition to this view Gadamer uses the Hegelian formula of the unity of identity and difference to describe the process of understanding as one in which the 'object' is part of the self and in which both develop in the course of cognition.

Gadamer deals with this aspect under the title *Wirkungs-geschichte* (effective-history) and outlines the emergence and content of the consciousness of it. This term eludes short definitions, but Gadamer, in a brilliant analysis, evidences its structural elements: awareness of one's hermeneutic situation and the 'horizon' that is characteristic of it; the dialogical relationship between interpreter and text; the dialectic between question and answer; openness for tradition. The awareness of effective-history Gadamer also identifies with 'hermeneutic consciousness' as one that overarches both historical and historic consciousness.

Effective-history represents the positive and productive possibility of understanding. In its context, the interpreter finds himself in his own 'situation' from where he has to understand tradition by means of the prejudices he derives from within it. Any cognition of historical phenomena is, therefore, always guided by the results of effective-history which determine in advance what is to be regarded as worth knowing. This force can either be ignored in the objectivist reliance on methods of interpretation – only that it will not go away as a result but makes itself felt 'behind the back' of the naive observer; but it could equally be harnessed for arriving at the truth which is attainable by us despite all the limitations imposed upon us by the finitude of our understanding.

To become conscious of the fundamental preconditions of our understanding of the effects of effective-history remains a necessary demand for truly scientific work. This would involve an awareness of the hermeneutic situation, i.e. the situation in which we find ourselves *vis-à-vis* the tradition we wish to understand. Like all reflection, this one too has to remain within the limits imposed by our historicality: 'to exist historically means that knowledge of oneself can never be complete. All self-knowledge proceeds from what is historically pregiven . . .' (pp. 285–6, 269). For this reason, any historical situation contains its own horizon. Historical consciousness recognizes different epochs which have to be understood in their own terms by attempting to enter into the position occupied by the original addressees of an author's intended meaning. But, paradoxically, the desire to reconstruct past situations for the purposes of objective knowledge aims straight past the real task; to find out the valid and comprehensible truth embodied in tradition, it turns a means into an end. The hermeneutic consciousness, by contrast, regards the conception of unitary epochs with a closed horizon as an abstraction: 'The historic movement that is human Dasein is characterized by the fact that it is not determined by any definite situation, and therefore does not possess a truly closed horizon. An horizon is, rather, something into which we wander and that moves with us' (p. 288). Both the interpreter and the part of tradition he is interested in contain their own horizon; the task consists, however, not in placing oneself within the latter, but in widening one's own horizon so that it can integrate the other. Gadamer terms the elevation of one's own particularity, and that of the 'object' onto a higher generality, the 'fusion of horizons'; this is what occurs whenever understanding takes place, i.e. our horizon is in a process of continued formation through the testing of our prejudices in the encounter with the past and the attempt to understand parts of our tradition. It is therefore inadequate to conceive of an isolated horizon of the present since it has already been formed through the contact with the past. This awareness of effective-history is to assist us in the controlled fusion of horizons.

Gadamer can in this way integrate Bultmann's pre-understanding, as the questioning approach, with Heidegger's projective conceptual *Vorgriff* in the concept of 'horizon'. The interpreter is, therefore, first aware of a distance between the text and his own horizon which leads, in the process of understanding, to a new, comprehensive horizon transcending the initial question and prejudices. The experience he makes in the course that leads to a new understanding is a hermeneutic one and essentially different from the experience that underlies the formulation of scientific methods. The objectivity of science has since Bacon been based on the possibility of constant, i.e. repeatable, experience which guarantees the intersubjectivity of findings. This approach is intent on eliminating all historic elements, as is exemplified by the experimental method in natural science. Husserl's analysis of the 'life-world' was directed against the monopoly of the experience gained within the 'world of science' – but with him experience, even in the pre-scientific sphere, carries a characteristic of the latter: it is directed at tangible phenomena.

The element of historicality in knowing has found its most emphatic acknowledgment with Hegel. Experience, as dialectical, feeds on determinate negation, and that indicates the fact that a new experience does not merely imply the overthrow of an earlier one but represents a new and higher stage of knowledge which comprehends both the new insight and an awareness of what had wrongly been regarded previously as a matter of fact: we now not only know more, but we know better. Dialectical experience does not capture the specifically hermeneutic element in the fusion of horizons, however. It is part of a scheme that finds its completion in absolute knowledge, the total identity of object and Knowledge. What is presumed – the system of total self-knowledge – precisely contravenes the central hermeneutic insight that self-knowledge can never be complete. Hermeneutic experience does not imply a desire for knowing everything, but being open to new experiences it 'has its own fulfilment not in definite knowledge, but in that openness to experience that is encouraged by experience itself . . . it refers to experience as a whole' (pp. 338, 319).

The experience we are here concerned with is one of human finitude; it does not mean to merely recognize what is just at this moment here in front of us, but to have insight into the limitations within which the future is still open to expectation. Thus, true experience is that of one's own historicality.

2. Understanding as a dialogical process

Hermeneutic experience is neither monological, as is science, nor is it dialectical, as is Hegel's universal history. Since

Gadamer explicates it on the model of human discourse I shall refer to it as 'dialogical' rather than 'dialectical'.

A dialogue can be treated as analogous to the interpretation of a text in that in both cases we experience a fusion of horizons:

> both are concerned with an object that is placed before them. Just as one person seeks to reach agreement with his partner concerning an object, so the interpreter understands the object of which the text speaks . . . in successful conversation they both come under the influence of the truth of the object and are thus bound to one another in a new community . . . [it is] a transformation into a communion, in which we do not remain what we were.
> (pp. 360, 341).

What, then, characterizes this hermeneutic experience?

The central task of the interpreter is to find the question to which a text presents the answer; to understand a text is to understand the question. At the same time, a text only becomes an object of interpretation by presenting the interpreter with a question. In this logic of question and answer a text is drawn into an event by being actualized in understanding which itself represents an historic possibility. The horizon of meaning is consequently unlimited, and the openness of both text and interpreter constitutes a structural element in the fusion of horizons. In this dialogical understanding the concepts used by the Other, be it a text or a thou, are regained by being contained within the interpreter's comprehension. In understanding the question posed by the text we have already posed questions ourselves and, therefore, opened up possibilities of meaning.

3. The linguisticality of understanding

The fusion of horizons is, however, inconceivable without the medium of language. It has already been pointed out that understanding has to be seen as an interpretation, and that interpretation is the explicit form of understanding. This insight is connected with the fact that the language used in interpretation represents a structural moment of interpretation – something that Bultmann had completely failed to take into account.

For Gadamer, the problem of language presents the central issue of hermeneutic philosophy. His concern with language even marks the point where he transcends the concerns of existential hermeneutics; it also provides a way out from Hegel's 'speculative chain of a philosophy of world history' (pp. 343, 323). Instead of a total mediation of universal history, and in the light of the awareness that a mediation is required in the fusion of horizons, Gadamer develops the theory of the universality of language. Linguisticality as the mediation of past and present has the additional advantage of providing a powerful argument against the ideal of objectivity advanced by the *Geisteswissenschaften*.

In his discussion of the linguisticality of all understanding, Gadamer gathers the insights so far accumulated in his book and provides them with a sharpened edge. The 'ontological turn of hermeneutics under the guidance of language' acquires its penetrative capacity through the incorporation of the work Heidegger produced after his own famous 'turn', which is best reflected in the single statement that 'language is the house of Being' (Heidegger, 1967, p. 145).

Heidegger's thought is now 'on the way to language', as a title of his work suggests. Hermeneutic philosophy is no longer seen as a theory but as the means of interpretation itself, the focus of which is not given in terms of an understanding of existence but in terms of understanding language, or rather, to understand existence itself in terms of a language that addresses us from inside it. Language cannot, therefore, be conceived of as an objectivation but is itself that which speaks to us. A text, consequently, should not be examined in respect of the author's intention but in view of the subject-matter contained within it which addresses itself at us and to which we respond with our words. Man's nature itself has to be defined as being linguistic: he exists, by *ant-worten*, responding with words, to the claims of Being. In *Identity and Difference*, the term 'hermeneutic' even refers back to its original meaning, as the message of the gods transmitted by Hermes. Gadamer develops the motive of Being 'being brought to language . . . Being comes to language by opening itself up' (Gadamer, 1967, p. 192), through determining the task of hermeneutic reflection in respect of language as the medium, the means, ground and 'middle' in and through which dialogue takes place. It cannot be used as a tool, as is the case in language considered as a system of signs; it already brings a situation, or the subject-matter of a text, to disclosure. It discloses our 'world', the space enclosing and uniting the participants of a 'game' in which they gamble with their prejudices. 'From language's relation to the world there follows its specific factuality. Matters of fact come into language' (pp. 421, 403). There is no world outside language:

> the linguistic analysis of our experience of the world is prior, as contrasted with everything that is recognized and addressed as beings. The fundamental relation of language and world does not, then, mean that the world becomes the object of language. Rather, the object of knowledge and of statements is already enclosed within the world horizon of language. The linguistic nature of the human experience of the world does not include making the world into an object. (pp. 426, 408)

The circularity apparent is again evaluated positively – it is impossible to look at linguistic existence for 'we cannot see a linguistic world from above in this way; there is no point of view outside the experience of the world in language from which it could itself become an object' (pp. 429, 410).

This line of argumentation is founded on the connection between language and understanding. Language does not produce a formulation of something we might have already understood pre-linguistically, but it is the mode of Being *qua* meaningful understanding as such. Its universal aspect consists in this: 'it is not the reflection of something given, but the coming into language of a totality of meaning . . . Being that can be understood is language' (pp. 450, 431–2). All understanding is linguistic and 'the linguisticality of understanding is the concretion of effective historical conscience' (pp. 367, 351); the agreement emerging from a dialogue, as in the interpretation of a text, i.e. of a subject-matter, takes place in the medium of language. The fusion of horizons can now be seen as 'the full realization of conversation, in which something is expressed that is not only mine or my author's, but common' (pp. 366, 350). The interpreter's horizon merges into the meaning of a text, or a partner's position, and is in this sense determining, without, however, assuming a fixed standpoint; it is, rather, an opinion and possibility that is open to changes when encountering those of an other 'object'. Only in this way can a subject-matter come to light.

Chapter 6

Conclusions: hermeneutic philosophy and hermeneutical theory

The hermeneutic philosophy developed by Heidegger and Gadamer includes two main elements: one (transcendental) philosophy, was established as a 'hermeneutic of facticity' (Heidegger), and a 'philosophical hermeneutic' (Gadamer); two, the theory of hermeneutics (Dilthey, Betti) was given a philosophical framework.

The central argument of hermeneutic philosophy can best be illustrated by reference to the title of Gadamer's book, *Truth and Method*. Method has, since Descartes, represented the royal road to truth in the sense of *veritas* and *adaequatio intellectus ad rem*: the correspondence between fact and proposition. The truth of the latter could be ascertained by reference to the former. Methodical procedures excluded the intrusion of external elements – e.g. Bacon's 'idols'. Verifiability came to be the measure of knowledge-claims, which themselves were based on the certainty accruing from adherence to a method. Apophantic logic lies at the heart of this conception, and guides the formulation of a 'judgment' in which something is predicated with an attribute, i.e. it is shown as it is.

Heidegger's monumental re-directing of philosophy rests on counterposing this propositional truth with another kind: *aletheia* (disclosure). Heidegger hereby opened up a dimension of experience more fundamental than that of the methodical acquisition of knowledge about beings. Modern science – herein paralleling metaphysical knowledge – concerned itself with things 'ready-at-hand' (*Vorhanden*) on the ontic level for the purpose of controlling and mastering them. The 'hermeneutic of facticity' gave an ontological explication of the Being of those beings by founding the transcendental basis of philosophy on a level far more fundamental than that of epistemology. Here, the hidden transcendental preconditions of the Logic of Science, i.e. the Philosophy of Science, in the form of the Cartesian–Kantian subject–object relation as well as the existential fore-structure of *verstehen* came to light. The latter contained those of *In-der-Welt-sein* (Being-in-the-world), *Mitsein* (Being-with), which Heidegger could draw on in his critique of epistemological idealism and methodological solipsism since they are presupposed in the constitution of the data of experience.

After his 'turn', language became the source of knowledge and language as logical was seen to be itself founded on language as disclosure. In its former use the subject strives for ultimate certainty through conceptual thought whereas in the latter he relies on language to unveil the Being of beings and he opens himself up to the meaning dwelling in historic existence.

The linguisticality of Being found expression with Gadamer in such concepts as *Wirkungsgeschichte* (effective-history), *Zugehörigkeit* (belongingness), *Spiel* (game), and *Gespräch* (dialogue) – which are almost completely interchangeable and point at the possibility of truth as disclosure, or *Horizontverschmelzung* (fusion of horizon) as Gadamer refers to it.

The linguisticality of our experience of the 'world' transcends all relativity and comprehends all things-in-themselves; it precedes everything that is recognized and pronounced as 'something'. Methodically derived experiences, consequently, merely represent a secondary form; they are abstracted from the totality of human existence and are characterized by their indifference towards capturing the essence of things through qualitative determinations. Such an approach to 'things' underlies methodical science, which concerns itself with phenomena that can be objectified and controlled by a, seemingly, autonomous subject. Scientistic conceptions, of course, regard this kind of experience as the only legitimate one and associate with it the independence of science from socio-historical processes. By referring to the universality of the hermeneutic experience, Gadamer was able to overcome both dogmatic metaphysics – which in the line from Descartes to Kant and Hegel had led to the absolutization of method – *and* scientistic restrictions of knowledge.

1. The universal aspect of hermeneutic philosophy

In the experience we gain through our involvement with art, philosophy and history Gadamer evidenced the possibility of truths that cannot be verified with the methodical means of science. The attempt to question their legitimacy involved a reflection upon the process of understanding and, with it, the hermeneutic problem exemplified by the circularity of understanding. Heidegger had already considered understanding as a mode of Being which underlies and guides all methodic scientific investigations – an insight Husserl expressed in reference to the pre-scientific 'life-world'. The experiences in that sphere Gadamer calls *Welterfahrung* (experience of the world) and they do not consist of the calculation and measuring of what is present-at-hand, but in becoming aware of the meaning of beings. This fundamental understanding represents the field of universal hermeneutic and takes the form of a dialectic between question and answer operating on the basis provided by language, as is apparent when the participants in a dialogue come to an agreement about a subject-matter. Another way of putting it would be to point at linguistic games in which the subjectivity of players is drawn into and subordinated to the game played by language itself which addresses them, suggests questions, questions us, lets itself be questioned by us. As in the language games Wittgenstein referred to,[9] it would be absurd to try and transpose one that is being played out in science onto experiences of the life-world, or to legislate for either. When we understand we do so by letting a subject-matter address us; it is an event in which something meaningful occurs to us. It also takes place within a context to which both listener and subject-matter belong: belongingness of recipient and message, of interpreter and text, characterizes the intimate relationship existing in this context – which now shows itself to be formed by 'tradition' and language.

All scientific activity is, consequently, guided by some pre-knowledge embedded in our language. It makes itself felt not only in the formulation of the aims of science, which necessitates normative discussions, but also in the communication between scientists concerning the criteria for a successful testing of hypotheses and, notably, in the formulation of scientific findings in everyday language – which is a precondition for their being put to use by 'outsiders'. The understanding taking place in science represents only one segment of the basic understanding that underlies all our activities and which contains conditions of truth preceding those of the logic of science. Can one derive from this an argument for the inadequacy of scientific methods to arrive at objective results?

Gadamer is at pains to dispel such a misleading view. His hermeneutic reflection brought to light the limitations of any striving for objectivity posed by the structural elements of understanding; all knowledge emerges from an historic situation in which the influence of tradition makes itself felt – even in science, in the form of preferred directions of research. But the recognition of this fact cannot be extrapolated into a questioning of the scientificity of its results. Science follows the laws of its subject-matter and can only be judged in relation to that. When it transgresses its legitimate sphere of activity – that of object-ifiable objects – and when it usurps the role of purveyor of all truth, hermeneutic consciousness will assert the legitimacy of a discipline of questioning and inquiry in which the methods of science cannot take hold; and it will re-affirm the fact that method cannot guarantee truth, but only secure degrees of certainty about controllable processes.

The universality of the hermeneutic problem not only refers to the historic situatedness of mathematical science but, *a fortiori*, also to the social sciences. With the latter, the element of belongingness of interpreter and object is, of course, of crucial importance for determining the possibility of objective knowledge in this sphere. It will be remembered that Betti saw his chief task in clarifying the relationship between understand-ing and interpretation and in defending the objectivity of the latter. Gadamer's hermeneutic philosophy, on the other hand, has provided us with insights into the structure of understand-ing that profoundly challenge the objectivist remnants not only in Betti's work but, at the same time, those in sociological approaches which take their starting-point in neo-Kantian philosophy – all of which fail to give an adequate account of the historicality of knowledge which Gadamer has explicated in terms of the consciousness of effective-history which seeks to reflect upon its own prejudices and to control its pre-under-standing.

Hermeneutic philosophy focuses not on the methodology of the *Geisteswissenschaften*, but on their relationship to the whole of our experience of the world; by evidencing understanding as a fundamental characteristic of existence it does not intend to restrict the disciplined and skilled understanding of texts, but only hopes to free it from a false self-understanding.

As is immediately apparent, the interpreter who is concerned with historical rather than ontic phenomena is himself part of tradition when he approaches segments of it; the subject–object dichotomy existing between the *res cogitans* and *res extensa* (Descartes) is therefore not applicable. Understanding is part of a game that is being played around him, an event which rep-resents nothing less than the precondition for his scientific activity.

From his hermeneutic situation the interpreter, or social

scientist, derives a comprehensive pre-understanding which guides the questions he formulates within a framework of societal norms. His standpoint is initially determining and it is only after reflecting upon his immediate preconceptions that he can exclude the more direct influence of his own environment. Value-freedom as envisaged by, for example, Max Weber is consequently from the outset unattainable and can only result in a blind decisionism as to the aims of research, an irrationalism that buries its head in the sand of inadequate notions about the role of the social scientist. It can be maintained only on the basis of a strict nominalism which is unable to take account of the use made of words in everyday life. Understanding is not a construct from principles but the development of knowledge we have gained of a wider context and which is determined by the language we use. The fact that the interpreter's technical concepts have to mediate between those apparent in the 'object' and his own puts the onus on him to subject them to continued reflection. He should avoid conceptions that may be current in his time and which express class or ethnic bias, and should allow himself to keep his own concepts open to correction in the course of his close acquaintance with the subject-matter.

The time-honoured distinction between natural science and *Geisteswissenschaften* gains a more plausible basis when considered in terms of the role pre-understanding plays in both: the linguisticality of our experience of the world enters the objectifying sciences in the form of undesirable prejudices which are largely rendered ineffective through adherence to a quantificatory methodology; but judgments and propositions are only a special form of linguistic activity and remain embedded within the totality of existence from where the human sciences derive their sphere of investigation; here, the role of prejudices is a positive one in that they open up possible fields of meaning in the object.

The historicality of understanding so far outlined refers to three aspects: the socio-historical mediation of pre-understanding, its constitution of possible objects and the value decisions formed by social praxis. Betti and Hirsch (1965) have attacked this notion and fear the unwarranted intrusion of subjective elements into, what could be, objective interpretation. Their views seem to rest, however, on a misconception of the role of pre-understanding in particular, and of philosophical hermeneutics in general. By failing to recognize that the latter does not attempt to meddle in the skilled interpretation of texts but only tries to show what happens in all understanding, both these authors have simply missed the point; in fact, the adequate conduct of hermeneutical research ought to be aware of both the 'negative' and 'positive' aspects of the role of pre-understanding.

2. The critique of method

The interpreter's thoughts have already fused with the subject-matter when he tries to arrive at the meaning of a text – but this initial function of his standpoint does not, of course, imply that he will stubbornly try and maintain his pre-notions in the face of unfolding textual meaning. As the description of the fusion of horizon and the notion of a 'game' indicates, understanding can be successful only in the constant revision of one's standpoint which allows the subject-matter to emerge. The prejudices held by the interpreter, therefore, play the important part of opening an horizon of possible questions and it is the hallmark of a truly scientific endeavour that it tries to bring them to consciousness.

Betti is, on the other hand, justified in fearing for the 'canon of the autonomy of the text'. The fixedness of the meaning of a text as the author intended it has already been recognized by Dilthey as the precondition for the objective interpretation of meaning. With Schleiermacher a similar conception led to the principle of an 'affinity of minds' that would do justice to the intellectual stature of the author. Hermeneutics has, therefore, always been tied to this specific conception of meaning as the author's intention that could be arrived at through the inversion of the process of creation. Closely connected with this view was the maxim that the author could be understood better than he had understood himself – which betrays the roots historism has in the Enlightenment and its conviction of the superiority of the present as the transitional apex of a development towards the self-determination of Reason.

Gadamer disagrees fundamentally. As he exemplified in reference to understanding as a dialogical event, such communication occurs only in the form of a mediation of past and present, the fusion of the horizon of a text and of the interpreter. Once completed, a work of art can no longer be tied to its creator but has to be seen as assuming an existence of its own which may embody insights the author may have been unaware of. In opposition to inverting the process of creation, understanding will try to shell-out the subject-matter contained in the text and bring it to expression. The interpreter's activity follows the logic of question and answer and provides the 'object' with the possibility to resonate with new and widened meaning. The context of tradition thereby comes to life again – not in the form of a repetition of the experience the original perceiver may have gained from it, but in a new way: something emerges that had not been there before. The conception of an existence-in-itself of a text is, therefore, quite incorrect and exhibits an element of dogmatism. This is what Gadamer means when he talks about the 'speculative' character of interpretations which are not restricted to the methodical approach. The words used by the interpreter have their origin in the context of language that comes to form an aura of meanings which are quite unique. The appropriation of textual meaning, consequently, has to be regarded not so much as a duplicative effort but as a genuine creation itself; each appropriation is different and equally valid. From here Gadamer can go on to suggest that to understand literature is not a referring back to past events, but a participating here and now in what is being said, the sharing of a message, the disclosure of a world.

What relevant insights can be derived from Gadamer's hermeneutic philosophy concerning Betti's other canons?

The need to participate in the event of understanding seems at first sight to be covered by the 'canon of the actuality of understanding'. A closer look will, however, evidence the crucial point that Betti cannot give a systematic account of the subject's constitutive role. While requiring his active interest in the author and his work – following thereby the hermeneutical maxim that one can only understand, and consequently should only attempt to interpret and translate, a work one is, at least potentially, in agreement with – Betti does not situate the subject historically as a participant in a tradition, universal discourse, etc., and can, therefore, conceive of the concepts he employs initially as instrumental and potentially detrimental to the objectivity of interpretation; in any case, it is the historicality of understanding that Betti sees negatively as the factor allowing only 'relative objectivity'. Paradoxically, Betti considers the process of interpretation in terms of a scheme that is apparent in all forms of cognition – just as Gadamer did; only Betti cannot escape from the subject–object relationship even where another mind addresses us. His historistic stand-point can approach the hermeneutic conception of the 'Other' only asymptotically; even the consideration of the process of interpretative understanding, as involving the re-cognition and re-construction of an author's intention and creational process, has to remain within a psychologistic conception that dismantles and then reassembles human expression in an almost mechanical way. The paradox referred to resides consequently in the fact that, despite his profoundly humanist stance, Betti remains unable to regard the Other as another subject with equally strong demands to be recognized, listened to and agreed with; in the process of understanding, subject and 'object' are irredeemably tied together for better or worse.

As far as the other two canons are concerned, it can be stated briefly that the one referring to the object of interpretation, i.e. that of the 'coherence of meaning', represents a secondary, methodologically diluted form of the hermeneutic circle already discussed, and can only be of heuristic use rather than leading to an awareness of effective-history. Finally, the 'canon of the adequacy of meaning' can most easily be dealt with by reference to Max Weber's ideal-type theory[10] where he counterposes a body of genetic concepts to causal explanation and deals with the questions surrounding the relationship between subject and historical meaning in terms of the demand for *sinnhafte Adäquanz* (meaningful adequacy), thereby neatly circumventing any confrontation with the issue of historism.

To conclude this chapter it may be worth asking what insights Gadamer's investigation into interpretation yield for a better conception of the process of understanding – remembering that Betti considered this question to be the rationale for his own work. The latter, put in a nutshell, found that both interpretation and understanding develop in a triadic process involving an author and a perceiving subject who are both mediated by meaning-full forms; (objective) interpretation, in relation to Understanding, serves as a means to an end.

How does Gadamer see it? In fact, he draws Betti's wrath by collapsing not only interpretation and understanding into one another but by even introducing 'application' as the third moment of what is, essentially, a unitary phenomenon.

Gadamer sets out to legitimate the truth-claims of knowledge derived from extra-scientific spheres of experience via reflection upon the phenomenon of understanding; he does so in the light of his view that science, both social and natural, is today, in the shape of the 'expert', filling the vacuum left by the disintegration of religious interpretations of human existence and the demise of tradition as a source of orientation. That is to say that the successful completion of his task would equally stake a claim for prudence and ensuing praxis in opposition to ever-encroaching technical knowledge and instrumental practice. It is obvious that the field of hermeneutics represents the proving-ground – or last bastion – for non-scientistic debates concerning values and norms. The sphere of interpretation acquires its significance for social development because it is here that communicative understanding about the aims and purpose of social existence is achieved.

The historistic *Geisteswissenschaften* have been characterized by their attempt at assimilating the research process in the field of objectivations of mind, especially in history, to the standards of the natural sciences. Betti has argued forcefully against a misconception in this view which fails to take account of the specificity of the object of the *Geisteswissenschaften* which requires an internal recognition and reconstruction and is, therefore, dependent on the spontaneity of the perceiving subject. In this sense Betti could reject the overtly objectivist nature of the 'historical school' around von Ranke. But it can be argued that his concern with salvaging at least 'relative objectivity' through the employment of a set of canons represents a residual of the scientistic approach to the non-natural sphere. Gadamer has rightly linked science with method – a development originating with Galileo – and its introduction into the hermeneutical process can only lead to the objectification of the 'object' and the subject's mastery over it; at the same time, it provides the basis for approaches that are 'value-free' in respect of their treatment of the subject-matter, and 'neutral' in regard to the use of its result, rendering the results open for re-examination by other interested parties who can ascertain their correctness by following the same routes of inquiry. In the theory of interpretation this conception gave rise to the distinction between interpretation and application, i.e. between theory and practice.

In contrast, the unity of understanding, interpretation and application can also be argued for and shown briefly.

Intellegere and *explicare* find their unity in the fusion of horizon that characterizes any true understanding. This event implies that, say, a text is created anew in an interpretation which is guided by an horizon of understanding that itself changes in the course of its activity; put in another way, the linguisticality of understanding renders interpretation speculative in that the content of an aspect of tradition is given voice and is empowered to communicate to us its truth in terms intelligible to us and consonant with our life experiences. Understanding tradition cannot be limited to the acquisition of knowledge concerning a specific text, but finds its fulfilment in the recognition of truths and insights; it is directed at, and based upon, effective-history and is, therefore, part of its object in such a way that the past is constantly re-interpreted or, what is the same, understood differently. To attribute to the former objective status and to regard the latter as a mere repository of items of knowledge is the consequence of narrowing dialogical experience down to monological research activity.

The distinction between normative application, re-cognitive and re-constructive interpretation and reproduction is equally rejected by Gadamer. Reproduction he considers to be, initially, interpretation aiming at a correct view and is, therefore, also a form of understanding – it does not constitute a re-creation but rather allows a work of art to come into its own. Since understanding always contains interpretation there can be no difference, in principle, between the interpretation of a musical and philological text: it is in both cases undertaken in the medium of language and merges into the immediacy of truth.

In the case of normative application Betti seems to stand on firm ground when he states that interpretation in jurisdiction and theology proceeds from a dogmatic point of view which requires the application of an objective meaning-context to a particular situation. Gadamer argues that it is impossible to clearly distinguish dogmatic from historical interpretation since, in the case of juridical hermeneutics, an historian of law and a jurist approach a legal text from the standpoint of the present legal situation and consider its relevance from this perspective; they both mediate between past and present: the former cannot exclude the contemporary effects of a law, the history of which he is tracing, whilst the jurist has to determine the original intention of the law-maker before he can draw conclusions for the present. Equally, a theologian's sermon represents the concretion of the Good News in that it explicates a received truth. 'Application', as the mediation of past and present, appears as the third moment of the unity of understanding, interpretation and application constituting the hermeneutic effort: adequate understanding of a text, which corresponds to its claim and message, changes with the concrete situation from which it takes place; it is always already an application.

That understanding and application are interwoven Gadamer further clarifies by reference to Aristotle's description of the opposition between *phronesis* on the one side, and *episteme* and *techne* on the other. *Phronesis* (prudence) as practical knowledge is internalized knowledge and cannot be forgotten if it is not needed at the moment. Practical knowledge can, consequently, not be accepted without prejudice. As action-oriented knowledge it is not directed at particular aims as is technical know-how; maxims of action have to be applied to changing situations whereby the original knowledge is itself further developed. This relationship between *phronesis* and applicative understanding underlies the work of the interpreter concerned with tradition; its unity is guaranteed by the dependency of understanding on the structure of prejudices.

Gadamer's hermeneutic philosophy represents obviously a gigantic re-orientation of hermeneutics by freeing it from the constraints it imposed upon itself in its narrow striving for methodically secured objectivity. At the same time, it provided a perspective for viewing scientific progress in general in terms of the universality of the hermeneutic aspect which was expounded on parallel lines by Kuhn's paradigm-oriented conception of scientific revolutions. Hermeneutic reflection upon the effective-history underlying all thought represents not only a critique of the objectivism of historism but also of the physicalism under-lying the ideal of a Unity of science – without for a moment impinging upon the scientific character of the result achieved under the auspices of historism and the positivist logic of science.

The next chapter will list criticisms of this part of Gadamer's work in conjunction with another. Habermas and Apel criticized Gadamer for his – what they considered uncritical – acceptance of the role of tradition as authoritative for present concerns, together with his 'ontologization of language', which fails to recognize its use as a medium of domination. The critique of ideology attempts to trace suppressed interests which have been excluded from the on-going dialogue of past and present; Reason is again reaffirmed as the restless agency for self-autonomy in conflict with tradition and authority.

Reading II

Hans-Georg Gadamer
The universality of the hermeneutical* problem

(translated by David Linge)

Why has the problem of language come to occupy the same central position in current philosophical discussions that the concept of thought, or 'thought thinking itself,' held in philosophy a century and a half ago? By answering this question, I shall try to give an answer indirectly to the central question of the modern age – a question posed for us by the existence of modern science. It is the question of how our natural view of the world – the experience of the world that we have as we simply live out our lives – is related to the unassailable and anonymous authority that confronts us in the pronouncements of science. Since the seventeenth century, the real task of philosophy has been to mediate this new employment of man's cognitive and constructive capacities with the totality of our experience of life. This task has found expression in a variety of ways, including our own generation's attempt to bring the topic of language to the center of philosophical concern. Language is the fundamental mode of operation of our being-in-the-world and the all-embracing form of the constitution of the world. Hence we always have in view the pronouncements of the sciences, which are fixed in nonverbal signs. And our task is to reconnect the objective world of technology, which the sciences place at our disposal and discretion, with those fundamental orders of our being that are neither arbitrary nor manipulable by us, but rather simply demand our respect.

I want to elucidate several phenomena in which the universality of this question becomes evident. I have called the point of view involved in this theme 'hermeneutical,' a term developed by Heidegger. Heidegger was continuing a perspective stemming originally from Protestant theology and transmitted into our own century by Wilhelm Dilthey.

What is hermeneutics? I would like to start from two ex-

*Editor's note: Following the terminology employed in this book, please read 'hermeneutic' for 'hermeneutical' throughout this essay.

128

periences of alienation that we encounter in our concrete existence: the experience of alienation of the aesthetic consciousness and the experience of alienation of the historical consciousness. In both cases what I mean can be stated in a few words. The aesthetic consciousness realizes a possibility that as such we can neither deny nor diminish in its value, namely, that we relate ourselves, either negatively or affirmatively, to the quality of an artistic form. This statement means we are related in such a way that the judgment we make decides in the end regarding the expressive power and validity of what we judge. What we reject has nothing to say to us – or we reject it because it has nothing to say to us. This characterizes our relation to art in the broadest sense of the word, a sense that, as Hegel has shown, includes the entire religious world of the ancient Greeks, whose religion of beauty experienced the divine in concrete works of art that man creates in response to the gods. When it loses its original and unquestioned authority, this whole world of experience becomes alienated into an object of aesthetic judgment. At the same time, however, we must admit that the world of artistic tradition – the splendid contemporaneousness that we gain through art with so many human worlds – is more than a mere object of our free acceptance or rejection. Is it not true that when a work of art has seized us it no longer leaves us the freedom to push it away from us once again and to accept or reject it on our own terms? And is it not also true that these artistic creations, which come down through the millennia, were not created for such aesthetic acceptance or rejection? No artist of the religiously vital cultures of the past ever produced his work of art with any other intention than that his creation should be received in terms of what it says and presents and that it should have its place in the world where men live together. The consciousness of art – the aesthetic consciousness – is always secondary to the immediate truth-claim that proceeds from the work of art itself. To this extent, when we judge a work of art on the basis of its aesthetic quality, something that is really much more intimately familiar to us is alienated. This alienation into aesthetic judgment always takes place when we have withdrawn ourselves and are no longer open to the immediate claim of that which grasps us. Thus one point of departure for my reflections in *Truth and Method* was that the aesthetic sovereignty that claims its rights in the experience of art represents an alienation when compared to the authentic experience that confronts us in the form of art itself.

About thirty years ago, this problem cropped up in a particularly distorted form when National Socialist politics of art, as a means to its own ends, tried to criticize formalism by arguing that art is bound to a people. Despite its misuse by the National Socialists, we cannot deny that the idea of art being bound to a people involves a real insight. A genuine artistic creation stands within a particular community, and such a community is always distinguishable from the cultured society that is informed and terrorized by art criticism.

The second mode of the experience of alienation is the historical consciousness – the noble and slowly perfected art of holding ourselves at a critical distance in dealing with witnesses to past life. Ranke's celebrated description of this idea as the extinguishing of the individual provided a popular formula for the ideal of historical thinking: the historical consciousness has the task of understanding all the witnesses of a past time out of the spirit of that time, of extricating them from the preoccupations of our own present life, and of knowing, without moral smugness, the past as a human phenomenon. In his well-known essay, *The Use and Abuse of History*, Nietzsche formulated the contradiction between this historical distancing and the immediate will to shape things that always cleaves to the present. And at the same time he exposed many of the consequences of what he called the 'Alexandrian,' weakened form of the will, which is found in modern historical science. We might recall his indictment of the weakness of evaluation that has befallen the modern mind because it has become so accustomed to considering things in ever different and changing lights that it is blinded and incapable of arriving at an opinion of its own regarding the objects it studies. It is unable to determine its own position vis-à-vis what confronts it. Nietzsche traces the value-blindness of historical objectivism back to the conflict between the alienated historical world and the life-powers of the present.

To be sure, Nietzsche is an ecstatic witness. But our actual experience of the historical consciousness in the last one hundred years has taught us most emphatically that there are serious difficulties involved in its claim to historical objectivity. Even in those masterworks of historical scholarship that seem to be the very consummation of the extinguishing of the individual demanded by Ranke, it is still an unquestioned principle of our scientific experience that we can classify these works with unfailing accuracy in terms of the political tendencies of the time in which they were written. When we read Mommsen's *History of Rome*, we know who alone could have written it, that is, we can identify the political situation in which this historian organized the voices of the past in a meaningful way. We know it too in the case of Treitschke or of Sybel, to choose only a few prominent names from Prussian historiography. This clearly means, first of all, that the whole reality of historical experience does not find expression in the mastery of historical method. No one disputes the fact that controlling the prejudices of our own present to such an extent that we do not misunderstand the witnesses of the past is a valid aim, but obviously such control does not completely fulfill the task of understanding the past and its transmissions. Indeed, it could very well be that only *insignificant* things in historical scholarship permit us to approximate this ideal of totally extinguishing individuality, while the great productive achievements of scholarship always preserve something of the splendid magic of immediately mirroring the present in the past and the past in the present. Historical science, the second experience from which I begin, expresses only one part of our actual experience – our actual encounter with historical tradition – and it knows only an alienated form of this historical tradition.

We can contrast the hermeneutical consciousness with these examples of alienation as a more comprehensive possibility that we must develop. But, in the case of this hermeneutical consciousness also, our initial task must be to overcome the epistemological truncation by which the traditional 'science of hermeneutics' has been absorbed into the idea of modern science. If we consider Schleiermacher's hermeneutics, for instance, we find his view of this discipline peculiarly restricted by the modern idea of science. Schleiermacher's hermeneutics shows him to be a leading voice of historical romanticism. But at the same time, he kept the concern of the Christian theologian clearly in mind, intending his hermeneutics, as a general doctrine of the art of understanding, to be of value in the special work of interpreting Scripture. Schleiermacher defined hermeneutics as the art of avoiding misunderstanding. To exclude by controlled, methodical consideration whatever is alien and leads to misunderstanding – misunderstanding suggested to us by distance in time, change in linguistic usages, or in the meanings of words and modes of thinking – that is certainly far from an absurd description of the hermeneutical endeavor. But the question also arises as to whether the phenomenon of understanding is defined appropriately when we saw that to understand is to avoid misunderstanding. Is it not, in fact, the case that every misunderstanding presupposes a 'deep common accord'?

I am trying to call attention here to a common experience. We say, for instance, that understanding and misunderstanding take place between I and thou. But the formulation 'I and thou' already betrays an enormous alienation. There is nothing like an 'I and thou' at all – there is neither the I nor the thou as isolated, substantial realities. I may say 'thou' and I may refer to myself over against a thou, but a common understanding [*Verständigung*] always precedes these situations. We all know that to say 'thou' to someone presupposes a deep common accord [*tiefes Einverständnis*]. Something enduring is already present when this word is spoken. When we try to reach agreement on a matter on which we have different opinions, this deeper factor always comes into play, even if we are seldom aware of it. Now the science of hermeneutics would have us believe that the opinion we have to understand is something alien that seeks to lure us into misunderstanding, and our task is to exclude every element through which a misunderstanding can creep in. We accomplish this task by a controlled procedure of historical training, by historical criticism, and by a controllable method in connection with powers of psychological empathy. It seems to me that this description is valid in one respect, but yet it is only a partial description of a comprehensive life-phenomenon that constitutes the 'we' that we all are. Our task, it seems to me, is to transcend the prejudices that underlie the aesthetic consciousness, the historical consciousness, and the hermeneutical consciousness that has been restricted to a technique for avoiding misunderstandings and to overcome the alienations present in them all.

What is it, then, in these three experiences that seemed to us to have been left out, and what makes us so sensitive to the distinctiveness of these experiences? What is the *aesthetic* consciousness when compared to the fullness of what has already addressed us – what we call 'classical' in art? Is it not always already determined in this way what will be expressive for us and what we will find significant? Whenever we say with an instinctive, even if perhaps erroneous, certainty (but a certainty that is initially valid for our consciousness) 'this is classical; it will endure,' what we are speaking of has already preformed our possibility for aesthetic judgment. There are no purely formal criteria that can claim to judge and sanction the formative level simply on the basis of its artistic virtuosity. Rather, our sensitive-spiritual existence is an aesthetic resonance chamber that resonates with the voices that are constantly reaching us, preceding all explicit aesthetic judgment.

The situation is similar with the historical consciousness. Here, too, we must certainly admit that there are innumerable tasks of historical scholarship that have no relation to our own present and to the depths of its historical consciousness. But it seems to me there can be no doubt that the great horizon of the past, out of which our culture and our present live, influences us in everything we want, hope for, or fear in the future. History is only present to us in light of our futurity. Here we have all learned from Heidegger, for he exhibited precisely the primacy of futurity for our possible recollection and retention, and for the whole of our history.

Heidegger worked out this primacy in his doctrine of the productivity of the hermeneutical circle. I have given the following formulation to this insight: It is not so much our judgments as it is our prejudices that constitute our being.* This is a provocative formulation, for I am using it to restore to its rightful place a positive concept of prejudice that was driven out of our linguistic usage by the French and the English Enlightenment. It can be shown that the concept of prejudice did not originally have the meaning we have attached to it. Prejudices are not necessarily unjustified and erroneous, so that they inevitably distort the truth. In fact, the historicity of our existence entails that prejudices, in the literal sense of the word, constitute the initial directedness of our whole ability to experience. Prejudices are biases of our openness to the world. They are simply conditions whereby we experience something – whereby what we encounter says something to us. This formulation certainly does not mean that we are enclosed within a wall of prejudices and only let through the narrow portals those things that can produce a pass saying, 'Nothing new will be said here.' Instead we welcome just that guest who promises something new to our curiosity. But how do we know the guest whom we admit is one who has something *new* to say to us? Is not our expectation and our readiness to hear the new also necessarily determined by the old that has already taken posession of us? The concept of prejudice is closely connected to the concept of authority, and the above image makes it clear that it is in need of hermeneutical rehabilitation. Like every image, however, this one too is misleading. The nature of the hermeneutical experience is not that something is outside and desires admission. Rather, we are possessed by something and precisely by means of it we are opened up for the new, the different, the

*Cf. *WM*, p. 261.

true. Plato made this clear in his beautiful comparison of bodily foods with spiritual nourishment: while we can refuse the former (e.g., on the advice of a physician), we have always taken the latter into ourselves already.

But now the question arises as to how we can legitimate this hermeneutical conditionedness of our being in the face of modern science, which stands or falls with the principle of being unbiased and prejudiceless. We will certainly not accomplish this legitimation by making prescriptions for science and recommending that it toe the line – quite aside from the fact that such pronouncements always have something comical about them. Science will not do us this favor. It will continue along its own path with an inner necessity beyond its control, and it will produce more and more breathtaking knowledge and controlling power. It can be no other way. It is senseless, for instance, to hinder a genetic researcher because such research threatens to breed a superman. Hence the problem cannot appear as one in which our human consciousness ranges itself over against the world of science and presumes to develop a kind of antiscience. Nevertheless, we cannot avoid the question of whether what we are aware of in such apparently harmless examples as the aesthetic consciousness and the historical consciousness does not represent a problem that is also present in modern natural science and our technological attitude toward the world. If modern science enables us to erect a new world of technological purposes that transforms everything around us, we are not thereby suggesting that the researcher who gained the knowledge decisive for this state of affairs even considered technical applications. The genuine researcher is motivated by a desire for knowledge and by nothing else. And yet, over against the whole of our civilization that is founded on modern science, we must ask repeatedly if something has not been omitted. If the presuppositions of these possibilities for knowing and making remain half in the dark, cannot the result be that the hand applying this knowledge will be destructive?

The problem is really universal. The hermeneutical question, as I have characterized it, is not restricted to the areas from which I began in my own investigations. My only concern there was to secure a theoretical basis that would enable us to deal with the basic factor of contemporary culture, namely, science and its industrial, technological utilization. Statistics provide us with a useful example of how the hermeneutical dimension encompasses the entire procedure of science. It is an extreme example, but it shows us that science always stands under definite conditions of methodological abstraction and that the successes of modern sciences rest on the fact that other possibilities for questioning are concealed by abstraction. This fact comes out clearly in the case of statistics, for the anticipatory character of the questions statistics answer make it particularly suitable for propaganda purposes. Indeed, effective propaganda must always try to influence initially the judgment of the person addressed and to restrict his possibilities of judgment. Thus what is established by statistics seems to be a language of facts, but which questions these facts answer and which facts would begin to speak if other questions were asked are hermeneutical questions. Only a hermeneutical inquiry would legitimate the meaning of these facts and thus the consequences that follow from them.

But I am anticipating, and have inadvertently used the phrase, 'which answers to which questions fit the facts.' This phrase is in fact the hermeneutical *Urphänomen*: No assertion is possible that cannot be understood as an answer to a question, and assertions can only be understood in this way. It does not impair the impressive methodology of modern science in the least. Whoever wants to learn a science has to learn to master its methodology. But we also know that methodology as such does not guarantee in any way the productivity of its application. Any experience of life can confirm the fact that there is such a thing as methodological sterility, that is, the application of a method to something not really worth knowing, to something that has not been made an object of investigation on the basis of a genuine question.

The methodological self-consciousness of modern science certainly stands in opposition to this argument. A historian, for example, will say in reply: It is all very nice to talk about the historical tradition in which alone the voices of the past gain their meaning and through which the prejudices that determine the present are inspired. But the situation is completely different in questions of serious historical research. How could one seriously mean, for example, that the clarification of the taxation practices of fifteenth-century cities or of the marital customs of Eskimos somehow first receive their meaning from the consciousness of the present and its anticipations? These are questions of historical knowledge that we take up as tasks quite independently of any relation to the present.

In answering this objection, one can say that the extremity of this point of view would be similar to what we find in certain large industrial research facilities, above all in America and

Russia. I mean the so-called random experiment in which one simply covers the material without concern for waste or cost, taking the chance that some day one measurement among the thousands of measurements will finally yield an interesting finding; that is, it will turn out to be the answer to a question from which someone can progress. No doubt modern research in the humanities also works this way to some extent. One thinks, for instance, of the great editions and especially of the ever more perfect indexes. It must remain an open question, of course, whether by such procedures modern historical research increases the chances of actually noticing the interesting fact and thus gaining from it the corresponding enrichment of our knowledge. But even if they do, one might ask: Is this an ideal, that countless research projects (i.e., determinations of the connection of facts) are extracted from a thousand historians, so that the 1001st historian can find something interesting? Of course I am drawing a caricature of genuine scholarship. But in every caricature there is an element of truth, and this one contains an indirect answer to the question of what it is that really makes the productive scholar. That he has learned the methods? The person who never produces anything new has also done that. It is imagination [*Phantasie*] that is the decisive function of the scholar. Imagination naturally has a hermeneutical function and serves the sense for what is questionable. It serves the ability to expose real, productive questions, something in which, generally speaking, only he who masters all the methods of his science succeeds.

As a student of Plato, I particularly love those scenes in which Socrates gets into a dispute with the Sophist virtuosi and drives them to despair by his questions. Eventually they can endure his questions no longer and claim for themselves the apparently preferable role of the questioner. And what happens? They can think of nothing at all to ask. Nothing at all occurs to them that is worth while going into and trying to answer.

I draw the following inference from this observation. The real power of hermeneutical consciousness is our ability to see what is questionable. Now if what we have before our eyes is not only the artistic tradition of a people, or historical tradition, or the principle of modern science in its hermeneutical preconditions but rather the whole of our experience, then we have succeeded, I think, in joining the experience of science to our own universal and human experience of life. For we have now reached the fundamental level that we can call (with Johannes Lohmann) the 'linguistic constitution of the world.'[1] It presents itself as the consciousness that is effected by history [*wirkungs-geschichtliches Bewusstsein*] and that provides an initial schematization for all our possibilities of knowing. I leave out of account the fact that the scholar – even the natural scientist – is perhaps not completely free of custom and society and from all possible factors in his environment. What I mean is that precisely *within* his scientific experience it is not so much the 'laws of ironclad inference' (Helmholz) that present fruitful ideas to him, but rather unforeseen constellations that kindle the spark of scientific inspiration (e.g., Newton's falling apple or some other incidental observation).

The consciousness that is effected by history has its fulfillment in what is linguistic. We can learn from the sensitive student of language that language, in its life and occurrence, must not be thought of as merely changing, but rather as something that has a teleology operating within it. This means that the words that are formed, the means of expression that appear in a language in order to say certain things, are not accidentally fixed, since they do not once again fall altogether into disuse. Instead, a definite articulation of the world is built up – a process that works as if guided and one that we can always observe in children who are learning to speak.

We can illustrate this by considering a passage in Aristotle's *Posterior Analytics* that ingeniously describes one definite aspect of language formation.[2] The passage treats what Aristotle calls the *epagoge*, that is, the formation of the universal. How does one arrive at a universal? In philosophy we say: how do we arrive at a general concept, but even words in this sense are obviously general. How does it happen that they are 'words,' that is, that they have a general meaning? In his first apperception, a sensuously equipped being finds himself in a surging sea of stimuli, and finally one day he begins, as we say, to know something. Clearly we do not mean that he was previously blind. Rather, when we say 'to know' [*erkennen*] we mean 'to recognize' [*wiedererkennen*], that is, to pick something out [*herauserkennen*] of the stream of images flowing past as being identical. What is picked out in this fashion is clearly retained. But how? When does a child know its mother for the first time? When it sees her for the first time? No. Then when? How does it take place? Can we really say at all that there is a single event in which a first knowing extricates the child from the darkness of not knowing? It seems obvious to me that we cannot. Aristotle has described this wonderfully. He says it is the same as when an army is in flight, driven by panic, until at last someone stops and looks around to see whether the foe is still dangerously close behind. We cannot say that the army stops when one soldier has stopped. But then another stops. The army does not stop by virtue of the fact that two soldiers stop. When does it actually stop, then? Suddenly it stands its ground again. Suddenly it obeys the command once again. A subtle pun is involved in Aristotle's description, for in Greek 'command' means *arche*, that is, *principium*. When is the principle present as a principle? Through what capacity? This question is in fact the question of the occurrence of the universal.

If I have not misunderstood Johannes Lohmann's exposition, precisely this same teleology operates constantly in the life of language. When Lohmann speaks of linguistic tendencies as the real agents of history in which specific forms expand, he knows of course that it occurs in these forms of realization, of 'coming to a stand' [*Zum-Stehen-Kommen*], as the beautiful German word says. What is manifest here, I contend, is the real mode of operation of our whole human experience of the world. Learning to speak is surely a phase of special productivity, and in the course of time we have all transformed the genius of the three-year-old into a poor and meager talent. But in the utilization of the linguistic interpretation of the world that finally comes about, something of the productivity of our beginnings remains alive. We are all acquainted with this, for instance, in the attempt to translate, in practical life or in literature or wherever; that is, we are familiar with the strange, uncomfortable, and tortuous feeling we have as long as we do not have the right word. When we have found the right expression (it need not always be one word), when we are certain that we have it, then it 'stands,' then something has come to a 'stand.' Once again we have a halt in the midst of the rush of the foreign language, whose endless variation makes us lose our orientation. What I am describing is the mode of the whole human experience of the world. I call this experience hermeneutical, for the process we are describing is repeated continually throughout our familiar experience. There is always a world already interpreted, already organized in its basic relations, into which experience steps as something new, upsetting what has led our expectations and undergoing reorganization itself in the upheaval. Misunderstanding and strangeness are not the first factors, so that avoiding misunderstanding can be regarded as the specific task of hermeneutics. Just the reverse is the case. Only the support of familiar and common understanding makes possible the venture into the alien, the lifting up of something out of the alien, and thus the broadening and enrichment of our own experience of the world.

This discussion shows how the claim to universality that is appropriate to the hermeneutical dimension is to be understood. Understanding is language-bound. But this assertion does not lead us into any kind of linguistic relativism. It is indeed true that we live within a language, but language is not a system of signals that we send off with the aid of a telegraphic key when we enter the office or transmission station. That is not speaking, for it does not have the infinity of the act that is linguistically creative and world experiencing. While we live wholly within a language, the fact that we do so does not constitute linguistic relativism because there is absolutely no captivity within a language – not even within our native language. We all experience this when we learn a foreign language, especially on journeys insofar as we master the foreign language to some extent. To master the foreign language means precisely that when we engage in speaking it in the foreign land, we do not constantly consult inwardly our own world and its vocabulary. The better we know the language, the less such a side glance at our native language is perceptible, and only because we never know foreign languages well enough do we always have something of this feeling. But it is nevertheless already speaking, even if perhaps a stammering speaking, for stammering is the obstruction of a desire to speak and is thus opened into the infinite realm of possible expression. Any language in which we live is infinite in this sense, and it is completely mistaken to infer that reason is fragmented because there are various languages. Just the opposite is the case. Precisely through our finitude, the particularity of our being, which is evident even in the variety of languages, the infinite dialogue is opened in the direction of the truth that we are.

If this is correct, then the relation of our modern industrial world, founded by science, which we described at the outset, is mirrored above all on the level of language. We live in an epoch in which an increasing leveling of all life-forms is taking place – that is the rationally necessary requirement for maintaining life on our planet. The food problem of mankind, for example, can only be overcome by the surrender of the lavish wastefulness that has covered the earth. Unavoidably, the mechanical, industrial world is expanding within the life of the individual as a sort of sphere of technical perfection. When we hear modern lovers talking to each other, we often wonder if they are communicating with words or with advertising labels and technical terms from the sign language of the modern industrial world. It is inevitable that the leveled life-forms of the industrial age also affect language, and in fact the impoverishment of the vocabulary of language is making enormous progress, thus bringing about an approximation of language to a technical sign-system. Leveling tendencies of this kind are irresistible. Yet in spite of them the simultaneous building up of our own world in language still persists whenever we want to say something to each other. The result is the actual relationship of men to each other. Each one is at first a kind of linguistic circle, and these linguistic circles come into contact with each other, merging more and more. Language occurs once again, in vocabulary and grammar as always, and never without the inner infinity of the dialogue that is in progress between every speaker and his partner. That is the fundamental dimension of hermeneutics. Genuine speaking, which has something to say and hence does not give prearranged signals, but rather seeks words through which one reaches the other person, is the universal human task – but it is a special task for the theologian, to whom is commissioned the saying-further (*Weitersagen*) of a message that stands written.

Notes

1 Cf. Johannes Lohmann, *Philosophie und Sprachwissenschaft* (Berlin: Duncker & Humbolt, 1963).
2 Aristotle, *Posterior Analytics*, 100a 11–13.

Part III

Critical hermeneutics

Introduction

Hermeneutics has so far been concerned with two interrelated aspects: the mediation of tradition and the understanding of subjectively intended meaning. Differences between hermeneutic philosophy and hermeneutical theory revolved around the question of how such understanding was possible and to what extent it could constitute objective knowledge. But while both approaches placed conflicting emphasis on the role of the interpreter, they share the exclusion of one dimension: the questioning of the content of the object of interpretation. Any reflection as to the truth of a text or of traditioned meaning was either excluded as falling outside the concerns of an epistemology and methodology of the understanding process – or it was outbid by the *a priori* assumption of the superiority of tradition and its all-encompassing quality.

The suspicion concerning the claims to truth contained in an author's work or in the tradition one is inhabiting that is lacking in idealist hermeneutics is, by contrast, the hallmark of critical hermeneutics. The experience of half-truths, lies, propaganda, manipulation and oppression of thought, censorship, etc., provide a prima facie case against the unquestioning acceptance of claims to knowledge or truth. On a more reflexive level, the existence of ideological structures, the force over people's minds exercised by 'false consciousness', has found its most exhaustive and damning exposition in the shape of historical materialism. It is here that false reflections of a 'false' reality have found their most penetrating critique – not in the sense of having an abstract set of ideas or values put against them, but by evidencing their origin in definite material conditions that add up to a state of unfreedom. The critique of the misunderstanding of self and others entailed the critique of the reality that gave rise to them.

As 'depth hermeneutics', critical hermeneutics seeks out the causes of distorted understanding and communication which operate underneath seemingly normal interaction. For Betti, intolerance and selfishness represented the main barriers to understanding, so that an exhortation to avoid these sins was all that was necessary and possible. Even in his 'critical-objective' approach we miss, therefore, an acceptance of the possibility of distorted meaning that can only be recognized and dissolved by assuming a standpoint *outside* this sphere of the creation and distribution of meaning, i.e. by leaving the ground that binds together all participants in understanding processes.

Because of its reference to empirical contingencies underlying intellectual processes, 'critical understanding' contains an element of causal explanation. It is this moment of objectification, that aims at theoretical truth, which links critical with hermeneutical understanding: the latter, after all, represented a move away from the uncritical, dogmatic acceptance of 'authoritative' texts and aimed at an unbiased rendering – even if the moral or intellectual content was itself never questioned.

The practical engagement on the side of historic truth and a better future brings critical hermeneutics into contact with hermeneutic philosophy – only that the 'anticipation of perfection' Gadamer evidences as a precondition of interpretation is no longer regarded as merely a contemplative act. In striving for practically relevant knowledge a mediation of the 'object' and the interpreter's own motives has to occur which is guided by the projective anticipation of the emergence of material conditions conducive to the self-knowledge of social actors.

Apel and Habermas have outlined an approach in which the meaning embedded in objectivations of human activity is understood objectively and then confronted with the 'author's' self-understanding of the intentions underlying them. By synthesizing explanatory and interpretative procedures it is hoped that it may be possible to demonstrate to social actors why they thought what they thought, why it may have been wrong, and how the mistake could be corrected. As a model for this task Apel, Habermas, and Lorenzer draw on psychoanalysis since it is here that 'distorted meaning' is interpreted in view of a patient's whole life-history and in reference to a theoretical system that can be used to explain the emergence of specific illnesses.

'Materialist' hermeneutics denotes here an emphasis on the empirical conditions underlying a patient's suffering, viz. the contradictions inherent in capitalist society.

'Materialistic hermeneutics', being based on a conception of intellectual representations as a reflection of economic conditions and relationships, can by-pass the hermeneutic intepretation of objectivations and recur directly to the material base of any such superstructural phenomena; 'hermeneutics' here takes the form of an explanation of the genesis and validity of human artefacts. Given its empirical-materialistic direction, this approach can reject all meaning-interpretative work as an outflow of bourgois ideology.

For those theorists who still adhere to an interpretative component in their critique of ideology, an important point emerges and demands clarification: how do they justify their own standpoint and their claim to know 'better'? Apart from having to evidence criteria for distinguishing 'true' from 'false' consciousness, their assumed position as arbiters over other people's conceptions contains an elitist undercurrent which an approach that lays claim to an 'emancipatory interest' would do well to reflect upon.

Chapter 7

Apel: critical hermeneutics in the form of an anthropology of knowledge

Heidegger's existential–ontological hermeneutic has been considered as a deepening of Kant's transcendental critique of knowledge. It was possible to show how the 'fore-structure' of understanding itself provided the basis on which the question of the conditions of the possibility of correct knowledge could be asked.

The figure of the hermeneutic circle was used by Gadamer to reject the objectivism inherent in the historical–hermeneutical *Geisteswissenschaften*. When challenged by Betti to evidence any criteria for judging the correctness or truth of proffered interpretations – the *quaestio iuris* – Gadamer answered that he was only concerned with 'showing what always happens when we understand', i.e. the *quaestio facti*.

Reference to the embeddedness of understanding in the historicality and finitude of Dasein was seen by Betti as a relapse into subjectivism. For critical hermeneutics it not only represents the forfeiting of the degree of autonomy from irrational social forces which thought acquired with the Enlightenment, but also precludes hermeneutic thought from assuming any methodological relevance. It is in this context that Apel's investigation into 'the possibility of a philosophical hermeneutic guided by the regulative principle of a progress in knowledge' (Apel, 1973, vol. I, p. 48) acquires its contour – which also marks it off from Betti's reactivation of traditional, romanticist hermeneutics.

The fulcrum of Apel's undertaking is nothing less than the 'transformation of philosophy'. By bringing together the dominant strands of contemporary philosophy: pragmatism (Peirce), linguistic philosophy (Wittgenstein), existential ontology.[1] The implications of the transformation of *a priori*, subject-oriented philosophy that has dominated Western philosophy since Descartes and certainly up to Husserl are fascinating enough to warrant attention.

1. Differences with Gadamer

Apel's programme is one of mediating the recognition of the existence of the hermeneutic circle underlying all thought-activity with the requirement of objective standards for the determination of truth-claims and the need for criteria for assessing the validity of proffered interpretations. This balancing act, which is undertaken with Heidegger's analysis of Dasein as the supporting rope, is hoped to lead to a 'methodologically relevant transcendental philosophy'.

This formulation pinpoints Apel's central criticism of Gadamer's hermeneutic philosophy: its claim to represent a transcendental philosophy in the Kantian sense is unjustified because it quite explicitly rejects the need to answer the *quaestio iuris*. The execution of Apel's ambitious task will immediately reveal the difference between his and Betti's approach: while both make the same point, Betti's corrective leads to a pre-Heideggerian position whereas Apel makes the historicality of understanding his point of departure.

Apel rejects the reasoning Gadamer employs in his response to Betti's critique: 'the task of a normatively relevant critique cannot be abandoned in favour of a mere *description* of that *which is*; and it is impossible to refer to a Critique of Pure Reason without attempting to answer the question after the conditions of the validity of science together with the question after its possibility' (1973, vol. I, pp. 35–6). In the context of the problem of 'how is understanding possible?' the whole issue presents itself as follows: the analysis of the 'fore-structure' of understanding cannot focus solely on the possibility of understanding at the exclusion of a concern for the validity of its results.

Gadamer evidences the structure of the fusion of past and present as underlying both accurate understanding and mis-comprehension – and feels no more is required for the purpose of demonstrating the possibility of understanding. In Apel's view, however, even this problematic cannot be adequately expounded unless one also asks about the *validity* of understanding; in fact, we require some criteria for distinguishing between understanding and misunderstanding *before* we can answer the question of the possibility of understanding.

In this sense, Apel calls for a 'normatively–methodologically relevant philosophical hermeneutic'. Such a conception would reassert the possibility of progress in interpretation – which Gadamer and Betti reduced to the emergence of 'different' interpretations. At the same time, the interpreter may be in a position to understand the author better than he had understood himself; his task to judge critically cannot be avoided by attributing some form of superiority to the 'object' or by pointing out that the interpreter himself necessarily proceeds from a dogmatic basis.[2]

Dialectical mediation of hermeneutic and explanatory approaches

The possibility and necessity of a progress in interpretative understanding arises from the field of hermeneutics itself when, for example, communication is impeded or rendered impossible. Such events are the domain of psychoanalysis and the critique of ideology, which both attempt to remove barriers to understanding that may be operative without the person or social group concerned being aware of them – as is the case in the behaviour of neurotic persons and groups acting with a 'false consciousness'. The 'interpreter', psychoanalyst or critical sociologist, is here in a position from where he understands the author better than he had understood himself on account of his ability to view instances of inadequate self-understanding in reference to a body of theory incorporating the life-history of individual and collective agents. Action originating from an inadequate or non-existent understanding of its motives becomes understandable with the help of an explanatory framework depicting its 'causes'. What may appear at first sight as the intrusion of a mode of cognition appropriate to the investigation of natural processes into the field of intersubjective communication and mediation of tradition is utilized in Apel's programme for the purpose of emancipation, i.e. that process of reflection through which individual and social processes are rendered transparent to the actors involved, enabling them to pursue their further development with consciousness and will – rather than remaining the end-product of a causal chain operative behind their backs.

These unconscious motivations, *qua* 'causes', represent a quasi-natural element in the history of the individual and the species and one which varies with the level of the interaction of man and nature achieved in a society – its economic development – and the form of political domination operative at given points of time. In conditions of scarcity the realm of necessity casts its shadow over that freedom, requiring men to follow economic imperatives rather than their desire for self-fulfilment.

The quasi-natural aspect of human action dominates in the 'pre-history' (Marx) of man – a state of affairs that still characterizes the present.

The idealist pre-supposition of hermeneutics can consequently be formulated as the neglect to attend to the material conditions under which history proceeds, which led to the failure to acknowledge the possibility that History, viz. the progress towards self-realization, is still hobbling along on crutches, deformed by outmoded forms of domination even in conditions where material want should already be an anachronism, and supported only by conceptions of human dignity which still have to be asserted defiantly in the face of an inhumane reality rather than being taken for granted. Put more positively, hermeneutics wrongly assumes that the step from pre-history to history proper has already been taken and that men are the conscious and self-determining creators of their own future, as philosophy has always promised.

These conditions, in which men act under the dictates not only of nature but also of a 'second nature',[3] that is of man's social environment appearing as unchangeable, uncontrollable and sometimes as menacing as 'first' or physical nature, provide the material basis for the introduction of causal and statistical methods into social science. Causal approaches imply that human behaviour has to be explained rather than 'understood', i.e. the motives underlying behaviour are operative in a causal way rather than being reasons that have been formed consciously and that are immediately intelligible as such to others; the application of statistics can only be successful if people do behave in regular, if not stereotyped, fashion – which is only another way of stating that all, or most, creativity and spontaneity has been driven out of them.

Since its 'object' is preformed in such a way that it incorporates both explanatory and interpretative moments, it would be the obvious task to consider them together in the context of the methodology of social science. Apel's approach differs from most other attempts in this field by avoiding any eclectic complementarity thesis by, instead, insisting on a dialectical synthesis that has its concrete correlate in the existence of a fundamental tension within the totality of social existence between forces that wish to confine man in his present state of unfreedom and those striving for something better; the synthesis of the two would be an 'apocalyptic'[4] event at the end of which man would emerge as the subject–object of history. On the methodological level, the constitution of its object as a

dialectical-contradictory one would lead to the following constellation for critical hermeneutics.

The methodology of the social sciences is characterized by the
clash between those wishing to achieve the standards of
objectivity and certainty apparent in the natural sciences[5] by
assimilating their methods on the one hand, and those who
insist on the irreducible and inalienably human aspect of social
life which defies generalization, prediction and control. But
whereas the interests in control and understanding underlying
these conflicting approaches exist in an uneasy relationship in
the social sciences, critical hermeneutics attempts a dialectical
mediation in the form of a critique of ideology. The paradigm
here is psychoanalysis, i.e. that process through which a patient
is helped to overcome his symptomatic behaviour through the
combined use of causal explanation and deepened self-understanding. The difference between critical hermeneutics in the
form of a critical sociology and positivist social science is
obvious: the former hopes to dissolve the causal, 'natural',
component in human action through making transparent their
mechanism and thereby enabling human actors to regain
mastery over their destiny; the latter continues and attempts to
extend the use of the methods of natural science which treat of
human individuals as mere objects of quantification, thereby
perpetuating the reign of 'second nature' in which social processes appear as natural events outside the scope of conscious
intervention, through providing the data required for the
technocratic-manipulative steering of social evolution.

2. The transformation of philosophy

The critical reconstruction of individual and social processes
supersedes the hermeneutic(al) interpretation of meaning. As
far as the latter is concerned, critical hermeneutics commits an
unjustifiable transgression by attempting to gain access to
meaning outside or behind the intentional self-understanding of
actors. Hermeneuticians regard the belief to 'know better' as
misguided and arrogant – contravening, for example, the 'fore-
conception of perfection' that, according to Gadamer, necessarily
guides interpretation.

How can the standpoint of critical hermeneutics be justified?
Asking after the conditions for the possibility of critical understanding requires an answer as fundamental as that which Kant
gave for the possibility of the natural sciences – without

starting from the hypostatization of a 'subject' or 'conscious-ness' as the metaphysical guarantor of the intersubjective validity of knowledge, but from the presupposition that we are – because of the fact that no one can follow a rule alone or only once (Wittgenstein) – destined *a priori* to intersubjective communication and understanding . . . . In this sense, a hermeneutically transformed transcendental philosophy starts from the *a priori* of an actual communicative community which is, for us, practically identical with the human species or society. (1973, vol. I, pp. 59–60)

It is clear that the imperfections apparent in existing communication, which are due to the intrusion of an element of force, necessitates the establishing of 'regulative principles' with the help of which actual states of affairs can be measured and judged and which provide the guideline for the endeavour to understand 'better' – which itself implies the emancipatory move towards a freer society. Apel, consequently, introduces the concept of an 'ideal communicative community'[6] which, while presupposed and anticipated in every communicative act, portrays a state of affairs that can only be approximated. The possibility of a freer society in which the ends and means of social progress can be discussed more openly and competently nevertheless remains a precondition for better understanding.

Ultimately, it is the anticipation of a truly human form of existence which provides the basis for the critique of present forms of life and of the distorted intersubjective communication and inadequate self-understanding that are co-extensive with it. Our understanding of texts and authors allows us to criticize and go beyond the 'truths' contained in them because we are in possession of the idea of a more truthful way of life. An idea, let it be re-emphasized, that is not 'a pie in the sky', but already presupposed as well as partially realized in contemporary communication and interaction.

Critical hermeneutics, therefore, recognizes that the conditions for the possibility of progress in human communication can only be established with the development towards a freer society.

Chapter 8

Habermas's programme of a dialectical–hermeneutical social science

Apel's work in the field of hermeneutics has been paralleled by that of Habermas. Both draw on the insights developed by hermeneutic philosophy which they find relevant for meta-theoretical considerations which are linked to a socio-political praxis that aims at the widening of communication about purposes and modes of social existence in the face of its gradual erosion by technocratic–manipulative social engineering; a further practical intention is the critical reconstruction of suppressed possibilities and desires for emancipation.

While different in some points of detail and approach, both theorists appear to be led to a formal and abstract ethics when it comes to evidencing the grounds of a critique of ideology. Having said this, it is also clear that, especially in Habermas's case, the formulation of 'regulative ideas' is increasingly embedded within a theory of language which, as a 'universal pragmatics', is promising to provide a confirmation of the view that the intention of arriving at a practical consensus, and the human interest in a society that furthers the free communication about aims and interests, is inherent in language itself.

As a dialectical social science, Habermas's critical hermeneutics attempts to mediate the objectivity of historical processes with the motives of those acting within it. As its aim is the freeing of emancipatory potential, i.e. the intentions of actors which have been 'forgotten' or repressed, it is not surprising that Habermas, too, should use psychoanalysis as a model for a dialectical–hermeneutical social science with an emancipatory intent.

This programme involves the adoption, critique and eventual overcoming-through-integration of hermeneutics. For outlining it, I shall focus on Habermas's appreciation and critique of Gadamer's work which, in a sense, contains the seeds of a number of related developments which culminate in a projected theory of communicative competence.

1. The 'hermeneutic dispute' between Habermas and Gadamer

Whereas the dispute between Betti and Gadamer revolved around the question of objective interpretation, the one that developed in terms of *Hermeneutics and the Critique of Ideology* (Apel *et al.*, 1971) concerns the possibility of 'depth' or 'critical' hermeneutics. In the latter dispute, which in the main was conducted between Gadamer and Habermas, some of the main insights of hermeneutic philosophy were accepted by both parties; their differences were more particularly concerned with the implications of, on the one hand, the nature of the 'fore-structure of understanding' and here especially with the status of language as its ultimate foundation, and with the justifiability of the critical stance *vis-à-vis* traditioned meaning which Habermas developed, on the other hand.

In retracing the steps of argument within the hermeneutic dispute I shall therefore give a mention to the aspects of hermeneutic philosophy which Habermas finds acceptable before outlining his criticism of the conservative tenor of Gadamer's views.

Habermas introduced hermeneutic thought into the methodology of the social sciences in order to exhibit the shortcomings of current interpretative approaches. Following on Gadamer's critique of the historistic assumptions underlying the *Geisteswissenschaften*, Habermas exhibits similar shortcomings in 'phenomenological' sociology and linguistic analysis of the Wittgenstein–Winch type. The traits shared by all these three, as approaches focusing on subjectively intended meaning, is the naive acceptance of the meaning of an act as defined by the actor, and the implicitly objectivist implications residing in the failure to consider both actor and interpreter as partners within a dialogical–dialectical situation.

The hermeneutic figure-of-speech of a 'fusion of horizon' at the same time serves to legitimate a critical component in the understanding of subjectively intended meaning on account of the need to continually revise the initial 'prejudices' which we brought to bear on a subject-matter that is characterized by its capacity to offer different definitions and accept or reject our interpretation. Critique, in the form of a co(r)-rection, constitutes an integral element in the dialectical process of understanding.

Gadamer's hermeneutic reflections bring to light the necessary limitations of behaviourist approaches to the social world:

part of the 'object' of social science can only be investigated by the researchers actively accepting the role of a 'reflective partner' in a communicative interaction. This situation also refers to another issue that arises out of the meaningful structure of the object: the categories used in the construction of theories and those used by the actor have to co(r)-respond in order to safeguard the adequacy of the results. In explaining behaviour, the scientist already has to know, and does know, how to categorize a certain manifestation of meaning, and it is only the closeness to his 'object', which is the result of sharing one 'life-world', that can to a large extent hide the problem of how we make sense of one another. As Habermas states, 'because of the radical limitation of the linguistic horizon to a few elementary and well operationalized meanings (need satisfaction, reward and punishment), the pre-understanding relied upon does not need to be thematized' (1970, p. 185).

A further difficulty arising out of the necessity to gain access to the data of social science through communication conducted in everyday language (e.g. in the use of questionnaires, participant observation, etc.) concerns the problem of how to measure meaning. Cicourel[7] has already shown that the transformation of communicative experience into data for scientific investigation contains an arbitrary element; there is no way in which we can be sure than an existing measurement system corresponds to the concepts used. Expressed in the terms of phenomenology, to which Cicourel recurs, 'life-world' and the 'world of science'[8] are linked together tentatively, whereby the latter assumes the character of a derivative, if not distorting, *demi-monde*.

The communication between subject and object essential for the possibility of social science is not without implication for the natural sciences. Here it is the communication *among* scientists which is evidenced by hermeneutic reflection as an important factor in the progress of science. While not directly affecting the results of their work, the modicum of understanding between scientists, which is necessary for the establishing of any sort of scientific community, secures a common opinion relating to worthwhile objects of research and to criteria for the elaboration and acceptance of findings within a scientific community. Habermas gives this fact a linguistic formulation by referring to the everyday language used in talking about the formal language of mathematical and scientific systems as 'metalanguage' or, rather, as the 'last metalanguage'.[9]

The inescapable link between everyday life and science is also apparent in the 'translation' of scientific findings into the language of practical affairs. Given Habermas's emphasis on the role played by the progress of science and technology in the continuance of highly developed societies – by providing both the material and political–ideological preconditions for the maintenance of technocratic-manipulative systems of domination – it is not surprising that he considers this sphere of interpretation as possessing great actuality.

The first publication in 1967 of Habermas's *Zur Logik der Sozialwissenschaften* initiated the hermeneutic dispute by providing the first counter-statements to Gadamer's conception.

To begin with, Habermas notes a reluctance on Gadamer's part to engage in any methodological considerations – a strand of thinking that is epitomized by the abstract opposition he establishes between hermeneutic and methical experience which, in a sense, 'involuntarily supports the positivist degradation of hermeneutics' (Habermas, 1970, p. 281). Underlying this approach, Habermas notices the Heideggerian self-conception of a philosophical hermeneutic as the 'inquiry into what happens with us beyond our willing and doing' (Gadamer, 1975, p. xv).

Tradition, as an on-going process, can never be completely objectified while at the same time providing the basis for all methical activity. Habermas now counterposes the idea of Reason to what he regards as the naturalization of tradition and, concomitantly, the re-affirmation of authority. In his opinion, Gadamer too readily accepts authority and tradition; his 'relative idealism', which regards language as the transcendental absolute, exhibits a lack of objectivity. A more adequate framework for the interpretation of meaning would, according to Habermas, refer to the systems of labour and domination which, in conjunction with language, constitute the 'objective context from within which social actions have to be understood' (Habermas, 1970, p. 289).

Hermeneutics merges into a social science in the form of a critique of ideology when traditioned meaning is interpreted in reference to given levels of societal labour, i.e. economic development, and existing forms of domination.

> Such a frame of reference would no longer leave tradition undetermined as some comprehensive entity, but it would allow us to grasp tradition as such and in its relationship to other moments of the totality of social existence, so that we are able to indicate those empirical conditions external to

tradition under which the transcendental rules of comprehension and action undergo changes. (ibid.)

On the basis of a theory of societal evolution, especially in terms of the emergence of class societies, it should be possible to systematically account for fundamental distortions operative in man's self-understanding. The 'dialogue' Gadamer referred to in order to depict the dialectic between past and present in the articulation of the individual's understanding of himself and his world need not be an 'open' one. By giving hermeneutical processes an ontological underpinning Gadamer is led to make light of economic and political factors which may drastically limit the 'horizon' of some or all of the participants.

Tradition, as a context that includes the systems of work and domination, enables as well as restricts the parameters within which we define our needs and interact in order to satisfy them. That socio-historical processes should occur over the heads and even behind the backs of those carrying them, who may systematically be unable to give an accurate account of their individual actions and the motivations underlying them, points to an approach to social phenomena which transcends the scope of merely meaning-interpretative investigations.

The assumption shared by Dilthey and Gadamer in the field of hermeneutical interpretation concerns the accessibility of meaning. Psychoanalysis, on the other hand, has evidenced the mechanism in which we repress socially unacceptable motives and channel them into acceptable forms of expression. This 're-definition', occurring under conditions of force, here represented by the demands of the Super-ego, provides the model for the critique of the self-delusion of groups within a class-society. The meaning that has been repressed can be retrieved with the help of a general interpretation that provides the frame for depicting the developmental history of a person or a social system in total, thereby allowing us to pinpoint the events and agencies behind 'distorted communication', and fill in any gaps in the self-understanding of the individual or group concerned.

In his reply Gadamer (1971a, 1971b) pitches his counter-arguments on the level that has emerged as the hub of the debate: the meta-theoretical status of hermeneutic reflection, i.e. its claim to universality. Should the 'hermeneutic problem' envelop all meaningful activity, then it would be impossible to argue from a position outside, or even against, it; there would be no Archimedean point since the attempt to unhinge one body of thought itself requires supporting ground, and with it a number of pre-suppositions and preconceptions that cannot all be clarified at once.

Gadamer argues for the universality of a philosophical hermeneutic on the basis of the Heideggerian conception of *verstehen* as an existentiale rather than the methodically trained procedure of the hermeneutical sciences; understanding and communication 'are modes of social co-existence which, in the last formalization, is a community of dialogue. Nothing is exempt from this community, no experience of any kind. Neither the specialization of modern science . . . nor material labour . . . nor political institutions of domination and administration . . . exist outside the universal medium of practical Reason (and un-Reason)' (1971b, p. 289).

In the linguistic formulation which Gadamer has given to the hermeneutic situatedness of all reflexive thought – 'Being that can be understood is language' – Heidegger's insight is expressed by reference to language as a mirror: 'everything that is, is reflected in the mirror of language' (1971a, pp. 71–2). Consequently, the assumption of sources of influence situated outside language can only seem absurd to Gadamer, as does the separating-off of material forces such as labour and domination – Gadamer uses Scheler's term of *Realfaktoren* – from the sphere of cultural tradition, and the restriction of the hermeneutic dimension to the latter.

Gadamer then goes on to reject the abstract antithesis of Reason[10] and authority, reflection and tradition, before finally addressing himself to the status of a critique of ideology *vis-à-vis* the universality of the hermeneutic problem. Here he recurs back to another metaphor, that of social life as a 'game', in order to construct a persuasive case against the transposition of the model of psychoanalysis onto social reality. By being a part of his object, the sociologist participates in this 'game' by playing out his various roles on the basis of a communally shared understanding. In trying to analyse social processes critically, he has to step outside this 'game' and treat his 'object' as a psychoanalyst would treat a patient, i.e. as someone who has to be unmasked, someone whose professed motives are not his real ones.

The point Gadamer makes here is that in the social context a sociologist acting in this way would be regarded as a 'spoil-sport' who is to be avoided by the other participants; furthermore, this 'analysis' itself occurs on the basis of a societal consensus rather than from an 'objective standpoint': the shared understanding – Gadamer refers to a 'societal consciousness' – that encompasses all human situations defines the limits within which an emancipatory social science can arrogate to itself the right to critique.

The issue now centres on the problem of how to provide standards which the critique of ideology can refer to in order to legitimize its procedure. The strategy Habermas adopts consists of, first, the attempt to discern the limits of hermeneutic consciousness and, second, to outline programmatically a theoretical framework in terms of which a critique of ideology can become a viable and justifiable undertaking.

2. Towards a theory of communicative competence

Habermas introduced hermeneutics into the methodology of the social sciences in order to combat the objectivism in scientistic approaches to the social world. The existence, and relative success, of objectifying methods at the same time indicate the limit of a sole concern with the interpretation of subjectively intended meaning: social existence is not only characterized by the intentions of those acting within it, but also by an 'objective' context that delimits the scope for the recognition and realization of intentions.

The dead weight of given socio-political interests and forces sedimented in social institutions and reflected in everyday language precludes the unrestricted self-clarification of these members subjected to its regime. The hiatus between subjectively intended and objectively realized meaning cannot be bridged by either hermeneutical or empirical–analytical sciences; both fortify their position at the opposite sides of a theoretical and practical divide and gaze at each other with incomprehension. Their apparent irreconcilability underlies the attempt at a dialectical mediation, once it is realized that they both represent legitimate modes of investigation; their contradictiveness stems from the fact that they focus on different realms of a disjointed reality.

As the result of both intention and constraint, social processes contain elements of spontaneity and regularity. Recognizing that, on the one hand, these intentions may partly be hidden from the actor himself or be re-defined for him by external, manipulative agencies, and that the regularities which form the basis of statistical–explanatory schemes more often than not represent structurally imposed constraints restricting rather than guaranteeing optimum social conduct, on the other hand, a dialectical social science has to aim at a theoretical framework which would allow the *objective understanding* of subjectively intended meaning. In contrast to earlier attempts, which ultimately ground to a halt in the shifting sands of historism, a dialectical–hermeneutical social science is not content with providing an inventory of past and present cultural objectives and achievements; instead, it is emphatically critical, not in the sense of voicing disapproval of contemporary arrangements, but in the sense that it tries to distil the meaning of historical processes and objectivations in relation to existing tendencies towards a freer society.

By introducing the concept of totality, tendencies towards a better society can be discerned and interpreted in relation to universal history. Subjectively intended meaning now acquires its objective complement without which it would not be meaningful. An objectively understanding hermeneutic of social existence is thereby both a theory and critique of socially distributed meaning.

Habermas arrives at an outline of a dialectical–hermeneutical theory of action through a *Aufhebung* of both hermeneutic philosophy and psychoanalysis. Before such a move was possible, the latter had to be freed from its scientistic self-misunderstanding before it could emerge as a general interpretation of self-formative processes occupying the same meta-theoretical status as general empirical theories and hermeneutical theory; as far as hermeneutic philosophy was concerned, the challenge from Gadamer still stood, which could be formulated as a rhetorical question: 'Is the critique of ideology not itself ideological?'

I shall deal with this point first and show how Habermas proceeds by dismantling the hermeneutic claim to universality on which such an objection to social criticism rests.

While acknowledging Gadamer's reservation against false universalist claims made by some critical viewpoints, and while realizing that 'under present conditions this may be more urgent than drawing attention to the universalist claim of hermeneutics' (Habermas, 1971, p. 159), Habermas nevertheless addresses himself to the latter in order to settle a meta-theoretical dispute; on its result will depend the legitimacy of critical hermeneutics. At the same time, hermeneutic consciousness itself 'has to remain incomplete as long as it has not reflected upon the limits of hermeneutical understanding' (1971, p. 133).

The hermeneutic claim to universality could be shown to be indefensible if it were possible to break through the context of everyday language. Of the three fields Habermas refers to as likely candidates, genetic epistemology, generative linguistics and systematically distorted communication, Habermas chooses to focus on the third one. Apart from the fact that he is most conversant with it,[11] psychoanalysis, as the explication of the structure of genuine communication, also provides a stepping-stone towards a theory of ordinary language.

Hermeneutic approaches have to consider speech as, in principle understandable – excluding, of course, pathological disturbances. Habermas's case is based, however, on the existence of 'patterns of systematically distorted communication which recur in "normal", i.e. pathologically inconspicuous, speech . . . . This is the case in pseudo-communication where the participants are not aware of a disturbance in their communication; only someone from outside realizes that they misunderstand one another' (1971, p. 134).

Transposed onto the social level, this view gives rise to the following insight.

Ideology, in the context of a capitalist system, provides an illusory account of a form of social existence that is characterized, in fact, by the domination of one section over another. Acting under the influence of 'false consciousness', members of the subjugated class may subordinate their interests to the continuance of an unjust social system that can hide its contradictions behind the veil of pseudo-scientific explanations and emotive appeals to some mythic entity or 'cultural ideal' (Freud). Passive acceptance of accounts of a 'false' reality given in terms of some 'harmonious' co-existence or certain needs and imperatives arising out of social development, or the alienated withdrawal from public affairs, may too easily be interpreted as indications of a fundamental assent to the status quo.

In any case, everyday experience of the existence of a 'false consensus' about important issues should sensitize us to the influence of dominant interests active behind the engineering of public opinion. On a more theoretical level, this awareness can be translated into a questioning of the body of shared assumptions that is handed down to us as 'tradition'.

Psychoanalysis provides Habermas with the model for a theoretical framework that allows us to transcend the communicative consensus meta-hermeneutically. As a 'depth-hermeneutic' it can decipher privatized forms of communication through 'scenic understanding'. Here the de-symbolization of conflict-generating needs is reversed. Through the reconstruction of the original conflictual situation, or 'scene' in early childhood, the patient is given the possibility to re-symbolize those areas in his life-history that have been kept semantically empty.

Scenic understanding is an explanatory understanding in that it can pinpoint the initial conditions that led to the systematic distortion of language. Hermeneutical understanding can only concern itself with reasonably well-functioning everyday communication and it serves to sanction the prevalent use of language. Depth-hermeneutics aims at explaining the emergence of patterns of speech which have to remain incomprehensible to hermeneuticians since they affect the organization of language itself.

The recognition of the intrusion of force into communication led Habermas to question the status of factually existing consensus as the last supporting ground of all communication, even of critique. By referring to the model of psychoanalysis he was able to explicate the framework of the critique of an individual's distorted self-understanding. Gadamer accepts the usefulness of this model on this level, but questions the legitimacy of its transference onto the social sphere.

He restates his objections to Habermas's programme, and in his 'Reply' makes the further point that the conditions under which processes of reflection occur in a psychoanalytic encounter are markedly different from that obtaining between contending classes: here, the dominant class would perceive emancipatory praxis rather more as a threat to its existence than as the freeing from self-imposed restrictions which a patient may actively seek.

Habermas clarifies. The model of emancipatory praxis is applicable to the relationship of a Communist party to the masses rather than to the antagonistic relationship between classes. 'Theories of the type of psychoanalysis and Marx's critique of ideology can be used to initiate processes of reflection and to dissolve barriers to communication'; 'they can also be used in order to deduce explanatory hypotheses without having (or taking) the opportunity to initiate communication with the people concerned and having one's interpretation confirmed by their processes of reflection' (1967: 1971, p. 36).

In any case, the use of critical–emancipatory knowledge need not necessarily exclude the direct dialogue with one's opponents: 'these are situations in which attempts at radical reformism – which tries not only to preach to the converted but also to convert – are more promising than revolutionary struggle' (1967: 1971, p. 37).

The interpretation Habermas offers of psychoanalysis as one component of a theory of communicative competence is used to out-manoeuvre both Gadamer and Freud: it enables him to reject the hermeneutic claim to universality by identifying the psychological, and eventually the action–theoretical, conditions of the exercise of communicative competence – which itself can only be improved but not explained by hermeneutical reflection. At the same time, it requires Habermas to separate Freud's scientistic self-understanding from his metapsychology before introducing the latter as part of a meta-hermeneutic.

The meta-hermeneutic Habermas is aiming for takes the form of a theory of communicative competence. Since the publication of *The Hermeneutic Claim to Universality* a number of papers have been published which inform us of the progress of Habermas's researches.[12]

The substantively oriented correlate to Habermas's meta-theoretical considerations follow the model of psychoanalysis as the critique of an individual's distorted self-understanding, which draws on a theoretical frame combining knowledge about general personality development and individual life-histories. Under the sway of ideology, social groups are prevented from recognizing and pursuing their common interests; the efficacy of these systems of interpretation depends on the erection of barriers to communication which block communicative processes directed at the formulation of socio-politically relevant aims and directives. The emergence of such barriers

> requires an explanation within the framework of a theory of systematically distorted communication. If that could be developed satisfactorily in connection with a universal pragmatics and combined with precisely formulated basic assumptions of historical materialism, then the systematic comprehension of cultural tradition could become possible. It may be that a theory of social evolution leads to testable assumptions concerning the logic of the emergence of systems of morals, of cosmologies and corresponding cultural practices. (1967: 1971, p. 19)

In the field of ordinary language, theoretical work undertaken here is hoped to make it possible to 'derive the principle of reasonable speech, as the necessary regulation of every actual speech, however distorted, from the logic of everyday language' (1971, p. 155).

His dispute with Gadamer left Habermas with the task of establishing a principle with the help of which it would be possible to distinguish between a true and a false consensus. This principle can be established via the description of a 'discourse'.

A discourse differs from interaction in that here the norms and opinions, which are 'taken-for-granted' in communicative action, are problematized; it is only discursively that the validity of these naively accepted norms can be ascertained consensually. Successful interaction pre-supposes that actors follow norms intentionally and that these norms appear to them as justified. It is thereby pre-supposed that actors are convinced that the norms underlying their actions can be justified at any time within a discourse.

But just as in interaction, so in discourse, too, there are pre-supposed a number of 'counterfactual' elements. In the course of a consensus theory of truth Habermas arrives at the view that the concept of truth provides no criterion for distinguishing between true and false consensus since truth itself can only be arrived at via a consensus in a discourse. It follows that in discourse we pre-suppose that any consensus arrived at within the framework of a discourse can be regarded as a true consensus.

This conception of truth as consensual in turn pre-supposes – or rather anticipates – the 'ideal speech situation' which is characterized by the exclusion of extraneous pressures, i.e. it is discussion free from domination. This situation provides a climate in which debates allow the formulation of the true interests of the participants and the eventual emergence and acceptance of the best argument.

Preconditions for successful interaction – such as the intelligibility and truth of what is said at an appropriate time by a sincere speaker – are thereby transposed onto discourse: the participants may not deceive themselves or others about their intentions, thereby excluding the possibility of a distortion of the communicative process. Just as full intentionality is pre-supposed in interaction, so the ideal speech situation counterfactually circumscribes the conditions in which true consensus may emerge.

It is here, in the conjoining of truth and conditions favourable to its emergence, i.e. freedom from constraints, that Habermas moves away most emphatically from the ontologization of language and tradition of a philosophical hermeneutic. As Habermas stated,

the idea of truth, which is measured against the idea of a

true consensus, implies the idea of a true existence – or, we could say, it includes the idea of *Mündigkeit* (being-of-age). Only the formal anticipation of the idealized dialogue, as a form of life to be realized, guarantees the ultimate, counter-factual agreement that already unites us and which allows us to criticize any factual agreement, if it is a false one, as such. (1971, p. 155)

Subjective understanding of meaning can be incorporated into a critical interpretation of distorted communication at a cost: its contemplative self-sufficiency will have to be given up in the demand for a freer society in which the roots of distortion are gradually eradicated; 'the enlightenment which follows from radical understanding is always political' (1971, p. 158).

Chapter 9

Materialist hermeneutics

The idealist basis of traditional hermeneutics has called forth two forms of response from Marxist theorists who ventured into this field. One, the development of a critical hermeneutics which recognizes the necessity to consider subjective intentions within a totality of social existence that is characterized by the level of economic development reached and the prevailing forms of political domination. As 'material forces' these impinge upon the process of intellectual production: they provide the parameters within which consciousness can objectivate itself, as well as the co-ordinates in relation to which the objective meaning of these creations can be ascertained. At the same time, these two factors 'intrude' into the activity of conscious actors as extraneous forces, barring it from finding its full and intended expression: they constitute a 'second nature' that exhibits all the resistance to man's striving for self-fulfilment which we are familiar with from our physical environment.

For critical hermeneutics, the idealist self-conception of an unimpeded exchange of meaning is, at best, the anticipation of a true state of human existence yet to be realized; the assumption that this state is already pertaining, which underlies objective-idealist methodologies, is in any case ideologically suspect.

A second strand of Marxist-oriented thinking would quite happily include critical hermeneutics under the rubric of 'idealism' and 'bourgeois ideology'. Suspicion is aroused in these quarters by the 'regulative idea' of 'communication free of domination' which to many appears simply as a utopia, a no-where. Sandkühler (1972, 1973) and Lorenzer (1972, 1973) make this point.

Sandkühler, a Marxist-Leninist, looks for 'actual alternatives as they are already realized in the socialized societies' (1973, p. 77) in order to concretize this utopia which would otherwise remain, as 'restored Enlightenment, an essential part of bourgeois ideology' (ibid.). What he finds instead of an existing alternative is a model of the utopia of communication free of domination: psychoanalysis.

It is here that the differences between Sandkühler and Lorenzer emerge. Sandkühler rejects Freud's unhistorical scheme of an unchanging drive-structure and, with it, psycho-analysis as a therapy – which he sees as pursuing the aim of re-integrating the patient into the sick society that is the cause of his complaint and which is represented by the analyst.

Lorenzer has moved away from his original theoretical agree-ment with Habermas towards the formulation of psychoanalysis as a materialist theory of socialization which would employ a 'materialist' hermeneutics as its method. Sandkühler similarly offers a 'materialistic hermeneutics' despite his grave reserva-tions against an idealist hermeneutic because 'it would be ruinous not to assure ourselves methodologically and theoretically of this hermeneutical instrument which has since been improved through materialist historism and through dialectical logic' (Sandkühler, 1973, p. 51).

1. Lorenzer: 'materialist' hermeneutics and psychoanalysis

Lorenzer, like Habermas, uses psychoanalysis as a model for a 'critical theory of the subject'. But whereas the latter draws on orthodox Freudian metapsychology as a step on the way towards a theory of communication, Lorenzer intends to inject an historical dimension into psychoanalysis – which is thereby transformed into a 'materialist theory of socialization'. As a theory of interaction, psychoanalysis is specifically concerned with structures of interaction that are distorted and consequently generate suffering in the individuals affected.

Psychoanalysis as a materialist theory of interaction
Habermas has already outlined the method of 'scenic under-standing' used for the re-introduction of privatized meaning into public language. The conception of the emergence of, for example, neuroses underlying this view contains the following line of argument in which the process of socialization is seen as a dialectical one.

Between the two poles represented by the child's 'inner nature', i.e. his bodily needs, and the satisfaction of them his mother is able to offer, given her social and cultural situation, there develop certain forms of interaction; initially, these forms are established unconsciously – until the child's capacity to acquire and use language allows them to become conscious ones. He is now able to attach predicates to certain interactions (e.g. 'mammy') which are learnt on the basis of these inter- actions: language enables the child to conceptualize his im- mediate experience and to partake in symbolic interaction. In ideal conditions there will exist a congruity between the child's needs that have found satisfaction in given forms of interaction, and the way he communicates them. In the course of a child's development there will occur instances in which his needs remain unsatisfied, i.e. in which the established forms of interaction fail to take place because of external barriers, such as the societal system of norms. Should the arising conflict remain insoluble, the only course open may be the withdrawal of the linguistic symbol representing the socially undesired inter- action. Splitting symbol and corresponding form of interaction allows the latter to sink back into a pre-linguistic state, thereby ceasing to molest the individual's conscious existence – with- out, however, losing its motivating force. The rejected form of interaction retains its initial virulence and now also acquires the compulsive character of unreflexive reactions which are triggered off by certain situational stimuli. Public language may well be adequate for camouflaging the area that was once occupied by the now banished symbolic representation of the rejected form of interaction; this is what we refer to as 'rationalization'. The persistence and intermittent actualization of the 'desymbolized' form of interaction may, however, conflict with the new, publicly acceptable definition to such an extent as to cause the kind of suffering known as 'neurosis'. It is the task of the psychoanalyst, consequently, to re-introduce the ex- communicated form of interaction into public language. In the course of this process, in which the analyst gains access to the structure of interaction through 'scenic understanding', the analysand may accept the interpreted form of interaction as a lost fragment of his own life-history, and consciously re-cognize its intended meaning and the genesis of its original, unconscious repression.

Lorenzer's 'materialist' hermeneutics

In what sense can the genesis and interpretation of repressed forms of behaviour be regarded as 'materialist'? Lorenzer states that 'subjective structures are products of the practical–dialectical process of socialization' (1973, p. 104). The dialectic involved is one that mediates the child's 'inner nature' with the 'outer nature' of his environment: the bodily needs with the societal praxis that is introduced into his 'world' through his mother. The interaction between mother and child that emerges in this dialectical relationship will, therefore, by necessity bear traces of social contradictions which enter the child's subjective structure through the socializing practices of the mother.

Psychoanalysis can be considered a 'materialist' hermeneutics in that the meaning objectivated in incomprehensible forms of behaviour, which awaits and calls for an interpretative analysis, is not seen as some emanation of an autonomous consciousness, but as the result of a form of interaction in which the material needs of a developing body and the material, socio-practical metabolism of man and nature in its historical-concrete form both find expression. It is important to note that Lorenzer not only sees external nature as the object of historical transformation which results in the naturalization of man and the humanization of nature: 'the development of drives is, on account of the inclusion of the symbolic structure of a concretely given society, not an ahistorical–asocial process, but from the outset a historically determined form' (1973, p. 163); 'because the organisation of bodily needs into concrete drive-requirements is already the product of a practical dialectic, not its basis' (1973, p. 105).

An individual's subjective structures, the object of psychoanalysis, are consequently not something that is determined ahistorically, but are the result of an historical process. Definitively formulated theories of personality consequently lead to the reification of dialectical processes. Lorenzer sees the Id as entering the structure and content of interaction constitutively. 'Id is that concrete bodily need that enters from the first moment of the still vegetative organism as interplay of child and environment into the structure of interaction in a determining way . . . . The dialectic of individual and society commences here concretely in evidencible mediations' (1973, p. 166).

Psychoanalysis, so conceived of as a theory of interaction, analyses the occurrence of distorted forms of interaction; as a materialist form of critical–hermeneutical interpretation it is directed at objectively determined relational structures. These forms of interaction are the product of the dialectical process of socialization and may in given socio-historical settings remain unrealizable in the course of an individual's life-history because they clash with existing social rules and acceptable formulations of needs and interests. The result is a 'splitting-off' of a symbolic representation from its corresponding forms of interaction – which the analyst will try to reverse.

Materialist hermeneutics and historical materialism

Lorenzer convincingly develops psychoanalysis as a social science by starting from Freud's insight that the kind of illness it deals with has to be seen as a conflict between nature and social norms.

The materialist–naturalist basis of such a science is guaranteed by its emphasis on the drive-structure – thereby pre-empting its fusion with an idealist-oriented approach to social phenomena. Developing this point, Lorenzer sees the social moment in a materialist theory of socialization to 'be pointing with immanent necessity to that other point of orientation: Historical materialism . . . . It is between this and the theory of drives that the theme of language has been developed by me' (1972, pp. 154–5).

Lorenzer does not attempt yet another synthesis of Marx and Freud, but merely tries to clarify the status of a 'critical theory of the subject' within a critique directed at the totality of social life. The point where both theoretical frameworks intersect is defined by the respective concepts of 'form of social interchange' and 'determinate form of interaction'. The former can be arrived at in objective data through the analysis of a political–economic situation; in its context, the derivation of subjective structures 'necessarily remains abstract in relation to the sensually experienceable suffering of atomized individuals here and now. The latter . . . is the point of departure for psychoanalysis' (1973, p. 147).

It is a prerequisite, therefore, of a fruitful relation between psychoanalysis and historical materialism that the former abandons its 'subjectivist' approach that abstracts from the historical totality and 'breaks through the veil of reified theory of personality by means of the category of "form of interaction"' (1973, p. 148). Marxist theorizing would, at the same time, be required to abandon objectivist tendencies apparent in recent trends.

Lorenzer earlier insisted that

> only in the concept of the subject can the dialectic between individual and society be thought of concretely. The asubjectivity of structuralism underlies also its ahistoricality and removes the point at which the individual is concretely mediated with *this* society. With the destruction of the subject, the relationship with everyday activity, with reality here and now, is cut-off. (1973, pp. 133–5)

It is only necessary to add that the 'subject' is here to be understood non-subjectivistically, i.e. as formed by socio-historical processes which he, in turn, influences.

Lorenzer's criticism of Habermas

These remarks provide a convenient bridge to Lorenzer's criticism of 'Habermas' subjectivism (to use this coarse label again)' (1973, p. 141).

'Subjectivist' does here not refer to the concept of 'reflection' which Lorenzer sees as the fundamental concept in Habermas's interpretation of psychoanalysis – especially so since the aim of hermeneutical understanding is here not directed at symbolic contexts as such but at self-reflection in which the patient re-integrates part of his own life-history into his improved understanding of himself. Lorenzer is, rather, directing our attention to Habermas's conception of metapsychology as a theory of subjectivity 'in which the subject is held at the level of reified structures' (1973, p. 142).

In other words, historically formed structures, such as the Id, have in this orthodox view turned into unchangeable constants. It is the lack of the moment of 'objectivity – or historical-material concreteness represented by the practical dialectic between inner and outer nature – that leads Lorenzer to term this approach 'subjectivist'.

This reliance on an ahistorical sub-stratum in the make-up of an individual is even in evidence in what, by all accounts, would seem to represent the objective–materialist moment in Habermas's scheme: the role of the sub-systems of work and domination in the understanding of meaning. According to Lorenzer,

> work, language and domination are joined here and held together by a concept of subjectivity and subjective competence which only maintains an abstract link with the material basis. Concomitant with a separation of work and interaction – dubious in itself because no human activity, not even libidinous attention, can be conceived of other than as a 'productive processing' within the context of societal relations. (1972, p. 9)

Lorenzer finds the fusion of interaction and communication equally unacceptable. 'This separates interaction from the concept of praxis (in the Marxian sense) and blocks the insight into the mechanism of the practical constitution of subjective structures within the field of tension of the historical–concrete interaction between outer and inner nature' (1973, p. 171).

2. Sandkühler's 'materialistic hermeneutics'

Lorenzer's conception of a 'materialist' hermeneutics remained within the framework of a theory of the interpretation of symbolic meaning and therefore on the level of linguistic communication and interaction. Hermeneutics was rendered 'materialist' by virtue of a re-formulation of Freudian meta-psychology which allowed for the consideration of material–historical factors in the formation of personality structures. The aim of psychoanalysis was, consequently, the evidencing of social contradictions as the cause of personal psychological suffering.

For Sandkühler, the efficacy of social contradictions in the process of intellectual creation is the starting-point of his analysis, which differs from Lorenzer's in the important point that the 'understanding' performed in 'materialistic hermen-eutics' is no longer tied to the subjective interpretation of symbolic meaning on account of the character of these symbols as the ideological reflection of an objective material base.

Lorenzer's conception, no less than that of critical hermen-eutics, would, from this perspective, still remain within the confines of idealist hermeneutics which misconceives of this material base in a subjectivist way.

It should be stated that Sandkühler does not intend to achieve an easy alliance between Marxism and hermeneutics in the sense that hermeneutics acquires a perspective for social totality, while Marxism opens itself up to individual experience – as Lorenzer had advocated. Sandkühler makes the point that 'hermeneutics and Marxism are concepts of differing classifica-tory levels, that hermeneutics as the methodology of the *Geisteswissenschaften* excludes "social totality" *a priori*, and that Marxism is *ex definitione* also a theory of individual experience' (1973, p. 53). His 'materialistic hermeneutics' is especially not intended to lead to the revision of some essential theoretical elements of Marxism! The exposition he gives 'asks, however, which place within materialistic dialectic is to be given to hermeneutics which cannot be a general theory of the under-standing of meaning with the sign "materialistic", but which has to be a method for the explanation of forms and contents of reflection appropriate to its documentary objects' (1973, p. 52).

Sandkühler considers 'materialistic hermeneutics' as a scien-tific sub-system of materialistic dialectics; its object is the 'intellectual reproduction of historical praxis' (1972, p. 1003). As a model for this science he refers to Marx's *Critique of Political*

Economy, which represents 'the hermeneutical exposition of that self-understanding, that categorical reflection of the capitalist mode of production the documentation of which Marx found in the sources of classical English economics' (1973, p. 51).

Materialistic hermeneutics attends to the intellectual reflection of actual history found in historical sources, texts, etc., and 'interprets' them by reconstructing the process of their creation. No longer is it, therefore, the task of hermeneutics to rethink what had been thought before: materialistic hermeneutics is aware of the non-identity of object and subject; it draws on 'history', as an intellectual product, in order to gain insight into real historical processes, and it attempts to discern the factors underlying the discrepancy between actual existence and its reflection in the heads of human agents.

The existence of 'false consciousness' requires an explanation as to the material conditions of its emergence – as Marx has achieved in relation to the reified structure of consciousness through the analysis of the fetishism of commodity production. As part of the instrumentarium of the critique of ideology, materialistic hermeneutics therefore does not aim at the investigation of the categorical formulation of socio-historical knowledge but has 'as its object . . . the analysis of the genesis of knowledge out of social existence, of real life' (1972, p. 1004). Materialistic hermeneutics derives its rationale, consequently, from the need to gain access to real life processes through the mediation of linguistic documents.

Reflection-theory of knowledge as the epistemological
underpinning of materialistic hermeneutics
The question of how the non-identity of interpreter and object can be bridged Sandkühler answers by reference to the use of 'the historical–logical analysis of the lawfulness of the process of cognition within the process of praxis' (1972, p. 1003), i.e. 'hermeneutical comprehension takes place as the dialectical reconstruction of the genesis [of its object, J.B.]' (1972, p. 980).

What are we to understand by this 'dialectical', or 'historical–logical' approach? Materialistic hermeneutics explicates the content of written documents in accordance with 'the historical material genesis of language as a function of the appropriation of reality' (1972, p. 978). It draws on the results of political economy, dialectical epistemology, materialist historism ('the science of the historical process as progress through class conflict'), and the critique of ideology. In the context of the present discussion, it is the 'dialectical epistemology' underlying materialistic hermeneutics that is of particular interest.

Sandkühler adheres to Lenin's 'reflection' – or 'copy' – theory of cognition which considers the content of consciousness as copying a reality that exists independent of it. Such an epistemology – or 'gnoseology' – is emphatically materialistic in affirming the primacy of 'matter' over 'mind', 'materialism' being here defined as 'the recognition of the objective lawfulness of nature and the approximately correct reflection of this lawfulness in the heads of men'.[13]

While this epistemology certainly opposes the idealist conception of a 'purely mental' immanence in the relationship of subject and object it is nevertheless difficult to see in what sense it does succeed in overcoming the 'undialectical mechanisation' (Sandkühler) of determinist conceptions.

Sandkühler is acutely aware of the danger of simplistic reductionism and places great hopes on a theory of personality that does justice to the complex structure of the determination of reflection as the transformation of something material into something intellectual. Above all, it is the work of Lucien Sève[14] that takes into account the socio-historical conditioning of thought. Sève asserts his 'theory of the concrete individual' in the face of Garaudy and Althusser and insists that personality is not the individual instance of a basic personality but that it is 'most essentially concrete and unique'.[15]

The distinction between the historical form of individuality and concrete, biologically and psychologically concrete, personality would allow it in Sandkühler's view to 'investigate this personality in its specific dynamic (which is the last necessary step in the reconstruction of the determinants of reflection)' (1972, p. 1001).

How Sandkühler will be able to express the unique in general categories, which is required by his explanatory use of materialistic hermeneutics, remains a puzzle. More immediately, the conception of it as 'an empirical science of the text . . . [which] transfers the method of historical and dialectical materialism onto its field of study: linguistic, textual documents of reflection' (1973, pp. 401–3) does not help us in solving any of the issues surrounding the interpretation of meaning.

The recognition that, as an 'organ' of the critique of superstructural elements – 'as history in the form of a critique' – it is itself subject to 'the laws of the formation of ideologies' (1973, p. 407) could almost be regarded as a development of the insight into the 'pre-judgmental structure of understanding' hermeneutic philosophy has alerted us to: only that in materialistic hermeneutics any revision of one's own 'prejudices' in the course of understanding a text is not deemed necessary – the interpreter is instead required to be aware of these laws and to pursue his partiality consciously. Being already in posession of the royal road to truth and standing on the right side of the march of History implies, of course, that there is precious little to be learned for one's own praxis from the study of 'ideological manifestations'; all that is left to do is to use the latter (a) as a means for getting to grips with the real processes that underlie them and which they merely reflect, and (b) to evidence their class-oriented limitations whenever it may assist in the development of a true proletarian consciousness (e.g. by criticizing the learning material offered to children in school).

Whatever its use an ideological weapon, the materialistic hermeneutics Sandkühler has formulated as a 'prolegomena' has yet to catch up with Dilthey's formulation of the problem of interpretation. Ultimately, it may be doomed to failure – as are all undialectical 'syntheses' in which one body of knowledge is merely superimposed on another.

Chapter 10

Conclusions: hermeneutics and Marxism

The place of critical hermeneutics within the field of the interpretation of meaning is an ambiguous one: while acknowledging the need for hermeneutics in non-empiricistic social science, it nevertheless takes account of empirical contingencies which delimit, if not determine, processes of communicative interaction. Habermas could therefore charge hermeneutics in its traditional and philosophic form with 'idealism' since it assumes the self-interpretation of actors to be the last and final arbiter of any account concerning their motives and interests. The idealizations[16] hermeneutics rests upon render it blind to the perception of material factors that assert themselves 'behind the backs' of social actors.

Its emphasis on the material sub-stratum of interaction in contemporary conditions is, consequently, the defining characteristic of critical hermeneutics – even though the perception of its status differs from that entertained by materialist hermeneutics. Is the creation and exchange of meaning the reflection of a material base, or is the latter the shifting ground upon which these activities take place – enabling and at the same time restricting them?

Habermas's position, which is closer to the second argument, is, in fact, regarded itself as 'idealist' by Lorenzer and Sandkühler – even if it is for different reasons – who both take a pronounced materialist perspective.

It is questionable whether Lorenzer does Habermas's conception justice when he mentions in his summary of his objections that 'the motor of the psychoanalytic process of cognition is not the interest in self-reflection, but the sensually experienceable suffering that demands alleviation' (1973, p. 142). Is it not the case that the the two are inseparable since the only way to achieve the freeing from unconscious motive-forces is through self-reflection – a process that is itself painful and is only undergone on the basis of acute suffering?

Since Lorenzer's critique of the contrasting conceptions of structuralism as represented by Lacan, Althusser and Foucault (pp. 120–34) and Habermas is undertaken with the aim of clarifying the relationship between psychoanalysis and historical materialism, two more comments may be appropriate.

Psychoanalysis, in Lorenzer's view, aims ultimately at the source of individual suffering: the contradictions within capitalist society. These contradictions enter the subjective structures of a child through the socializing practices of the mother. Unfortunately, Lorenzer leaves us in the dark as to how this process of the transformation of objective into subjective structures does occur – apart from saying that they 'enter into language' (1973, p. 107).

One would, furthermore, like to ask whether there does not, in fact, exist a slight confusion as to the place of 'contradictions' within psychoanalysis. Is it not the case that the cause of an analysand's suffering is the conflict between his inner nature and an outer reality that blocks the gratification of his desires and needs – rather than class-based conflict within this reality itself? Within the perspective of a theory of socialization, social conflicts can surely only appear in the form of differing socialization patterns based on differing life-chances, access to experiences, etc., which are characteristic of members of different classes. As a consequence, differing results of the socialization process are the reflection of the existence of differing groups in society. The fact that their intra-societal relationship may be an antagonistic one can, by itself, hardly account for conflicts generated between individual and societal needs; it can only account for class-specific variations in the propensity to be afflicted by a certain kind of psychological illness – but not the cause of it.

What does seem to occur in this argumentation is a two-fold reversal of what Lorenzer takes to be Habermas's position, where, one, 'the Freudian materiality of nature and the material –historical processes reach into the utopian ideality of "communicative action" only "from below"' (1973, p. 140). It can be said that, in Lorenzer's scheme, the material factors specifiable as socio-economic reality are 'imposed from above' onto the individual's developing forms of interaction in a dogmatic fashion. Two, Lorenzer appears to re-translate the approach of the critique of ideology, which had psychoanalysis as its initial paradigm, back onto individual processes: class domination, as the repression of one group by another which owns the means of the material, and thereby of intellectual, reproduction of society, prevents the subjugated class from defining and achieving their interests and needs by physical force or, more often than not, by attacks on people's minds through ideologies. This model, which is plausible in the discussion of the generation of social conflict borne by groups or classes, seems to be transposed by Lorenzer onto the repression of needs inflicted upon the individual by society as a whole ('civilization'); the difference being, of course, that in the latter case the agent of repression is society as such rather than a particular segment within it: reference to class domination can again only explain variations in the form and intensity of the suffering inflicted by society but not its genesis; in the end, *both* capitalists *and* proletarians suffer from a society organized along the principle of the accumulation of profit rather than the satisfaction of needs.

Lorenzer relies too uncritically upon the central tenet of historical materialism for his explanation of the societal causes of psychological illness in terms of 'contradictions' within it. If, for example, the assumption of the existence of an antagonistic class relationship in contemporary Western societies were in need of modification, how would this affect Lorenzer's analysis?

Where Lorenzer exhibits a latent dogmatism, Sandkühler professes an open one. His unquestioning, affirmative support of Marxism as codified in the DiaMat is at the bottom of his materialistic conception. Here the materialist character of his 'dialectical epistemology' – which, as has been noted, forms the basis of a materialistic hermeneutics – is clarified as asserting (a) 'the primacy of matter and of materiality as the signum of the unity of reality', and (b) 'the dialectic not only as a categorial methodology but also as the real principle of the movement of the whole of material and intellectual reality' (1972, p. 98).

It is not here the place to enter into a debate with the Engels–Lenin conception that is based on the identity-theory of the late Hegel and in which the simplistic inversion of the primacy of mind over matter gives rise to a metaphysical materialism in which knowledge is absorbed into Being. The difference implied in the use of the terms 'materialist' and 'materialistic' – which signify a change from a focus on material, i.e. concrete-historical, processes, in the investigation of political and intellectual phenomena to a deterministic view that sees the latter as a mere reflection of the former – this difference has a crucial bearing on what the term 'ideology' means to us, and with it on the status of 'critique'.

In contradistinction to the other critical approaches, Sandkühler's orthodox Marxism does not allow him to see ideology as 'false consciousness' but only as the socially necessary consciousness of social existence: 'the characterization of all forms and qualities of social consciousness as merely "ideological" would be the result of a differentiating theory of knowledge' (1973, p. 318). By referring to all intellectual production as 'ideology', the term loses its critical edge and becomes descriptive.

As a further consequence, the treatment of these phenomena in the context of hermeneutics has to differ radically, and with it the form and content of hermeneutics itself. Since the ideological products of the bourgoisie, which are dominating intellectual activity at present are, *a priori*, inadequate reflections of reality, there is nothing that can be gained by trying to integrate the content of this particular tradition into the body of Marxist thought. Being suspect by definition, *qua* product of the class enemy, the appropriation of it in a hermeneutic(al) process has to give way to the task of evidencing the distortions that are being foisted upon the working-class through it.

It is clear that, following the programme outlined by Sandkühler, materialistic hermeneutics has to take the form of an explanation of the genesis and validity of products of consciousness rather than that of a critique – which would, at least, acknowledge a partial truth within the object which was worth being salvaged. The spectre of a reduction of concrete individuals and their work to abstract generalities ('bourgeois') looms large here. The economic conditioning of a person's motivation and rationality is subject to a number of mediations which may profoundly alter their course. As Sartre's poignant formulation puts it, 'Valéry is a petit-bourgeois intellectual, no doubt about it. But not every petit-bourgeois intellectual is Valéry. The heuristic inadequacy of contemporary Marxism is contained in these two sentences' (Sartre, 1963, p. 56).

Hermeneutic(al) interpretation and Marxism

Sandkühler's argumentation leads, of course, to a questioning of the Marxian scheme in which all emanations of consciousness are seen as representations of an alienated practice; as a consequence, all thought has hitherto been false and only serves to mask reality.

How a Marxist thinker may arrive at truth himself has remained a puzzle at least since Mannheim made it the starting-point of a

sociology of knowledge – unless, of course, one accepts identification with the potential subject–object of history as a
sufficient condition or adheres to a reflection theory of knowledge which would guarantee the proletariat and its spokesmen
privileged access to truth on account of their 'possession' of
dialectical materialism which, we are told, reflects both the laws
of history *and* nature.

Interestingly enough, the problem of what Marx's work
'means' to us today again throws open the problem of hermeneutics in its entirety. It is, in fact, possible to find all the various
forms of hermeneutics indicated in this book practised by the
differing ways of applying Marx's work to present circumstances. The conflict of interpretations may, therefore, usefully
be demonstrated by referring to the use that has been made of
Marx.

Dogmatic, orthodox Marxism adheres to Marx's writings, as
codified in the DiaMat almost to the letter. Contemporary reality
is seen here in Marxian terms: Marxism here takes the form of a
Weltanschauung;[17] all that is needed is the elucidation of, and
comment on, difficult theoretical points in the direct application
of it to given problems. In relation to the history of hermeneutics, this position would correspond to the pre-Enlightenment
interpretation of authoritative texts, the truth-content of which
was in no way to be questioned.

The next stage in hermeneutical theory, the objective–critical
interpretation of a text in view of what the author really meant,
would compare with the work of academic marxologists and
their neutral, historistic clarification of 'issues in Marxian
theory'. Such a treatment is close to the consideration of Marx as
a 'classic' (as Merleau-Ponty advocated in his late work) from
which all areas of the social sciences could derive specific aspects
and integrate them into their own perspective.

A further possibility, the 'fusion of horizons' between Marx's
and present-day concerns with authentic human existence
largely takes the form of an attentive reading of the 'early Marx';
it is clear from the recent growth in this field that the insights of
the 'humanist Marx' into the problem of alienation accord with
our experiences and help us to understand ourselves better by
giving a name to, and an analysis of, the profound disquiet, if
not anxiety, many of us feel today.[18]

Leading on from a 'dialogue' with Marx about specific, or,
rather, fundamental–existential concerns, which we approach
his work with, or have sparked off by reading certain passages in
it, we arrive at a further stage in the hermeneutical appropriation

of Marx: the critical acceptance of Marx's work as a whole which is, wherever necessary, modified so as to accord with changed circumstances – itself a precondition for allowing the emancipatory interest underlying it, which is shared by the 'interpreter', to take its maximum effect. The objectifying moment apparent in the claim to understand Marx better than he had understood himself is here mediated with the need to reformulate basic assumptions of historical materialism.[19]

Reading III

Jürgen Habermas
The hermeneutic claim to
universality

I

Hermeneutics refers to an 'ability' we acquire to the extent to
which we learn to 'master' a natural language: the art of understanding linguistically communicable meaning and to render it
comprehensible in cases of distorted communication. The
understanding of meaning is directed at the semantic content of
speech as well as the meaning-content of written forms or even
of non-linguistic symbolic systems, in so far as their meaning-
content can, in principle, be expressed in words. It is no
accident that we speak of the art of understanding and of making-
oneself-understood, since the ability to interpret meaning,
which every language-user possesses, can be stylized and
developed into an artistic skill. This art is symmetric with the art
of convincing and persuading in situations where decisions have
to be reached on practical questions. Rhetoric, too, is based on
an ability which is part of the communicative competence of
every language user and which can be stylized into a special
skill. Rhetoric and hermeneutics have both emerged as teachable arts which methodically discipline and cultivate a natural
ability.

This is not so in the case of a philosophical hermeneutic:[1] it is
not a practical skill guided by rules but a critique, for its
reflexive engagement brings to consciousness experiences of
our language which we gain in the course of exercising our
communicative competence, that is, by moving within language.
It is because rhetoric and hermeneutics serve the instruction and
disciplined development of communicative competence that
hermeneutic reflection can draw on this sphere of experience.
But the reflection upon skilled understanding and making-
oneself-understood on the one hand (1), and upon convincing
and persuading on the other (2), does not serve the establishing

of a teachable art, but the philosophical consideration of the structures of everyday communication.

(1) The art of understanding and making-oneself-understood provides a philosophical hermeneutic with its characteristic insight that the means of natural language are, in principle, sufficient for elucidating the sense of any symbolic complex, however unfamiliar and inaccessible it may initially appear. We are able to translate from any language into any language. We are able to make sense of objectivations of the most remote epoch and the most distant civilization by relating them to the familiar, i.e. pre-understood, context of our own world. At the same time, the actual distance to other traditions is part of the horizon of every natural language. In addition, the already understood context of one's own world can at any time be exposed as being questionable; it is, potentially, incomprehensible. Hermeneutic experience is circumscribed by the conjunction of these two moments: the intersubjectivity of everyday communication is principally as unlimited as it is restricted; it is unlimited because it can be extended *ad libitum*; it is restricted because it can never be completely achieved. This applies to contemporary communication both within a socio-culturally homogeneous language community and across the distance between different classes, civilizations and epochs.

Hermeneutic experience brings to consciousness the position of a speaking subject *vis-à-vis* his language. He can draw upon the self-referentiality of natural languages for paraphrasing any changes metacommunicatively.

It is, of course, possible to construct hierarchies of formal languages on the basis of everyday language as the 'last meta-language' which would relate to one another as object – to meta, to metametalanguage, etc. The formal construction of such language systems excludes the possibility that for individual sentences the rules of application be determined ad hoc, commented on or changed; and the type-rule prohibits meta-communication about sentences of a language on the level of this object language. Both these things are, however, possible in everyday language. The system of natural language is not closed, but it allows the rules of application for any utterance to be determined ad hoc, commented on or changed; and metacom-munication has to employ the language which itself is made the object: every natural language is its own metalanguage. This is the basis for that reflexivity which, in the face of the type-rule, makes it possible for the semantic content of linguistic utter-ances to contain, in addition to the manifest message, an indirect message as to its application. Such is, for example, the case in a metaphoric use of language. Thanks to the reflexive structure of natural languages, the native speaker is provided with a unique metacommunicative manoeuvring space.

The reverse side of this freedom of movement is a close bond with linguistic tradition. Natural languages are informal; for this reason, speaking subjects cannot confront their language as a closed system. Linguistic competence remains, as it were, behind their backs: they can make sure of a meaning-complex explicitly only to the extent to which they also remain tied to a dogmatically traditioned and implicitly pregiven context. Hermeneutical understanding cannot approach a subject-matter free of any prejudice; it is, rather, unavoidably pre-possessed by the context within which the understanding subject has initially acquired his interpretative schemes. This pre-understanding can be thematized and it has to prove itself in relation to the subject-matter in the course of every analysis undertaken with hermeneutic awareness. But even the modification of these unavoidable pre-conceptions does not break through the objectivity of language *vis-à-vis* the speaking subject: in the course of improving his knowledge he merely develops a new pre-understanding which then guides him as he takes the next hermeneutical step. This is what Gadamer means when he states that the 'awareness of effective-history is unavoidably more being than consciousness'.[2]

(2) The art of convincing and persuading, in turn, provides a philosophical hermeneutic with the characteristic insight that it is possible not only to exchange information through the medium of everyday language, but also that, through it, action-orienting attitudes are formed and changed. Rhetoric is traditionally regarded as the art of bringing about a consensus on questions which cannot be settled through compelling reasoning. This is why the classical age reserved the realm of the merely 'probable' for rhetoric, in contrast to the realm in which the truth of statements is discussed theoretically. We are consequently here dealing with practical questions which can be traced to decisions about the acceptance or rejection of standards, of criteria for evaluation and norms of action. These decisions, if arrived at in a rational process, are made neither in a theoretically compelling nor in a merely arbitrary way: they have, in effect, been motivated by convincing speech. The peculiar ambivalence between conviction and persuasion, which attaches to any consensus arrived at through rhetorical means, not only evidences the element of force which to this day has not been removed

from the determination of socio-political objectives – however much it is based on discussion. More importantly, this equivocality is also an indication of the fact that practical questions can only be resolved dialogically and for this reason remain within the context of everyday language. Rationally motivated decisions can be arrived at only on the basis of a consensus that is brought about by convincing speech; and that means depending on the both cognitively and expressively appropriate means of everyday language.

We can also learn from our experience of rhetoric about the relationship between a speaking subject and his language. A speaker can make use of the creativity of natural language to respond spontaneously to changing situations and to define new situations in principally unpredictable statements. A formal prerequisite for this is a language-structure which makes possible the generation and understanding of an infinite number of sentences by following general rules and by drawing on a finite number of elements. This productivity extends, however, not only to the immediate generation of sentences in general, but also to the long-term process of the formation of interpretative schemes which are formulated in everyday language and which both enable and pre-judge the making of experiences. A good speech which leads to a consensus about decisions on practical questions merely indicates the point where we consciously intervene in this natural–innate process and attempt to alter accepted interpretative schemes with the aim of learning (and teaching) to see what we pre-understood through tradition in a different way and to evaluate it anew. This type of insight is innovatory through the choice of the appropriate word. Thanks to the creativity of natural language the native speaker gains a unique power over the practical consciousness of the members of a community. The career of sophistry reminds us that it can be used for mind-fogging agitation as well as for enlightening people.

There is, however, another side to this power: the specific lack of power of the speaking subject *vis-à-vis* habitualized language-games; they cannot be modified unless one participates in them. This in turn can be successful only to the extent that the rules which determine a language-game have been internalized. To enter into a linguistic tradition necessitates, at least latently, the efforts of a process of socialization: the 'grammar' of language-games has to become part of the personality structure. The sway of a good speech over practical consciousness rests with the fact that a natural language cannot be adequately comprehended as a system of rules for the generation of systematically ordered and semantically meaningful symbolic contexts; an immanent necessity ties it, in addition, to the context of action and bodily expressions. Rhetoric experience teaches us, in this way, the interconnection of language and praxis. Everyday communication would not only be incomplete but impossible outside the, grammatically ruled, connection with normatively guided interaction and accompanying, intermittent expressions of experiences. The insight that language and action mutually interpret each other is, of course, developed in Wittgenstein's concept of a language-game which is, at the same time, a life-form. The grammar of language-games, in the sense of a complete lifepraxis, regulates not only the combining of symbols but, at the same time, the interpretation of linguistic symbols by actions and expressions.[3]

These remarks should serve as a reminder that a philosophical hermeneutic develops those insights into the structure of natural languages which can be gained from the reflexive use of communicative competence: *reflexivity and objectivity are fundamental traits of language, as are creativity and the integration of language into life-praxis.* Such reflexive knowledge, which is comprised by the 'hermeneutic consciousness', is obviously different from a skill in understanding and speech. A philosophical hermeneutic differs equally from linguistics.

Linguistics is not concerned with communicative competence, that is the ability of native speakers to participate in everyday communication through understanding and speaking; it restricts itself to linguistic competence in the narrower sense. This expression was introduced by Chomsky[4] to characterize the ability of an ideal speaker who has a command of the abstract system of rules of natural language. The concept of a language system in the sense of *langue* leaves out of account the pragmatic dimension in which *langue* is transformed into *parole*. It is precisely experiences a speaker makes in this dimension that a philosophical hermeneutic is concerned with. Furthermore, linguistics aims at a reconstruction of the system of rules that allows the generation of all the grammatically correct and semantically meaningful elements of a natural language, whereas a philosophical hermeneutic reflects upon the basic experiences of communicatively competent speakers whose linguistic competence is tacitly presupposed. This distinction between rational reconstruction and self-reflection I would like to introduce by just giving one intuitive example.

Through *self-reflection* a subject becomes aware of the unconscious pre-suppositions of completed acts. Hermeneutic consciousness is thus the outcome of a process of self-reflection in which a speaking subject recognized his specific freedom from, and dependence on, language. This leads to the dissolution of a semblance, both of a subjectivist and an objectivist kind, which captivates naive consciousness. Self-reflection throws light on experiences a subject makes while exercising his communicative competence, but it cannot explain this competence. The rational *reconstruction* of a system of linguistic rules, in contrast, is undertaken with the aim of explaining linguistic competence. It makes explicit those rules which a native speaker has an implicit command of; but it does not as such make the subject conscious of suppositions he is not aware of. The speaker's subjectivity, constituting the horizon within which reflexive experience can be gained, remains excluded in principle. One could say that a successful linguistic reconstruction makes us conscious of the apparatus of language that is functioning without us being aware of it. This would, however, be an inauthentic use of language, since the consciousness of the speaker is not changed by this linguistic knowledge. What, then, is the relevance of hermeneutic consciousness if a philosophical hermeneutic is as little concerned with the art of understanding and of speech as it is with linguistics, i.e. if its usefulness is equally limited in relation to the pre-scientific exercise of communicative competence as it is for the scientific study of language?

It is nevertheless possible to cite four aspects in which a philosophical hermeneutic is relevant to the sciences and the interpretation of their results. (1) Hermeneutic consciousness destroys the objectivist self-understanding of the traditional *Geisteswissenschaften*. It follows from the hermeneutic situatedness of the interpreting scientist that objectivity in understanding cannot be secured by an abstraction from preconceived ideas, but only by reflecting upon the context of effective-history which connects perceiving subjects and their object.[5] (2) Hermeneutic consciousness furthermore reminds the social sciences of problems which arise from the symbolic pre-structuring of their object. If the access to data is no longer mediated through controlled observation but through communication in everyday language, then theoretical concepts can no longer be operationalized within the framework of the pre-scientifically developed language-game of physical measuring. The problems that arise on the level of measuring recur on the level of theory-construction: the choice of a categorical framework and of basic theoretical predicates has to correspond to a tentative pre-conception of the object.[6] (3) Hermeneutic consciousness also affects the scientistic self-understanding of the natural sciences but not, of course, their methodology. The insight that natural language represents the 'last' metalanguage for all theories expressed in formal language elucidates the epistemological locus of everyday language within scientific activity. The legitimation of decisions which direct the choice of research strategies, the construction of theories and the methods for test-ing them, and which thereby determine the 'progress of science', is dependent on discussions within the community of scien-tists. These discussions, which are conducted on the level of meta-theory, are nevertheless tied in principle to the context of natural language and to the explicative forms of everyday com-munication. A philosophical hermeneutic can show the reason why it is possible to arrive at a rationally motivated but not at a peremptory consensus on this theoretic level. (4) Hermeneutic consciousness is, finally, called upon in one area of interpret-ation more than in any other and one which is of great social interest: the translation of important scientific information into the language of the social life-world. 'What would we know of modern physics which so visibly alters our existence from physics alone? Its portrayal, which aims beyond the circle of experts, is dependent on a rhetorical element for its impact . . . . All science that hopes to be of practical use is dependent on rhetoric.'[7]

The objective need to rationally relate technically utilizable knowledge to the practical knowledge of the life-world is explained by the function which scientific–technological pro-gress has acquired for the maintenance of the system of developed industrial societies. It is my opinion that a philo-sophical hermeneutic tries to satisfy this need with its claim to universality. Hermeneutic consciousness can open the path towards 'integrating again the experience of science into our own general and human life-experience'[8] only when it is possible to consider 'the universality of human linguisticality as an element that is itself unlimited and that supports everything, not just linguistically transmitted cultural objects'.[9] Gadamer refers to Plato's saying that he who considers objects in the mirror of speech arrives at their whole and uncurtailed truth – 'in the mirror of language everything that exists is reflected'.[10]

This specific historical theme, which itself led to the efforts of a philosophical hermeneutic, does not, however, correspond to Plato's statement. It is obviously the case that modern science

can legitimately claim to arrive at true statements about 'things'
by proceeding monologically instead of considering the mirror
of human speech: that is, by formulating theories which are
monologically constructed and which are supported by controlled observation. It is because hypothetic–deductive systems
of propositions of science do not form an element of everyday
speech that the information derived from them is removed from
the life-world which is articulated in natural language. Of
course, the transference of technically utilizable knowledge into
the context of the life-world requires that monologically
generated knowledge be made intelligible within the dimension
of speech, i.e. within the dialogue of everyday language; and
this transference does, of course, represent a hermeneutic
problem – but it is a problem that is new to hermeneutics itself.
Hermeneutic consciousness does, after all, emerge from a
reflection upon our own movement *within* natural language,
whereas the interpretation of science on behalf of the life-world
has to achieve a mediation *between* natural language *and* monological language systems. This process of translation transcends
the limitations of a rhetorical–hermeneutical art which has only
been dealing with cultural products that were handed down and
which are constituted by everyday language. Going beyond
hermeneutic consciousness, that has established itself in the
course of the reflective exercise of this art, it would be the task of
a philosophical hermeneutic to clarify the conditions for the
possibility to, as it were, step outside the dialogical structure of
everyday language and to use language in a monological way
for the formal construction of theories and for the organization
of purposive rational action.

At this stage I would like to include, parenthetically, some
considerations. Jean Piaget's[11] genetic epistemology uncovers
the non-linguistic roots of operative thought. It is certainly the
case that the latter can only reach maturity through the integration of cognitive schemes, which emerge pre-linguistically
within the sphere of instrumental action, with the linguistic
systems of rules. But there is sufficient indication that language
merely 'sits upon' categories such as space, time, causality and
substance, and rules for the formal–logical combination of
symbols which possess a *pre*-linguistic basis. With the help of
this hypothesis it is possible to understand the monological use
of language for the organization of purposive–rational action and
for the construction of scientific theories; in these cases, natural
language is, in a manner of speaking, removed from the structure of intersubjectivity; without its dialogue-constitutive

elements and separated from communication it would be solely under the conditions of operative intelligence. The clarification of this issue is still to be completed; it will, in any case, be of relevance for deciding upon our question. If it is the case that operative intelligence goes back to pre-linguistic, cognitive schemes, and is therefore able to use language in an instrumental way, then the hermeneutic claim to universality would find its limit in the linguistic systems of science and the theories of rational choice. On the basis of this pre-supposition it could be made plausible why monologically constructed systems of language, even though they cannot be interpreted without recourse to natural language, can nevertheless be 'understood' while by-passing the hermeneutic problem; the conditions for understanding would not, at the same time, be the conditions for everyday communication. That would only be the case once the content of rigorously constructed theories were to be translated into the context of the life-world of speech.

I cannot deal with this problem now, but I would like to put the question concerning the validity of the hermeneutic claim to universality in a different way. Can there be an understanding of meaning in relation to symbolic structures formulated in everyday language that is not tied to the hermeneutic pre-supposition of context-dependent processes of understanding, an understanding that in this sense by-passes natural language as the last metalanguage? Since hermeneutical understanding always has to proceed in an ad hoc way and cannot be developed into a scientific method – it can at best be developed into an art – this question is equivalent to the problem of whether there can be a theory appropriate to the structure of natural languages on which a methical understanding of meaning can be based.

I can envisage two ways which promise success in looking for a solution.

On the one hand we hit upon a non-trivial limit to the sphere of hermeneutical understanding in cases which are dealt with by psychoanalysis – or the critique of ideology where collective phenomena are concerned. Both deal with objectivations in everyday language in which the subject does not recognize the intentions which guided his expressive activity. These manifestations can be regarded as parts of systematically distorted communication. They are comprehensible only to the extent to which the general conditions of the pathology of everyday communication are known. A theory of everyday communication would first of all have to beat a path through to the pathologically blocked meaning-context. If the claim to represent such a theory were justified, then an explanatory understanding would be possible which transcended the limit of the hermeneutical understanding of meaning.

On the other hand, representatives of generative linguistics have for more than a decade been working on a renewed programme of a general theory of natural languages. This theory is meant to provide a rational reconstruction of a regulative system that adequately defines general linguistic competence. If this claim could be fulfilled in such a way that each element of a natural language can definitely be attached to structural descriptions formulated in theoretical language, then the latter could take the place of the hermeneutical understanding of meaning.

I cannot deal with this problem either in the present context. In the following, I shall only consider the question whether a critical science such as psychoanalysis can by-pass the way skilful interpretation is tied to the natural competence of everyday communication with the help of a theoretically based semantic analysis – and thereby refute the hermeneutic claim to universality. These investigations will help us to establish more precisely in what sense it is nevertheless possible to defend the basic hermeneutic tenet that we cannot transcend 'the dialogue which we are', to use Gadamer's romanticist formulation.

II

Hermeneutic consciousness remains incomplete as long as it does not include a reflection upon the limits of hermeneutic understanding. The experience of a hermeneutical limitation refers to specifically incomprehensible expressions. This specific incomprehensibility cannot be overcome by the exercise, however skilful, of one's naturally acquired communicative competence; its stubbornness can be regarded as an indication that it cannot be explained by sole reference to the structure of everyday communication that hermeneutic philosophy has brought to light.

In this case it is not the objectivity of linguistic tradition, the finite horizon of a linguistically articulated understanding of life, the potential incomprehensibility of what is implicitly regarded as self-evident, that stands in the way of the interpretative effort.

In cases where understanding proves difficult owing to great cultural, temporal or social distance it is still possible for us to state in principle what additional information we require in order to fully understand: we know that we have to decipher an alphabet, get to know a vocabulary or rules of application which are specific to their context. Within the limits of tolerance of normal everyday communication it is possible for us to determine what we do not – yet – know when we try to make sense of an incomprehensible complex of meaning. This hermeneutic consciousness proves inadequate in the case of systematically distorted communication: incomprehensibility is here the result of a defective organization of speech itself. Openly pathological speech defects which are apparent, for example, among psychotics, can be disregarded by hermeneutics without impairment of its self-conception. The area of applicability of hermeneutics is congruent with the limits of normal everyday speech, as long as pathological cases are excluded. The self-conception of hermeneutics can only be shaken when it appears that patterns of systematically distorted communication are also in evidence in 'normal', let us call it pathologically unobtrusive, speech. This is the case in the pseudo-communication in which the participants cannot recognize a breakdown in their communication; only an external observer notices that they misunderstand one another. Pseudo-communication generates a system of misunderstandings that cannot be recognized as such under the appearance of a false consensus.

Hermeneutics has taught us that we are always a participant as long as we move within the natural language and that we cannot step outside the role of a reflective partner. There is, therefore, no general criterion available to us which would allow us to determine when we are subject to the false consciousness of a pseudo-normal understanding and consider something as a difficulty that can be resolved by hermeneutical means when, in fact, it requires systematic explanation. The experience of the limit of hermeneutics consists of the recognition of systematically generated misunderstanding as such – without, at first, being able to 'grasp' it.

Freud has drawn on this experience of systematically distorted communication in order to demarcate a sphere of specifically incomprehensible expressions. He always regarded dreams as the 'standard model' for those phenomena which themselves extend innocuous pseudo-communication and parapraxes in everyday life to the pathological manifestations of neuroses, mental illness and psychosomatic complaints. In his writings on the theory of civilization Freud extended the sphere of systematically distorted communication and he used the insights gained in dealing with clinical phenomena as a key for pseudo-normality, i.e. the hidden pathology of societal systems. We shall first of all focus on the sphere of neurotic manifestations that has received the fullest explanation.

There are available three criteria for demarcating neurotically distorted, which here means specifically incomprehensible, forms of expression. On the level of linguistic symbols, distorted communication is apparent in the application of rules which deviate from the publicly accepted rule-system. It is possible for an isolated semantic content or complete fields of meaning, in extreme cases even the syntax, to be affected. Freud examined the content of dreams mainly in relation to condensation, displacement, a-grammaticality and the role of contraries. On the level of the behaviour, a deformed language game is noticeable because of its rigidity and compulsion to repeat. Stereotyped patterns of behaviour recur in situations with the same stimuli which give rise to affective impulses. This inflexibility is an indication that the semantic content of a symbol has lost its specifically linguistic situational independence. When we consider the system of distorted communication as a whole it becomes apparent that there exists a characteristic discrepancy between the levels of communication: the usual congruence between linguistic symbols, actions and accompanying expressions has disintegrated. Neurotic symptoms are merely the most stubborn and manifest evidence of this dissonance. No matter on what level of communication these symptoms appear – in linguistic expression, body-language or compulsive behaviour – it is always the case that a content, which has been excommunicated from its public usage, assumes independence. This content expresses an intention which remains incomprehensible according to the rules of public communication, and is, in this sense, privatized; but it also remains inaccessible to its author. There exists within the self a barrier to communication between the 'I' who is linguistically competent and who participates in intersubjectively established language-games, and that 'inner exile' (Freud) that is represented by the symbolic system of a private or protogenal language.

Alfred Lorenzer has examined the analytical dialogue between doctor and patient from the point of view of psychoanalysis as a linguistic analysis.[12] He conceives of the depth-hermeneutical decoding of the meaning of specifically incomprehensible objectivations as an understanding of analogous scenes. The aim of analytical interpretation, seen hermeneutically, consists of the clarification of the incomprehensible meaning of symptomatic expressions. As far as neuroses are concerned, these expressions represent part of a deformed language-game within which the patient 'acts': he enacts an incomprehensible scene by contravening, in a conspicuous and stereotyped way, existing expectations of behaviour. The analyst tries to render understandable the meaning of a symptomatic scene by relating the latter to analogous scenes in a situation which contains the key to the coded relationship between the symptomatic scene which the adult patient enacts outside his treatment on the one hand, and to the original scene of his early childhood on the other, in the transfer situation. This is because the analyst is pushed into the role of the conflict-charged primary object. In his role as reflective partner the analyst can interpret the transference as a repetition of scenes of early childhood and can thereby draw up a lexicon of the meanings of these symptomatic expressions which are formulated in a private language. Scenic understanding proceeds, therefore, from the insight that the patient behaves in his symptomatic scenes as he does in certain transference scenes; it aims at a reconstruction of the original scene which the patient validates in an act of self-reflection.

As Lorenzer has demonstrated by reference to the phobia of Little Hans whom Freud examined, the reconstructed original scene is typically a situation in which a child suffers an intolerable conflict which he then represses. This defence is connected with a process of desymbolization and of symptom-formation. The child excludes the experience of conflictive object-relations from public communication (and thereby renders it inaccessible even to his own Ego); it splits off the part of the representation of the object that is charged with conflict and, in a way, desymbolizes the meaning of the relevant object. The gap that appears in the semantic field is closed by a symptom, in that an unsuspicious symbol takes the place of the symbolic content that has been split off. This symbol is, however, as conspicuous as a symptom since it has gained a private meaning and can no longer be used in accordance with the rules of public language. Scenic understanding establishes an equivalence of meaning between the elements of three patterns: everyday scene, transference scene and original scene; it thereby breaks through the specific incomprehensibility of the symptom and assists in the re-symbolization, i.e. the re-introduction into public communication of a symbolic content that has been split off. The latent meaning underlying the present situation is rendered comprehensible by reference to the unmutilated meaning of the original scene in infancy. Scenic understanding makes possible the 'translation' into public communication of the sense of a pathologically petrified pattern of communication which has so far remained inaccessible, but which determined behaviour.

Scenic understanding is distinguishable from the elementary hermeneutical understanding of meaning by its explanatory potential; it makes accessible the meaning of specifically incomprehensible forms of expression only to the extent to which it is possible to clarify the conditions for the emergence of nonsense in conjunction with the reconstruction of the original scene. The 'what', the meaning-content of systematically distorted expressions, can only be 'understood' when it is possible to answer, at the same time, the 'why' question, i.e. to 'explain' the emergence of the symptomatic scene by reference to the initial conditions of the systematic distortion itself.

This understanding can acquire an explanatory function in the narrow sense only if the analysis of meaning does not rely solely on the skilled application of communicative competence but is guided by theoretical assumptions. I name two points of evidence to show that scenic understanding relies on theoretical pre-suppositions which in no way follow automatically from the natural competence of a native speaker.

Scenic understanding is, first of all, tied to a specific hermeneutical form of experimentation. The analytical rule introduced by Freud guarantees a form of communication between doctor and patient which, as it were, fulfils experimental conditions; virtualization of an actual situation and free association on the part of the patient, and goal-inhibited reaction and reflective participation by the analyst, make it possible that a transference occurs which can be used as a foil for the task of 'translation'. Secondly, the analyst's pre-understanding is directed at a small segment of possible meanings: viz. early, conflictive object-relations. The linguistic material that emerges in talks with the patient is classified within a closely circumscribed context of possible double meaning. This context consists of a general interpretation of infant patterns of interaction which is correlated with a theory of personality that exhibits specific phases of development. Both these aspects show that scenic understanding cannot be regarded in the same way as hermeneutical understanding, i.e. as a non-theoretical application of communicative competence which makes theorizing possible in the first place.

The theoretical assumptions tacitly underlying depth-hermeneutical language analysis can be developed in relation to three aspects. The psychoanalyst has a pre-conception of the structure of undistorted everyday communication (1); he traces the systematic distortion of communication back to the confusion of pre-linguistic and linguistic organization of symbols which are separated as two stages in the developmental process (2); he explains the emergence of deformations with the aid of a theory of deviant processes of socialization which extends onto the connection of patterns of infant interaction with the formation of personality (3). I need not here develop these theoretical assumptions in a systematic way; but I would like to illustrate briefly the aspects just mentioned.

(1) The first set of theoretical assumptions refers to the structural conditions that have to be met when talking about 'normal' everyday communication.

(a) In non-deformed language-games there exists a congruence of expression on all three levels of communication; those utterances symbolized linguistically, those that are presented in actions, and those embodied in physical expressions do not contradict but complement one another metacommunicatively. Intended contradictions, which themselves contain a message, are, in this sense, regarded as normal. It is a further aspect of the normal form of everyday communication that a part of extra-verbal meanings, which varies with its socio-cultural context but which remains constant within a language-community, is intentional, i.e. in principle verbalizable.

(b) Normal everyday language follows intersubjectively valid rules: it is public. Communicated meanings are, in principle, identical for all members of a language-community. Verbal utterances are formed in agreement with the valid system of grammatical rules and are applied in a specific context; there also exists a lexicon for all extra-verbal utterances not following grammatical rules which varies within limits between socio-cultural contexts.

(c) In normal speech, the speakers are aware of the categorical difference between subject and object. They differentiate between outer and inner speech and separate private and public existence. The differentiation between reality and appearance is, in addition, dependent on the difference between linguistic symbol, its meaning-content (signification) and the object referred to by the symbol (referent, denotation). Only on this basis is it possible to use linguistic symbols independently of a given situation (decontextualization). The speaking subject becomes capable of distinguishing between reality and appearance to the extent to which language acquires for him an existence separate from the denoted objects and the represented state of affairs as well as from private experiences.

(d) It is in normal everyday communication that the inter-subjectivity of relations which secures the identity of individuals who mutually recognize one another is formed and maintained. Whereas the analytical use of language allows the identification of states of affairs (i.e. the categorization of objects by means of the identification of the specific, the subsumption of elements under classes, and the inclusion of aggregates), the reflexive use of language secures the relationship of speaking subject to a language-community, which is something that cannot be adequately represented with the mentioned analytical operations. The intersubjectivity of a world, which the subjects can inhabit on the strength of their communication in everyday language alone, is not a generality under which individuals are subsumed in the same way as elements under a class. It is, rather, the case that the relations between I, You (other I) and We (I and the other Is) are established through an analytically paradoxical achievement. The speakers identify themselves with two mutually incompatible dialogic roles and thereby secure the identify of the I as well as that of the group. The one (I) affirms his absolute non-identity *vis-à-vis* the other (You); but at the same time both recognize their own identity by accepting one another as irreplaceable individuals. In this process they are connected by something they share (We), i.e. a group which itself affirms its individuality *vis-à-vis* other groups, so that the same relations are established on the level of intersubjectively united collectives as exist between individuals.[13]

The specific point about linguistic intersubjectivity is that individuated persons can communicate on the basis of it. In the reflexive use of language we formulate what is inalienable and individual in general categories; we do this in such a way that we, as it were, metacommunicatively retract (and confirm with reservation) our direct message in order to express indirectly that part of the I that is non-identical and that cannot be represented by general determinations – even though they are the only means for expressing it.[14] The analytical use of language is embedded within the reflexive use, since the inter-subjectivity of everyday communication cannot be maintained without the reciprocal self-representation of speaking subjects. A speaker can distinguish between reality and appearance to the extent to which he has a mastery of those indirect means of communication on the level of metacommunication. It is pos-sible for us to communicate directly about states of affairs, but the subjectivity we encounter in the course of talking to one another appears only as a surface-phenomenon in direct forms of communication. The categorial meaning of indirect forms of communication which give expression to that which is individualized and unsayable is merely ontologized in the concept of an entity that exists in its appearances.

(e) Finally, it is characteristic of normal speech that the sense of substance and causality, space and time differs depending on whether these categories are applied to objects in the world or to the linguistically constituted world of speaking subjects itself. The interpretative scheme 'substance' has a different sense in the identity of objects which can be categorized in an analytically unequivocal way from the one it has for speaking and acting subjects whose Ego-identity cannot be captured in analytically unequivocal operations. The causal interpretative scheme leads to the concept of physical 'cause' if applied to the empirical consequences of events, and also to the concept of 'motive' in the context of intentional action. Space and time are, analogously, schematized differently in respect of the physically measurable properties of objects and events than in respect of the intersubjective experience of contexts of symbolically mediated interaction. In the first case categories are employed as a system of co-ordinates for observations which are checked by the success of instrumental action; in the second case they serve as a frame of reference for subjective experiences of social space and historical time. The parameter of possible experiences in the field of intersubjectivity changes complementarity to the parameter of possible experiences about objectivated objects and events.

(2) The second set of assumptions refers to the relationship between two genetically consecutive stages of the human organization of symbols.

(a) The earlier organization of symbols which does not allow the transposition of its contents into grammatically regulated communication can only be investigated through data about the pathology of speech and on the basis of an analysis of the content of dreams. We are here concerned with symbols which direct behaviour and not just with signs since symbols possess an authentic meaning-function; they represent experiences gained in interaction. This layer of paleo-symbols is, however, devoid of all the properties of normal speech.[15] Paleo-symbols are not integrated into a system of grammatical rules. They are unordered elements and do not arise within a system that could be transformed grammatically. It is for this reason that the functioning of pre-linguistic symbols has been compared with that of analogy computers in contrast to digital computers.

Freud had already noticed the lack of logical connections in his analyses of dreams. In particular, he points to contraries which have preserved, on the linguistic level, the genetically earlier characteristic of an ensemble of logically irreconcilable, that is contrary, meanings.[16] Pre-linguistic symbols are highly charged affectively and are tied to specific scenes; there is also no separation between linguistic symbol and bodily expression. They are tied to a specific context so closely that symbols cannot vary freely in relation to actions.[17] Even though paleo-symbols represent the pre-linguistic basis for the intersubjectivity of co-existence and collective action they do not lend themselves to public communication in the strict sense. This is because the constancy of meaning is low while the proportion of private meanings is, at the same time, high: they cannot yet guarantee an intersubjectively binding identity of meaning. The privatism of the pre-linguistic organization of symbols, which is apparent in all forms of pathological speech, can be traced back to the fact that the distance which is maintained in everyday speech between addressor and addressee has not yet been developed, and neither has the distinction between symbolic sign, semantic content and referent. Nor is it as yet possible, by means of paleo-symbols, to differentiate clearly between the level of reality and that of appearance, and between public and private world (adualism).

Pre-linguistic organization of symbols does not, finally, allow any satisfactory categorization of the experienced world of objects. Among the disorders of communication and thought processes apparent in psychotics[18] one can find two extreme forms of malfunctioning; in both cases, the analytical operation of classification is disturbed. There exists, firstly, a structure of fragmentation that does not allow the comprehension of disintegrated individual elements into classes by following general criteria. Secondly, one can find an amorphous structure that does not allow any analysis of aggregates of objects which resemble each other superficially and which are vaguely grouped together. The use of symbols has not become impossible in its entirety. But the inability to form hierarchies of classes and to identify elements of classes indicates in both cases the collapse of the analytical use of language. It is, of course, possible to conclude on the basis of the second variation that an archaic formation of classes is possible by means of pre-linguistic symbols. In any case, we can find so-called primary classes, which are not formed on the abstract basis of the identity of properties, in the early stages of ontogenetic and phylogenetic development and in cases of speech-pathology. The aggregates in question, in fact, comprehend concrete objects in view of an overarching, subjectively convincing context of motivation irrespective of their identifiable properties. Animistic cosmologies are organized in accordance with such primary classes. Since comprehensive intentional structures cannot be developed without any experience of interaction one can assume that early forms of intersubjectivity are already developed in the pre-linguistic stage of symbol-organization. Paleo-symbols are, apparently, formed in contexts of interaction before they are incorporated into a system of grammatical rules and connected to operative intelligence.

(b) The organization of symbols described above, which is genetically prior to language, is a theoretical construction. It can nowhere be observed. The psychoanalytic decoding of systematically distorted communication pre-supposes such a construction, however, since depth-hermeneutics comprehends confusions of normal speech either as forced regression to earlier stages of communication or as the intrusion of an earlier form of communication into language. Basing himself on an analyst's experience of neurotic patients, Alfred Lorenzer sees the essence of psychoanalysis, as has been already shown, as the attempt to re-integrate split-off symbolic contents, which led to a privatistic narrowing of public communication, into the general usage of language. Analysis helps to achieve a 'resymbolization' by retracing, and thereby undoing, the process of repression; the latter can, therefore, be regarded as a process of 'desymbolization'. The patient reacts against the analyst's cogent interpretation by the defence mechanism of repression, which is analogous to a taking to flight; this is an operation that takes place through and against language – otherwise it would be impossible to undo the defensive process by hermeneutical means, i.e. through the analysis of language. The fleeing Ego that in situations of conflict is forced to submit to the claims of external reality hides before itself by removing the representatives of the claims of unwelcome drives from the text of its everyday self-understanding. By means of this censorship, the representation of the tabooed object of love is excommunicated from the public use of language and, as it were, pushed back into the genetically earlier stage of paleo-symbols.

The assumption that neurotic behaviour is guided by paleo-symbols and is only subsequently rationalized by linguistic interpretation also provides an explanation for the characteristics of this form of behaviour: for its status as pseudo-communication, stereotyped and compulsive behaviour, emotional attachment, expressive content and inflexible situational tie.

If repression can be regarded as desymbolization then it is possible to provide a language-analytical interpretation for a complementary defensive mechanism that is not directed at the self but at external reality, viz. projection and disavowal. Whereas in the first case the public use of language is mutilated by symptoms that have been formed in place of excommunicated linguistic elements, distortion in the second case is directly attributable to the uncontrolled intrusion of paleo-symbolic derivatives into language. Language analysis does not aim here at the re-transformation of desymbolized contents into linguistically articulate meaning, but at a consciously undertaken excommunication of pre-linguistic elements. In both instances, systematic distortion of everyday communication can be explained by reference to semantic contents which are tied to paleo-symbols and which encyst within language like alien bodies. It is the task of language analysis to dissolve these syndromes, i.e. to isolate both levels of language.

In processes of linguistic creation, however, there occurs a genuine integration; the meaning-potential tied to paleo-symbols is publicly retrieved in the creative use of language, and is utilized for the grammatically guided use of symbols.[19] The transference of semantic contents from the pre-linguistic to the linguistic state of aggregation widens the sphere of communicative action at the expense of the unconsciously motivated one. The moment of successful, creative use of language is one of emancipation.

This is not so in the case of jokes. The laughter with which we almost compulsively respond to a joke is witness to the liberative experience of the transition from the stage of paleo-symbols to that of linguistic thought; the funny element consists in the demasking of the ambiguity of the joke which resides in the teller enticing us to regress to the stage of pre-linguistic symbolism, i.e. to confuse identity and resemblance, and at the same time to convict us of the mistake of this regression. The ensuing laughter is one of relief. In our response to a joke, which leads us to retrace, virtually and experimentally, the dangerous passage across the archaic boundary between pre-linguistic and linguistic communication, we become reassured of the control we have achieved over the dangers of a superseded stage of consciousness.

(3) Depth-hermeneutics, which clarifies the specific incomprehensibility of distorted communication, can, strictly speak-

ing, no longer be considered in relation to the model of translation, as is the case with ordinary hermeneutical understanding. This is because the controlled 'translation' or pre-linguistic symbolism into language removes obscurities which do not arise within language but through language itself; it is the structure of everyday communication, which provides the basis of translation, which is itself affected. Depth-hermeneutical understanding requires, therefore, a systematic pre-understanding that extends onto language in general, whereas hermeneutical understanding always proceeds from a pre-understanding that is shaped by tradition and which forms and changes itself within linguistic communication. The theoretical assumptions which relate, on the one hand, to two stages in the organization of symbols and, on the other hand, to processes of de- and re-symbolization, to the intrusion of paleo-symbolic elements into language and the conscious excommunication of these interspersals, as well as to the integration of pre-linguistic symbolic contents – these theoretical assumptions can be integrated into a structural model which Freud derived from his experiences gained in the analysis of the mechanism of defence. The constructions of the 'Ego' and the 'Id' interpret the analyst's experience of resistance on the part of the patient.

'Ego' is the portion of the personality that fulfils the task of examining reality and of censuring drives. 'Id' is the name for those parts of the self which have been separated from the Ego and the existence of which becomes accessible in connection with the mechanism of defence. The 'Id' is indirectly represented by symptoms which fill the gaps in normal discourse that appeared in the course of de-symbolization; It is directly represented by those delusory paleo-symbolic elements which enter language through projection and disavowal. The same clinical experience of 'resistance' which led to the construction of the structures Ego and Id now also shows that defensive processes occur mainly unconsciously. This is why Freud introduced the category of 'Super-ego': an agency of defence unknown to the Ego which is formed through the open-ended identification with the expectations of the primary object. All three categories, Ego, Id and Super-ego, are consequently tied to the specific sense of a systematically distorted communication which analyst and patient enter into with the aim of initiating a dialogical process of enlightenment, and to encourage and guide the patient towards self-reflection. Metapsychology can only be established as meta-hermeneutics.[20]

The structural model implicitly relies upon a model of the

deformation of everyday intersubjectivity; the dimensions of Id and Super-ego within the structure of personality clearly correspond to the deformation of that structure of intersubjectivity which is apparent in communication free from domination. The structure model which Freud introduced as the categorial frame of metapsychology can, consequently, be traced back to a theory of the distortion of communicative competence.

Metapsychology consists, in the main, of assumptions about the formation of personality structures which, too, can be explained by reference to the meta-hermeneutical role of psychoanalysis. The understanding of the analyst derives, as we have seen, its explanatory force from the fact that the clarification of systematically inaccessible sense can succeed only to the extent that the origin of this non-sense can itself be explained. The reconstruction of the original scene can do both at the same time; it makes it possible to understand the meaning of deformed language-games and, together with it, to explain the origin of this deformation. This is why scenic understanding pre-supposes a metapsychology in the sense of a theory of the formation of the structures of Ego, Id and Super-ego.

On the sociological level, this finds its correspondence in the theory of the acquisition of the basic qualifications for role-guided behaviour. But both theories are part of a meta-hermeneutic which traces back the psychological development of personality structures and the acquisition of the basic qualifications for role-guided behaviour to the development of communicative competence; this is the socializing introduction into, and practising of, forms of the intersubjectivity of everyday communication. It is now possible to answer our original question: explanatory understanding, in the sense of the depth-hermeneutical decoding of specifically inadequate expressions, does not only necessitate the skilled application of naturally acquired communicative competence, as it is the case with elementary hermeneutical understanding, but also pre-supposes a theory of communicative competence. The latter covers the forms of the intersubjectivity of language and causes of its deformation. I cannot say that a theory of communicative competence has up until now been attempted in a satisfactory way, never mind been explicitly developed. Freud's metapsychology would have to be freed of its scientistic self-miscomprehension before it could be utilized as a part of a meta-hermeneutic. I would say, however, that each depth-hermeneutical interpretation of systematically distorted communication, irrespective of whether it appears in an analytic encounter or informally, implicitly relies on those demanding theoretical assumptions which can only be developed and justified within the framework of a *theory of communicative competence.*

III

What follows from this hermeneutic claim to universality? Is it not the case that the theoretical language of a meta-hermeneutic is subject to the same reservation as all other theories: that a given non-reconstructed everyday language remains the last metalanguage? And would not the application of general interpretations, which are deducible from such theories, to material given in everyday language still require basic hermeneutical understanding which is not replaceable by any generalized measuring procedure? Neither of these questions would any longer have to be answered in accordance with the hermeneutic claim to universality if the knowing subject, who necessarily has to draw on his previously acquired linguistic competence, could assure himself explicitly of this competence in the course of a theoretical reconstruction. We have so far bracketed this problem of a general theory of natural language. But we can already refer to this competence, which the analyst (and the critic of ideologies) has to employ factually in the disclosure of specifically incomprehensible expressions, in advance of all theory construction. Already the *implicit knowledge of the conditions of systematically distorted communication,* which is pre-supposed in an actual form in the depth-hermeneutical use of communicative competence, *is sufficient for the questioning of the ontological self-understanding of the philosophical hermeneutic* which Gadamer propounds by following Heidegger.

Gadamer turns the context-dependency of the understanding of meaning, which hermeneutic philosophy has brought to consciousness and which requires us always to proceed from a pre-understanding that is supported by tradition as well as to continuously form a new pre-understanding in the course of being corrected, to the ontologically inevitable primacy of linguistic tradition.[21] Gadamer poses the question: 'Is the phenomenon of understanding adequately defined when I state that to understand is to avoid misunderstanding? Is it not, rather, the case that something like a 'supporting consensus' precedes all misunderstanding.[22] We can agree on the answer, which is to be given in the affirmative, but not on how to define this preceding consensus.

If I understand correctly, then Gadamer is of the opinion that the hermeneutical clarification of incomprehensible or misunderstood expressions always has to lead back to a consensus that has already been reliably established through converging tradition. This tradition is objective in relation to us in the sense that we cannot confront it with a principled claim to truth. The pre-judgmental structure of understanding not only prohibits us from questioning that factually established consensus which underlies our misunderstanding and incomprehension, but makes such an undertaking appear senseless. It is a hermeneutical requirement that we refer to a concrete pre-understanding which itself, in the last analysis, goes back to the process of socialization, i.e. the introduction into a shared tradition. None of them is, in principle, beyond criticism; but neither can they be questioned abstractly. This would only be possible if we could examine a consensus that has been achieved through mutual understanding by, as it were, looking into it from the side and subjecting it, behind the backs of the participants, to renewed demands for legitimation. But we can only make demands of this kind in the face of the participants by entering into a dialogue with them. In this case we submit, yet again, to the hermeneutic demand to accept, for the time being, the clarifying consensus which the resumed dialogue might arrive at, as a supporting agreement. It would be senseless to abstractly suspect this agreement, which, admittedly, is contingent, of being false consciousness since we cannot transcend the dialogue which we are. This leads Gadamer to conclude to the ontological priority of linguistic tradition over all possible critique; we can consequently criticize specific traditions only on the basis that we are part of the comprehensive context of the tradition of a language.

On first sight, these considerations seem plausible. They can, however, be shaken by the depth-hermeneutical insight that a consensus achieved by seemingly 'reasonable' means may well be the result of pseudo-communication. Albrecht Wellmer has pointed out that the Enlightenment tradition generalized this insight which is hostile to tradition. However much the Enlightenment was interested in communication, it still demanded that Reason be recognized as the principle of communication, free from force in the face of the real experience of communication distorted by force: 'The Enlightenment knew what a philosophical hermeneutic forgets – that the "dialogue" which we, according to Gadamer, "are", is also a context of domination and as such precisely no dialogue . . . . The universal claim of the hermeneutic approach [can only] be maintained if it is realized at the outset that the context of tradition as a locus of possible truth and factual agreement is, at the same time, the locus of factual untruth and continued force.'[23]

It would only be legitimate for us to equate the supporting consensus which, according to Gadamer, always precedes any failure at mutual understanding with a given factual agreement, if we could be certain that each consensus arrived at in the medium of linguistic tradition has been achieved without compulsion and distortion. But we learn from depth-hermeneutic experience that the dogmatism of the context of tradition is subject not only to the objectivity of language in general but also to the repressivity of forces which deform the intersubjectivity of agreement as such and which systematically distort everyday communication. It is for this reason that every consensus, as the outcome of an understanding of meaning, is, in principle, suspect of having been enforced through pseudo-communication: in earlier days, people talked about delusion when misunderstanding and self-misunderstanding continued unaffected under the appearance of factual agreement. Insight into the prejudgmental structure of the understanding of meaning does not cover the identification of actually achieved consensus with a true one. It, rather, leads to the ontologization of language and to the hypostatization of the context of tradition. A critically enlightened hermeneutic that differentiates between insight and delusion incorporates the meta-hermeneutic awareness of the conditions for the possibility of systematically distorted communication. It connects the process of understanding to the principle of rational discourse, according to which truth would only be guaranteed by *that* kind of consensus which was achieved under the idealized conditions of unlimited communication free from domination and could be maintained over time.

K.-O. Apel rightly emphasized that hermeneutical understanding can, at the same time, lead to the critical ascertainment of truth only to the extent to which it follows the regulative principle: to try to establish universal agreement within the framework of an unlimited community of interpreters.[24] Only this principle can make sure that the hermeneutic effort does not cease until we are aware of deceptions within a forcible consensus and of the systematic distortion behind seemingly accidental misunderstanding. If the understanding of meaning is not to remain *a fortiori* indifferent towards the idea of truth then we have to anticipate, together with the concept of a kind of truth which measures itself on an idealized consensus achieved in unlimited communication free from domination, also the structures of solidary co-existence in communication free from force. Truth is that characteristic compulsion towards unforced universal recognition; the latter is itself tied to an ideal speech situation, i.e. a form of life, which makes possible unforced universal agreement. The critical understanding of meaning thus has to take upon itself the formal anticipation of a true life. This has already been expressed by G. H. Mead:[25]

> Universal discourse is the formal ideal of communication. If communication can be carried through and made perfect, then there would exist the kind of democracy . . . in which each individual would carry just the response in himself that he knows he calls out in the community. That is what makes communication in the significant sense the organising process in the community.

The idea of truth, which measures itself on a true consensus, implies the idea of the true life. We could also say: it includes the idea of being-of-age (*Mündigkeit*).* It is only the formal anticipation of an idealized dialogue, as the form of life to be realized in the future, which guarantees the ultimate supporting and contra-factual agreement that already unites us; in relation to it we can criticize every factual agreement, should it be a false one, as false consciousness. It is, however, only when we can show that the anticipation of possible truth and a true life is constitutive for every linguistic communication which is not monological that we are in a position not merely to demand but to justify that regulative principle of understanding. Basic meta-hermeneutic experience makes us aware of the fact that critique, as a penetrating form of understanding which does not rebound off delusions, orients itself on the concept of ideal consensus and thereby follows the regulative principle of rational discourse. But to justify the view that we not only do, but indeed have to, engage in that formal anticipation in the course of every penetrating understanding, it is not enough to merely refer to experience alone. To attempt a systematic justification we have to develop the implicit knowledge, that always and already guides the depth-hermeneutical analysis of language, into a theory which would enable us to deduce the principle of rational discourse from the logic of everyday language and regard it as

Mündigkeit (originally, *Mund* = mouth), here refers to one's ability as a competent, self-determining speaker.

the necessary regulative for any actual discourse, however distorted it may be.

Even without anticipating a general theory of natural language, the above considerations would suffice to criticize two conceptions which follow not so much from hermeneutics itself but from what seems to me to be a false ontological self-understanding of it.

(1) Gadamer deduced the rehabilitation of prejudice from his hermeneutic insight into the pre-judgmental structure of understanding. He does not see any opposition between authority and reason. The authority of tradition does not assert itself blindly but only through its reflective recognition by those who, while being part of tradition themselves, understand and develop it through application. In response to my criticism,[26] Gadamer clarifies his position once again:[27]

> I grant that authority exercises force in an infinite number of forms of domination . . . . But this view of obedience to authority cannot tell us why these forms all represent ordered states of affairs and not the disorder of the brachial use of force. It seems to me to follow necessarily when I consider recognition as being determined in actual situations of authority . . . . One only needs to study such events as the loss or decay of authority . . . to see what authority is and what sustains it; it is not dogmatic force but dogmatic recognition. But what is dogmatic recognition, however, if it is not that one concedes to authority a superiority of knowledge.

The dogmatic recognition of tradition, and this means the acceptance of the truth-claims of this tradition, can be equated with knowledge itself only when freedom from force and unrestricted agreement about tradition have already been secured within this tradition. Gadamer's argument pre-supposes that legitimizing recognition and the consensus on which authority is founded can arise and develop free from force. The experience of distorted communication contradicts this pre-supposition. Force can, in any case, acquire permanence only through the objective semblance of an unforced pseudo-communicative agreement. Force that is legitimated in such a way we call, with Max Weber, authority. It is for this reason that there has to be that principle proviso of a universal agreement free from domination in order to make the fundamental distinction between dogmatic recognition and true consensus. Reason, in the sense of the principle of rational discourse, represents the rock which factual authorities have so far been more likely to crash against than build upon.

(2) If, then, such opposition between authority and reason does in fact exist, as the Enlightenment has always claimed, and if it cannot be superseded by hermeneutic means, it follows that the attempt to impose fundamental restrictions upon the interpreter's commitment to enlightenment becomes problematic, too. Gadamer has, in addition, derived the re-absorption of the moment of enlightenment into the horizon of currently existing convictions, from his insight into the pre-judgmental structure of understanding. The interpreter's ability to understand the author better than he had understood himself is limited by the accepted and traditionally established certitudes of the socio-cultural life-world of which he is part:[28]

> How does the psychoanalyst's knowledge relate to his position within the social reality to which he belongs? The emancipatory reflection which he initiates in his patients necessitates that he inquires into the more conscious surface interpretations, breaks through masked self-understanding, sees through the repressive function of social taboos. But when he conducts this reflection in situations which are outside the legitimate sphere of an analyst and where he is himself a partner in social inter-action, then he is acting out of part. Anyone who sees through his social partners to something hidden to them, i.e. who does not take their role-acting seriously, is a 'spoil-sport' who will be avoided. The emancipatory potential of reflection which the psychoanalyst draws on therefore has to find its limit in the social consciousness within which both the analyst and his patient are in agreement with everyone else. As hermeneutic reflection has shown us, social com-munality, despite existing tensions and defects, always refers us back to a consensus on the basis of which it exists.

There is, however, reason to assume that the background consensus of established traditions and of language-games may be a forced consensus which resulted from pseudo-communication; this may be so not only in the individual, pathological case of disturbed family systems, but also in societal systems. The range of a hermeneutical understanding that has been extended into critique must, consequently, not be tied to the radius of convictions existing within a tradition. A depth-hermeneutic which adheres to the regulative principle of rational discourse has to seek out remaining natural–historical traces of distorted

communication which are still contained even within fundamental agreements and recognized legitimations; and since it
can find them there, too, it follows that any privatization of its
commitment to enlightenment, and the restriction of the
critique of ideology to the role of a treatment as it is institutionalized in the analyst–patient relationship, would be incompatible with its methodic point of departure. The enlightenment, which results from radical understanding, is always
political. It is, of course, true that criticism is always tied to the
context of tradition which it reflects. Gadamer's hermeneutic
reservations are justified against monological self-certainty
which merely arrogates to itself the title of critique. There is no
validation of depth-hermeneutical interpretation outside of the
self-reflection of all participants that is successfully achieved in a
dialogue. The hypothetical status of general interpretations
leads, indeed, to *a priori* limitations in the selection of ways in
which the given immanent commitment of critical understanding to enlightenment can at any time be realized.[29]
     In present conditions it may be more urgent to indicate the
limits of the false claim to universality made by criticism rather
than that of the hermeneutic claim to universality. Where the
dispute about the grounds for justification is concerned, however, it is necessary to critically examine the latter claim, too.

Notes

1 H. G. Gadamer, 'Rhetorik, Hermeneutik und Ideologiekritik', in
   Kleine Schriften, I, Tübingen, 1967, pp. 113–30.
2 Ibid., p. 127.
3 Cf. J. Habermas (1968a), p. 206.
4 N. Chomsky, *Aspects of the Theory of Syntax*, MIT Press,
   Cambridge, Mass., 1965.
5 Gadamer shows this in the second part of *Truth and Method*.
6 Cf. J. Habermas, 'Zur Logik der Sozialwissenschaften', in *Phil-
   Rundschau*, Supplement 5 (1967), ch. III.
7 H. G. Gadamer, 'Rhetorik, Hermeneutik und Ideologiekritik',
   p. 117.
8 H. G. Gadamer, 'Die Universalität des hermeneutischen
   Problems' in *Kleine Schriften*, I, p. 109 (translated in this book as
   'The universality of the hermeneutical problem').
9 H. G. Gadamer, 'Rhetorik, Hermeneutik und Ideologiekritik',
   p. 118.
10 Ibid., p. 123.
11 Cf. H. G. Furth's excellent examination, *Piaget and Knowledge*,
    Prentice-Hall, Englewood Cliffs, N.J., 1969.

12 A. Lorenzer, *Symbol und Verstehen im psychoanalytischen Prozess. Vorarbeiten zu einer Metatheorie der Psychoanalyse*, Suhrkamp, Frankfurt, 1970.

13 This is also apparent in our relationship with foreign languages. We can, in principle, learn every foreign language since all natural languages can be traced back to a general system of generative rules. But, yet, we acquire a foreign language only to the extent to which we, at least potentially, undergo at a late stage the process of socialization of native speakers – and, thereby, again at least potentially, grow into an individual language community; natural language can be general only as something concrete.

14 For the concept of non-identity, see T. W. Adorno, *Negative Dialektik*, Frankfurt, 1966 (translated as *Negative Dialectics*, Routledge & Kegan Paul, London, 1973).

15 Cf. S. Arieti, *The Intrapsychic Self*, Basic Books, New York, 1967, especially ch. 7 and ch. 16; also H. Werner and B. Kaplan, *Symbol Formation*, Wiley, New York, 1967; P. Watzlawick, J. H. Beavin, D. D. Jackson, *Pragmatics of Human Communication*, Norton, New York, 1967, especially ch. 6 and ch. 7.

16 Cf. A. Gehlen, *Urmensch und Spätkultur*, Bonn, 1956; A. S. Diamond, *The History and Origin of Language*, London, 1959.

17 Lorenzer (op. cit., p. 88) finds the same characteristics in the unconscious representatives which direct neurotic modes of behaviour: the confusion of living expression and symbol, the close co-ordination with a particular mode of behaviour, the scenic content, context-dependency.

18 Cf. S. Arieti, op. cit., p. 286; Werner and Kaplan, op. cit., p. 253, and L. C. Wynne, 'Denkstörung und Familienbeziehung bei Schizophrenen', in *Psyche*, May 1965, p. 82.

19 S. Arieti, op. cit., p. 327.

20 Cf. J. Habermas (1968a), p. 290.

21 Cf. C. V. Bormann, 'Die Zweideutigkeit der hermeneutischen Erfahrung', in *Philosophische Rundschau*, vol. 16 (1969), p. 92 (also in Apel *et al.*, *Hermeneutik und Ideologiekritik*, Suhrkamp, Frankfurt, 1971, pp. 83–119) for Gadamer's meta-critique to my objections to the third part of *Truth and Method*, where he gives an ontological interpretation of the hermeneutic consciousness.

22 H. G. Gadamer, 'Die Universalität des hermeneutischen Problems', p. 104.

23 A. Wellmer, *Kritische Gesellschaftstheorie und Positivismus*, Frankfurt, 1969, p. 48 (translated as *Critical Theory of Society*, Seabury, New York, 1974).

24 K.-O. Apel, 'Szientismus oder transzendentale Hermeneutik?' in Bubner *et al.*, *Hermeneutik und Dialektik*, Mohr, Tübingen, 1970, vol. II, p. 48; also in Apel, *Transformation der Philosophie*, Suhrkamp, Frankfurt, 1973, vol. II.

25 G. H. Mead, *Mind, Self and Society*, University of Chicago Press, 1934, p. 327.

26 J. Habermas, 'Zur Logik der Sozialwissenschaften', p. 174.
27 H. G. Gadamer, 'Rhetorik, Hermeneutik und Ideologiekritik', p. 124.
28 Ibid., p. 129.
29 Cf. Habermas, *Protestbewegung und Hochschulreform*, Suhrkamp, Frankfurt, 1969, Introduction, p. 43, note 6.

Part IV

Summary and new perspectives

Introduction

The consideration of contemporary hermeneutics has so far led to the differentiation of three mutually incompatible strands.

Hermeneutical theory attempts a solution to the problem of how meaning can be understood objectively – or, as Schleiermacher put it, how to avoid misunderstanding. The methodical direction of these discussions link hermeneutical theory closely to sociology. Once Dilthey asserted the need to reconstruct the meaning of intentional actions in order to understand human behaviour, a problematic emerged that has occupied sociology, especially in Germany, ever since.

Weber's theory of action grappled with the problem, ultimately left unanswered by Dilthey, of how to render accounts of subjective meaning provided by the human or cultural sciences objective. Following on Weber, but inverting the relationship between the theory of action and objectivations of human activity, Parsons tried to reduce intentional meaning to the objective context of social systems.

The experience of the situatedness of understanding contained in the formation of 'historical consciousness' had already led Mannheim to the formulation of methodological devices in which the 'relativism' inherent in Dilthey's historicism was 'overcome with the help of a sociology of knowledge which evidenced the essential 'relatedness' of all knowledge to its social base.

Coming from American Pragmatism and having studied in Germany for a number of years, G. H. Mead insisted on the intersubjectivity of expectations of behaviour as the origin of the identity of the intended meaning of an action, thereby laying the cornerstone for 'symbolic interactionism'. Phenomenological sociology and ethnomethodology developed the insight that both the 'object' of sociology and its investigation are characterized by their directedness at meaning-complexes. As 'interpretative sociology' these approaches provide an alternative to, as well as a critique of, scientistic accounts of social phenomena that treat of them as if they were natural objects that could be investigated through the use of largely quantitative means alone.

This dichotomy of interpretative and explanatory approaches has found its most recent and emphatic formulation in Habermas's conception of the duality of hermeneutical and empirical–analytical science that could only be superseded in the form of a critique of ideology.

This split, which is most pronounced in sociology, is also apparent in the original domain of hermeneutical theory: philology, literary criticism, and the theory and philosophy of art and language, where hermeneutic(al) thought finds itself opposed by structuralist semiology. The differences here are fundamental ones: on the one side the mediation of the interpretation of meaning through a subject that is itself located within a context of traditioned meaning; on the other side, the investigation of structures within a system of signs that functions according to objective laws and independently of an understanding subject.

Betti had already drawn on neo-Kantian philosophy and Husserlian phenomenology with the hope of introducing a methodically secure path towards the explication of objectivations of mind – without, however, giving sufficient weight to the existential dimension apparent in the anticipation and application of meaning contained in a text. The figure of the hermeneutic circle may destroy the self-misconception of objectivist approaches of intentional meaning – but in itself it cannot give us any clarification as to their relative merits.

To pursue the problem of the relationship of objectifying and existential forms of interpretation I am able to draw on another contemporary hermeneutician who set out to define the respective limits and interrelations of hermeneutic claims and the objective mode of interpretation *par excellence*: structuralism. Any insights accruing from this investigation would automatically be relevant to the relationship between a philosophical hermeneutic and the objective–hermeneutical interpretation of texts.

Chapter 11

Ricoeur's phenomenological hermeneutic

Hermeneutical theory and hermeneutic philosophy have so far only been considered in contrasting terms. Gadamer, of course, frequently made the point that his theory of understanding did not detract from the validity of a disciplined interpretation of human artefacts. His arguments were, rather, designed to improve the self-understanding of this practice. Betti, however, felt called upon to rescue the ideal of objectivity from what he considered the subjectivistic implications of Gadamer's work.

It may well be that Betti too readily transposed his criticisms of Bultmann[1] onto Gadamer. It would, consequently, be useful to separate the latter's philosophical exposition from Bultmann's methodological tenets, which guided his demythologization, and subject them to some scrutiny – in the hope of leading to new insights into the relationship between the interpretation of objective meaning and the historicality of personal decision.

Ricoeur's work is of great value in this context, and I shall draw on it in the following way: the critique of Bultmann's theological hermeneutic leads me to Ricoeur's theory of the symbol and, through it, to his theory of interpretation. This will then lead immediately to some considerations concerning the relationship between hermeneutics, phenomenology and structuralism, the outcome of which is nothing less than the mediation of what seem, at first sight, irreconcilable approaches; and, finally, the new formulation of the relationship of understanding and explanation, which itself is based on a 'theory of the text' that draws on the major strands of contemporary philosophy.

1. The conflict of interpretations

Ricoeur's important contribution to hermeneutic thought centres on his theory of the conflict of interpretations; that is to say, Ricoeur mediates between theories of hermeneutics so far advanced by considering the reconstructive determination of objective sense and the existential appropriation of traditioned meaning as equally justified and operating on different strategic levels. It is necessary to note that hermeneutics, which for Betti provided the rules for the interpretation of all objectivations of mind, is restricted by Ricoeur to the interpretation of texts.

Their differences are, of course, apparent on the methodological level and have epistemological implications; at the same time they are an expression of differing intentions or 'interests'. Ricoeur would, however, go even further and trace these differences to another, more fundamental, precondition: the structure of their object which is given in symbolic form. It would, therefore, be appropriate to outline Ricoeur's theory of the symbol.

2. Bultmann and Lévi-Strauss

Symbolizations contain not only a semantic level, or a self-contained system of signs, but also refer to an extra-linguistic reality: symbols, in the form of symptoms, furthermore indicate a hidden state of affairs. These aspects have been made the subject-matter of linguistic, existential and critical investigations.

I shall first deal with Ricoeur's dialectical treatment of the conception of myth underlying the work of Lévi-Strauss and Bultmann.

The relationship between myth and symbol is one of secondary elaboration in that symbols, such as 'sin' and 'guilt', appear in a mythical form as 'myths of evil' and as the myth of Adam which narrates man's fall.

Bultmann's focus on theological hermeneutic had led him to consider the interpretation of myth as dependent upon man's self-understanding. As a corollary of this view it became necessary to demythologize myth so as to render it comprehensible to modern man, who can no longer accept cosmological accounts of natural phenomena. To arrive at the *kerygma* contained in myth, it was therefore necessary to transpose its content from mythical language into existential categories. As a consequence, descriptions of the life of faith or of sin appeared, once stripped of their mythical form, as the call to authentic existence. Bultmann's theory of myth, therefore, relies on a distinction between invalid and valid languages, between myth and a scientific world view, between primitive and modern mentality. As such it is close to Lévi-Bruhl's[2] view and is diametrically opposed to the one advanced by Lévi-Strauss, who finds that 'the kind of logic in mythical thought is as rigorous as that of modern science' (1963, p. 229). The difference between modern and primitive mind is rather one of the object it is applied to than one of intellectual process.

This view of myth as a product of the human mind characteristic of mankind as such, and not just of a particular historical epoch, is shared by Ricoeur. His strategy in mediating both views is to acknowledge the validity of mythical language and to introduce phenomenological procedures into its investigation, i.e. 'grafting phenomenology on to hermeneutic theory' – while at the same time complementing Lévi-Strauss's structuralist scheme with an existential–hermeneutic dimension. I shall deal with the former point first.

3. Phenomenology and hermeneutics

Betti, basing himself partly on the early Husserl, strongly insisted on the *Ansich* (in-itself) of the object of hermeneutics. Ricoeur's phenomenological starting-point leads to an amplification of this view and to the reconsideration of the relationship between phenomenology and hermeneutics, especially in its ontological–existential form.

Phenomenology and hermeneutics had, in a sense, already been fused by Heidegger when he introduced the latter term from Dilthey's writings in order to distinguish his own approach from Husserl's phenomenology which had been the starting-point of his philosophical career. Heidegger did not follow Husserl from eidetic to transcendental phenomenology and remained with the interpretation of phenomena in relation to their essence: as 'hermeneutic', his phenomenology still proceeds from a given Dasein for the determination of the meaning of existence – but now takes the form of a fundamental ontology.

Ricoeur, too, follows Husserl only to the 'second period', the eidetic phenomenology that superseded descriptive phenomenology – as his abiding interest in the Cartesian *Meditations* and the *Ideen*, which he translated into French, shows. Here Husserl referred all human activity back to a transcendental ego, the Cogito. Husserl's achievement here resides in his bringing together the problem of language with ontology – but the way this ontology is developed Ricoeur cannot agree with; nor can he, for this matter, accept the position of Heidegger or Merleau-Ponty, since they all short-circuited the problem by giving a direct description of Dasein – or Husserl's *Lebenswelt*. This kind of interpretation in a sense still remains in a state of naive self-assurance as regards the transparency of self-consciousness – which, since Marx, Nietzsche and Freud, should have been profoundly shaken. Man can know himself only through his expressions and he can deal with his illusions in a dialectic of distantiation and appropriation.

So the route which Ricoeur decides upon is an arduous one and commences with distantiation and with the determination of the objectivity of sense which is embedded in a text.

What role can eidetic phenomenology play here? Again, Ricoeur takes the longer route by first letting hermeneutic philosophy have its say against the methodical approach to the text, and he lists five objections levelled against it by hermeneutic philosophy: one, 'the ideal of scientificity . . . encounters its fundamental limit in the ontological condition of comprehension' (1975b, p. 88); this refers to the hermeneutic experience of *belonging-to* (*apparetenance*, *Zugehörigkeit*). Two, Husserl's reference to intuition remains on the level of epistemology and consequently that of the *Geisteswissenschaften*; hermeneutic philosophy, by contrast, has already pointed out the universality of understanding in the figure of the hermeneutic circle. The object of interpretation, the text, furthermore, takes on an autonomous character once produced, so that it is no longer adequate to merely refer to its original meaning; instead of containing a fixed meaning, a text invites plural reading and interpretation. It is on this basis an open, unlimited process. Three, Ricoeur cites the reservation against an ultimate foundation in subjectivity, as the immanence of the Cogito, provided by psychology and the critique of ideology. Since, fourth, hermeneutics has to aim for the subject-matter of a text which projects a world and not for the psychology of the author, the implication for Husserl's conception is that 'phenomenology, which was born with the discovery of the universal character of intentionality, has not remained faithful to its own discovery, namely that consciousness has its meaning beyond itself. The idealist theory of the constitution of meaning has thus "hypostasized subjectivity"' (1975b, p. 94). Five, the initial relegation of subjectivity allows it to be re-accepted in a more modest role as a disciple of a text rather than its master; rather than being the starting-point, it represents the fulfilling agency through which hermeneutics leads to self-comprehension.

Despite these fundamental objections, Ricoeur feels able to vindicate his thesis that 'phenomenology remains the indispensable pre-supposition of hermeneutic theory (1975b, p. 95).

First, hermeneutic theory can explicate the conditions for hermeneutical understanding only through reference to its linguisticality – which itself pre-supposes a general theory of 'sense' in which the notion of meaning has the same extension as intentionality and thereby includes Frege's logical notion of sense. This, for Ricouer, 'can establish the eminence of meaning above self-consciousness' (1975b, p. 97).

Second, the epoché which shuts out the empirical, linguistic world can be regarded as a movement of distantiation. In this act, the way we exchange signs for things, i.e. signify, is itself made thematic, and this allows meaning to emerge through being interpreted. As such it constitutes the critical moment within the subject's belonging-to.

Third, Ricoeur affirms the primacy of the structure of experience in relation to linguisticality; he can here point to the parallel between the noematic analysis of the pre-linguistic sphere and then to the experience of art in the form of a game, referred to by Gadamer. In both cases linguistic considerations are preceded by the presentation of what it is that is brought to language.

Further, another parallel developing from the pre-predicative aspects of phenomenology and hermeneutic philosophy concerns the relationship between the 'world of science' and the 'world of life' on the one side, and that of the objectivating approach of the *Geisteswissenschaften* to artistic, historic, linguistic experience on the other. Both *Lebenswelt* and Dasein designate 'the surplus of meaning of life-experience, which make possible the objectifying and explicative attitude' (1975b, p. 100).

After the experience of the various ways phenomenology and hermeneutic philosophy are linked, Ricoeur summarizes his argument as a fifth point, when he states that the case of the former implies the 'necessity for phenomenology to conceive of its method as an *Auslegung*, an exegesis, an explication, an interpretation' (1975b, p. 102).

These reflections on the eidetic method of phenomenology can be traced in Riceour's criticisms of Bultmann. This method opens up basic structures within a particular sphere proceeding from immediately, intuitively given phenomena; it distils their essence by freely varying them in all their possible forms: that which remains invariant is regarded as their essence. It is this stability of an ideal 'sense' which Betti placed such great emphasis on in his debate with Bultmann and which Ricoeur now subscribes to. Existential interpretation pre-supposes the appropriation of sense – in Frege's term – as an 'ideal' moment that has no place in reality.

The semantic level has to precede that of personal decision – in fact, it is a necessary precondition for the latter. In his translation of biblical myths Bultmann fails to do justice to this level since he cannot approach the *kerygma* embedded in it as the 'initiative of sense, the arrival of sense which establishes the text *vis-à-vis* the existential decision' (1973, p. 195).

Without attention to the sense of a text, demythologization may terminate in fideism. Drawing on the phenomenology of religion, Ricouer puts forward the view that symbols and myths invite thought; they give meaning and have, therefore, to be interpreted on their own level with a specific set of rules. In his seminal essay, 'Existence et Hermeneutique',[3] Ricoeur refers to the 'enumeration of symbolic forms' and a 'criteriology'. This level of analysis corresponds to the eidetic approach and brackets any existential significance.

It is here that phenomenology comes into close contact with structuralism, which provides the most elaborate counter-position to Bultmann's existential interpretation. While re-affirming the importance of objective interpretation prior to existential appropriation, structural analysis suffers from a shortcoming paralleling that of eidetic phenomenology: its exclusion of the existential dimension of meaning.

4. Structuralism and hermeneutics

Husserl can, in a way, be regarded as a precursor of structural analysis.[4] His early work attempted to establish the preconditions for 'philosophy as a strict science' by analysing the givenness of objects of knowledge in consciousness. In the course of this task he arrived at 'structures' and evidenced them in their necessary character and, as a consequence, opened up the possibility of nomological knowledge in areas so far restricted to the *verstehen* approach.

Structuralism has come to stand both for a particular form of analysis and for a *Weltanschauung*. Saussure's linguistic theory did not employ the term 'structure' but only referred to 'system'. *Parole* (speech) as actualized language is the concern of psychology and sociology, while *langue* represents the constitutive rules of the code which enables the free combination of linguistic elements; it is the object of scientific investigations centring on a closed system of signs which derive their meaning only in relation to one another. This focus on *langue* as a system furthermore leads to the primacy of synchronic considerations over the diachronic development of language; the latter, in this respect, can only be rendered comprehensible if viewed as a transition from one synchronic state to another.

The application of this scheme to areas outside linguistics has been fruitful – even though it may be restricted, according to Ricoeur, to cases where it is possible to work on a closed system, establish inventories of elements, place these elements in relation of opposition and construct a calculus of possible combinations. The possibly most renowned field of application outside linguistics of the structural method may well be anthropology and here especially Lévi-Strauss's towering achievements. This theorist, in fact, unites in his work the two strands mentioned above: structural analysis and *Weltanschauung*.[5]

To return to my theme, Lévi-Strauss's (1963) investigation of myths centres on precisely that dimension which Bultmann disregarded, i.e. their sense-structure, and which Lévi-Strauss treats as a linguistic entity. The constitutive units of myths he refers to as 'mythemes' in analogy to the phonemes, morphemes and semantemes of language. As a result of his investigations, Lévi-Strauss is able to explain how a myth 'works', by showing how its elements fit together as sets of contradictions.

In keeping with the relevance he had attributed to eidetic phenomenology, Ricoeur accredits structural analysis with the same importance for the understanding of human expressions: it is not only legitimate but necessary, since it establishes the inner logic operative within them. Its limit is, however, co-extensive with its merit and constitutes the reversal of Bultmann's case. Whereas the latter failed to do justice to the inherent sense of a myth, while seeing it in relation to existential concerns, so structural analysis can explain a myth but not interpret it. It excludes the primary intention of language: to say something about something; as speech (*parole*) it adds real reference to ideal sense. By methodically excluding the former, structural analysis does violence to aspects of language which even the theorists of language rely on, if and when they reflect upon the epistemological commitment they have entered into, and when communicating among themselves. Language as disclosure, choice, actualization, remains outside the perspective of structural linguistics.

In the field of mythical thought this approach excludes the investigation of what it has to say to us. In the case of Lévi-Strauss's *The Savage Mind*, the focus on internal logic has become even more exclusive and provokes Ricoeur's critique in 'Structure and Hermeneutic'.[6]

The object now is the mind of the 'savage', again an object amenable to structuralist procedures by constituting an unconscious order, a system of differences which can be studied in independence of the observer. Again, 'understanding' is not directed at existing intentions of meaning in the attempt to incorporate them into a different tradition – and thereby give them a new life; it is, instead, directed at the rationality embedded in a code of transformative rules which underlies the homologies between structural arrangements as they are apparent on the various levels of social reality.

While acknowledging the efficacy of this approach, especially its highlighting of the importance of arrangements, Ricoeur nevertheless voices a number of misgivings.

He notes a lack of reflectivity, which is already evident in earlier writings, concerning the conditions of the validity of one's findings, and the price that has to be paid in opting for syntax rather than semantics. The lack of reflectivity permits the formulation of generalizations concerning the minds of savages – and the step from structuralist science to structuralist philosophizing, which constitutes a transgression of its self-imposed limits.

The selection of totemism may have provided Lévi-Strauss with an unrepresentative form of myth and one that is favourable to his kind of investigation since, in 'totemistic illusion', the arrangement of myths assumes greater importance than their content and the thought contained in them can indeed be characterized as *bricolage*, i.e. the handling of heterogeneous elements of meaning.

When Ricoeur counterposes the treasure of myths in the Semitic, Hellenistic and Indo-germanic spheres, he does so not in order to suggest that here the structural approach is inappropriate, but only to question whether these myths are completely exhaustible by it. The price to be paid for the use of the structural method is here higher than in totemism, where the content is in any case nowhere near as productive as the arrangement, so that it provides most nearly the ideal object for such methods. In the case of the Jewish *kerygma*, however, the interpretation of the activity of Yahweh provided Israel with an historic interpretation of itself. It enabled its people to form an identity by re-incorporating accounts of a unified people that had initially been projected into tradition. Israel's history became the object of belief and of believed accounts. It is, therefore, possible to detect an element of historicality in the interpretation of the *kerygma* which necessitates an excess of meaning that could be appropriated differently over time.

The symbols the interpreter is here concerned with are characterized by containing a 'temporal energy' (*charge temporelle*) and a meaning-surplus; because, as expressions of 'objective spirit', they always contain more meaning than they express verbally, they give rise to a continued production of new statements and therefore necessitate an interpretative endeavour which is directed at the existential, spiritual meaning underlying their literal, profane sense. Their historicality marks them off from myths, which represent a narrative of events that occurred 'long ago' and, in addition, veil the 'temporal potential' of symbols to a certain extent – a consequence of the integral place they occupy in the social structure of a society.

This characteristic underlies the peculiar ineffectiveness of structural analysis in the case of true and effective tradition. 'Because here the semantic relation emerges from the excess of potential of meaning over its use and function within a given synchronic system, the hidden time of symbols can convey the historicality of tradition, which passes on and sediments tradition, as well as the historicality of tradition which keeps tradition alive and renews it' (1973, p. 64).

For this reason, Ricoeur is justified in considering totemistic myths and the *kerygma* as occupying the extreme ends of the spectrum of myths – which also represents the gradual diminution of the efficacy of structural analysis.

At this point Ricoeur addresses himself to the question how structural analysis and hermeneutic appropriation are related to one another. He briefly summarizes their characteristics (p. 72): structural explanation refers to (a) an unconscious system, (b) constituted by differences and opposites, that is (c) independent of the observer; the interpretation of traditioned meaning occurs as (a) the re-appropriation of (b) an over-determined wealth of symbols through (c) an interpreter, who proceeds under the conditions of the hermeneutic circle.

So far, the attempt to distinguish between the two approaches does not seem to meet with great difficulty – but how can they be related?

The hermeneutic pre-supposition of structural analysis
The neo-positivistic undertones of structuralism are nowhere more apparent than in the question of 'meaning'. The hermeneutic circle asserts its effectiveness in particular whenever we are dealing with human authorship – the scientifically minded investigator will at one point have to recur to his own pre-understanding of the phenomena he objectivated; he can face up to the fact that he is part of his object – or ignore it – but it will not go away.

Myths can, to a large extent, be considered in respect of their inner logic (*langue*), thereby suspending the referential aspect, the thing they talk about. The distinction Frege made within 'meaning' between *Sinn* and *Beduetung*, sense and reference, is clearly pertinent here. For one, myths cannot merely be regarded as an algebra of constitutive units; even Lévi-Strauss's 'mythemes' have to be expressed as sentences which contain sense and reference. The oppositions one is dealing with, furthermore, derive their significance from the fact that they do refer to something; if they did not, structural analysis would merely reproduce and arbitrarily combine meaningless elements of discourse. But because myths contain a subject-matter, because they talk about birth and death, etc., we are able to interpret them, i.e. allow their world-decoding potential to address us. Structural analysis may wish to relegate the hermeneutic pre-understanding underlying the typology of, for example, 'high' and 'low' as a residual element – residual it may be to varying degrees, but the pre-understanding of the meaning-potential of 'high' and 'low' which the anthropologist has inherited from his own culture can never be 'meaningless'. 'There can be no structural analysis . . . without a hermeneutically enlightened comprehension of the transfer of meaning (without "metaphor", without *translatio*), without this indirect meaning-attribution, which constitutes the semantic field, from which one then distils structural homologies' (1973, p. 79).

If the hermeneutic dimension apparent – but pushed to the side – in structural analysis is faced fully in all its implications, then the path has been opened for appropriating the meaning-content of myths and for conjoining Bultmann's concern.

*The necessity of structural analysis prior to existential
interpretation*

But the short-cut the latter had taken by failing to consider the
objectivity of sense – and which Ricoeur had attempted to
remedy through the introduction of eidetic phenomenology into
hermeneutic interpretation – can equally provide a justification
for the use of structuralist methods in order to acquire that
element of distantiation *vis-à-vis* the object which is necessary
for an appropriation that does not do violence to it. Ricoeur
consequently states that 'there can be no re-acquisition of
meaning without a minimum of structural understanding' (1973,
p. 76). Symbols, myths, texts, words, i.e. elements of discourse,
are characteristically polysemic. 'Fire', for example, warms,
purifies, renews, destroys – and can symbolize the Holy Spirit.
Structural analysis, through its consideration of differentiated
elements within a whole, brings into play an economy and order
that sets limits to polysemic meaning and, at the same time,
allows symbolism to achieve its significant character: 'symbols
can only symbolize within the framework of a whole that limits
and articulates their meaning' (1973, p. 79).

The account of this structural analysis forms a necessary
mediating link between naive understanding, that accepts
symbols in their surface-meaning, and hermeneutic understanding proper. Only in mediating the objectivity of sense and the
historicality of personal decision does Ricoeur see a possibility
for the interpretation of the *kerygma* that remains faithful to the
origin of Judaic–Christian belief and, at the same time, can
address contemporary man. The case involving belief can be
extrapolated to cover all understanding of texts in which both
'sense' and 'event' are joined in mutually enhancing harmony.

5. Psychoanalysis and interpretation

I have dwelt on Ricoeur's debate[7] with structuralism because it
provides a sophisticated re-affirmation of the 'subject' in the face
of its wilful elimination in the context of an anti-historic and
anti-humanist *Weltanschauung*. In relation to Ricoeur's work so
far, the significance of this debate, which occurred on the whole
in the first half of the nineteen-sixties, may lie in his attempt to
develop a phenomenological hermeneutic and an 'archaeology of
the subject'. I can, however, only refer to his work on Freud
published in 1965 as *De l'Interpretation. Essai sur Freud* in the
briefest way before going on to draw together some of the

threads so far established in terms of Ricoeur's theory of the text.

Ricoeur, at this stage, restricts the concept of interpretation to the investigation of meaning hidden in its literal and apparent sense; at a later stage this conception merges into that of the 'hermeneutic arch' that includes a theory of language as interpretation and a theory of the interpretation of texts.

The starting-point for Ricoeur's approach is the insight that man is not transparent to himself – which leads him to a position more critical than Gadamer, who seemed to be content with stating that 'Being is more than consciousness' and with the exhortation to take account of 'consciousness exposed to the effects of history' – as Ricoeur translates *wirkungsgeschichtliches Bewusstsein.*

Interpretation leads to indirect knowledge about existence. It not only aims at the sense of a text; the text is, rather, interpreted with a given intention:[8] to understand existence which comes to expression in a text. Interpretation is, therefore, both intentional and existential. Psychoanalysis uncovers hidden or distorted meaning – but it cannot represent interpretation as such since the illusions it deals with cannot be dispelled without the commitment to seek the truth behind them. Hermeneutics will have to combine a distrust of accepted meaning with an attitude of active and sincere sympathy with the message, a desire to listen to what is being said. As the investigation of symbols has evidenced, it can never be sufficient to mistrust their false explanatory claims; in order to do justice to their essence it is also necessary to attend to the message embodied in them.

Ricoeur can hereby follow Lacan's structuralist psychoanalysis that considers the unconscious as a language. Psychoanalysis mediates existential concerns and the absolute knowledge of Hegelian Reason by considering man as a creation of language, as a linguistic being. Symbols express man's desires in a language that has to be brought to light before he can begin to take possession of himself – they can certainly not be discarded as illusory, in the sense of having no correlate in reality as Freud's partially positivistic self-understanding to some extent implies.

Chapter 12

Ricoeur's theory of interpretation

As has already been indicated, a later conception[9] of 'hermeneutics' in terms of the *arc herméneutique* (hermeneutic arch) sees hermeneutics as the theory of textual interpretation. It now merges with a theory of 'language as interpretation' into a hermeneutic that exhibits an affinity with Gadamer's philosophical hermeneutic. The methodological implications of this interesting development are clearly and succinctly formulated in his paper on 'The Model of the Text': Meaningful Action Considered as a Text'.

1. What is a text?

Throughout his work Ricoeur adheres to Dilthey's conception of hermeneutics as the interpretation of 'linguistically fixed expressions of life'; at the same time, his concern with the existential aspect of intellectual activity – which informed his critical appraisal of structural analysis – leads him away from any psychologistic reconstruction of the author's intellectual meaning and towards the consideration of the content of a text as the 'opening-up' of possible existence. The duality apparent here guarantees a very interesting reformulation, or rather supersession, of the *verstehen–erklären* dichotomy through a synthesis of the objective and existential moments of interpretation.

In his discussion of the structural analysis of language Ricouer re-affirmed the necessity to consider language as an event (*parole*) in addition to language as a system of signs (*langue*). In case of the former, language is usually considered as speech or discourse and distinguished from the latter by a number of traits: it is realized temporally; it is self-referential; it is about something, i.e. it refers to a world outside it; it is aimed at an addressee. One can, of course, differentiate within speech between spoken and written discourse, depending on the way in which the mentioned traits are actualized. Following these distinctions Ricoeur establishes the paradigm of a text which also constitutes its 'objectivity': first, writing represents the fixation of meaning in which the 'said' assumes greater importance than the act of speaking.[10] He illustrates this point by reference to Austin's and Searle's theory of the speech-act and shows how the force of locutory, illocutory and perlocutory acts diminishes, in this order, if meaning is committed to writing.

This is due to the fact that the locutionary act, the act of saying, lends itself more readily to exteriorization than that which we do *in* saying (giving a command, requesting) or that which we do *by* saying (inducing effects, e.g. fear, hope).

Second, following Gadamer against Betti, Ricoeur considers that 'with written discourse, the author's intention and the meaning of the text cease to coincide . . . the text's career escapes the finite horizon lived by the author' (1971a, p. 532).

Third, a text surpasses the ostensive references of spoken discourse by opening-up possible modes of being, a whole new 'world', over and above the restricted 'situation' the partners of a dialogue find themselves in. Through its display of non-ostensive references the text, in a way, frees the meaning of discourse from the dialogical situation.

Fourth, through being permanently fixed, a text can achieve a universal range of its addressees in contrast to the often limited number of partners in spoken discourse.

Ricoeur interestingly inverts the relationship between spoken and written discourse which, since Dilthey, was characterized by the primacy of the former over the latter. Immediate contact with a speaker had always been regarded as paradigmatic for successful understanding. It not only allowed the listener to gain direct access to the intended meaning, but provided him with the possibility of discerning any attempts at misleading him, which may become apparent if there exists an incongruency between the content of speech and accompanying features such as voice-intonation and gestures.

The loss of immediacy and ostensive reference Ricoeur seems to consider as being outweighed by the gain derivable from such a conception: it aims at freeing the 'said' from the author's in-tention and attributes it with non-ostensive references.

Ricoeur follows Gadamer in affirming the 'autonomy of the text' but still adheres to the hermeneutical pre-supposition of the fixedness of the expressions of life which, in his hands, acquires a dimension that links him closely with Betti's theory when he extends the character of fixedness even to meaning. Ricoeur here exempts the meaning of a text from the dialectic of question and answer with which Gadamer had identified dialogue and goes so far as to state that dialogue 'finds its deepest wish fulfilled in written speech'.[11]

2. Meaningful action considered as a text

Taking his cue from Max Weber, Ricoeur asks to what extent meaningful action exhibits characteristics of a text, i.e. represents objectivations of meaning, which would render it open to scientific investigation. He finds that in analogy to texts, meaningful actions can assume a fixed form, possibly, in habitual patterns of action in which the meaning becomes detached from the event, the intention from the consequences of action.

'Unintended effects' have always been associated with social action and it is this aspect which answers to the second criterion, viz. the autonomy of meaning.

Flowing from this autonomy is the ability for the meaning of an action to transcend the social context in which it originated so that it may be re-appropriated differently in new social conditions. Superstructural phenomena can consequently be viewed not only as a mirror of economic relationships, but as an opening-up of a new world which is contained within the old one in embryonic form. This conception of 'autonomy', which provides the meaning of actions with its non-ostensive reference, could, accordingly, supply Marxist theorists of culture with a useful tool for mediating between a work of art and the socio-economic situation of its author.

This feature equally allows the potentially unlimited re-appropriation of the meaning of human action, i.e. their continual practical interpretation, in the course of present praxis. Just as the meaning of a text, the meaning of an action is open-ended and awaits to be determined ever anew.

On the methodological level, the conception of the fixedness of meaning provides, of course, the pre-supposition of any attempt at objective interpretation – a notion Ricoeur strenuously adheres to. He suggests a semiological model of explanation in order to transcend the fruitless dichotomy of *verstehen* and explanation, and, at the same time, to dialectically mediate truth and method.

In the course of his exposition of meaning-full forms and the triadic process of Understanding revolving around them Betti referred to Peirce's 'theory of signs'. For Peirce 'representation is that character of a thing by virtue of which, for the production of a certain mental effect, it may stand in place of another thing . . . the thing having this character I term a "representamen", the mental effect or thought its "interpretant", the thing for which it stands, its object'.[12] This triadic relationship of sign, interpretant and object is used by Ricoeur, too, for explicating the possibility of objective interpretation. The object in textual interpretation, viz. the world-disclosing potential of a text, is explained through the employment of 'depth-semantics' and is then appropriated in understanding, viz. in the submission to what the text has to say to us about ourselves. This explication, which could take the form of structural analysis, provides the means for progressing from naive to critical, or 'depth' interpretation and to interpretation as appropriation; these are the two pillars that form the 'hermeneutic arch', the bridge from explanation to understanding, and the mediation of truth and method.

Subjectivist and psychologizing interpretation can only be avoided through the mediatory employment of depth-semantics which releases the 'dynamic meaning' of the world-disclosing potential of the text for authentic appropriation: 'the theory of hermeneutics consists of the mediation of interpretation-appropriation by the series of interpretants' (1970, p. 200).

Ricoeur's theory of interpretation indeed succeeds in overcoming Dilthey's dichotomy of *verstehen* and explanation. In contrast to critical hermeneutics his use of objectifying techniques remains within the overarching 'fusion of horizon'. They serve the appropriation of meaning rather than represent a moment in the emancipatory dissolution of a 'false consciousness', and are thereby still tied to the idealizations concerning the communicative process that characterize idealist hermeneutic thought.

At the same time, Ricoeur provides an account of the interpretation of texts that is already prefigured in Schleiermacher's theory of interpretation which had achieved the integration of the hermeneutic(al) interpretation of meaning and of grammatical analysis – only that now it takes place on the level of a sophisticated, contemporary development of the subject–object problematic.

Chapter 13

Conclusions: Ricoeur and the hermeneutic dispute

With Gadamer, Ricoeur shares the view of all philosophy as being hermeneutic. Where he differs from him, in detail rather than in fundamental conception, is in the rejection of Gadamer's dichotomy of truth and method, which prevents him from 'doing justice to a critique of ideology as the modern and post-Marxist expression of the critical approach' (Ricoeur, 1973, p. 52).

Since Ricoeur tries to mediate in the hermeneutic dispute by trying to do justice to both critical and existential–phenomenological viewpoints it is by referring to his writings again that I should like to draw my introduction to contemporary hermeneutics to an end.

In the dispute between hermeneutic philosophy and critical hermeneutics the latter rejected the hermeneutic claim to universality – which would regard the critique of ideology as merely one specific form of the hermeneutic reflection directed at evidencing the pre-understanding that guides our thinking and doing – as yet another form of pre-Enlightenment affirmation of tradition and authority.

Hermeneutic philosophy could counter with the persuasive point that criticism is dependent on the object of its attack for its own motives; in the light of this insight, the claim to be able to proceed from a position free of prejudice appears as naive or as entangled in the illusion of absolute enlightenment.

In the course of the hermeneutic debate, therefore, two clearly demarcated positions emerged that can be counterposed in the following way: hermeneutic philosophy attempts the mediation of tradition and is thereby directed at the past in the endeavour to determine its significance for the present; critical hermeneutics is directed at the future and at changing reality rather than merely interpreting it. These contrasting intentions are related to equally contrasting modes of foundation. The former takes as its bedrock the existence of a 'supportive consensus' given in and through language; further knowledge is acquired on the basis of prejudices which are subjected to learning processes in the course of the 'fusion of horizons'. This transcendental element finds its contrasting correlate in the role played by 'interests' and communicatively established values; the 'emancipatory interest', for example, underlies the critique of the present and the anticipation of a free society. Critical hermeneutics is here characterized by its use of formal guidelines, i.e. the regulative idea of a true consensus. Where this approach has to feed on hope, however well supported it may be cognitively, as the price for wanting something better than can be found at present, the philosophical hermeneutic of human existence bases itself on language and tradition – at the cost of their ontologization.

Ricoeur's mediatory efforts arrive at the conclusion that to the extent to which hermeneutic philosophy and critique of ideology insist on their radically different interests, they are *both* ideological, which in Ricoeur's use of the term means illusory.

In order to bridge the gap of mutual self-miscomprehension it is necessary to recognize that hermeneutic philosophy, too, contains a number of critical elements.

First, the 'autonomy of the text' *vis-à-vis* the author's intention, its socio-cultural context and its original addressees, allows for the precondition of the distantiation of the interpreter and the text. Second, the reading of a text implies a reconstructive element to be envisaged in the form of a semiological analysis that precedes the appropriation of its content and aims at the sense contained in it, i.e. its internal organization, rather than its reference to a 'world' outside it. Finally, given the superiority of the text over the reader, the latter has to open himself up to its messsage and enter with it into a process of mutual metamorphosis. In 'trying-out' a number of possible interpretations, the reader has to remain in a state of distantiation with the text and it is this element of manoeuvring space allowed which makes it possible for him to test and critically review his own preconceptions, illusions, prejudices.

Having shown that the existential appropriation of the 'world' displayed in a text necessitates some element of critique – a view which Gadamer surely would not object to – Ricoeur now turns to the critique of ideology in order to attempt a symmetrical result by evidencing *its* hermeneutic situatedness. By transposing the problem of the justification of critique from its transcendental level to the consideration of the actual ideology of science and technology, Ricoeur arrives at the question not of the conditions for the possibility of critique but at the point: how can the atrophy of communicative action in the face of the advance of instrumental action be averted. He answers that, unless it is content with remaining a pious wish, the interest in emancipation would have to recur to cultural heritage as the basis upon which the re-affirmation of communicative action has to be based.

But apart from relying on tradition in general as a kind of reservoir from which emancipatory action has to draw in the re-affirmation of its own interest, the critique of ideology rests upon a particular tradition: the Enlightenment. Since 'critique, too, is a tradition' it is subject to 'that dialectic of the recalling of tradition and the anticipation of liberation' (1973, p. 61).

Ricoeur's conception is open to a number of objections, however. The main points that spring to mind are, first, the apparent failure to take note of the difference between a particular tradition such as the Enlightenment and tradition as that enveloping entity from within which even the consideration of a particular tradition has to proceeed. The important difference in the context of the hermeneutic debate is that the latter cannot be questioned as such, since it provides the basis for even the formulation of the first criticism directed at it; traditions in the former sense have, however, been criticized by Gadamer himself – viz. the Enlightenment and Romanticism. It follows that the fact that critical hermeneutics derives its inspiration from a particular tradition cannot be used as an argument against its claim to be able to break through the universality of the hermeneutic problem.

Secondly, Ricoeur restricts critical hermeneutics to a re-membrance of the past; 'in theological terms: eschatology is nothing without the recitative of past acts of deliverance' (1973, p. 61). While this conception would come close, in some respects, to the one held by Adorno and Benjamin it does not capture adequately recent developments even within the Frankfurt School; critical hermeneutics is today characterized by its attempt to develop an explanatory framework, such as the universal pragmatics Habermas is hoping to formulate, that is radically future-oriented in its anticipation of something new and better.

Reading IV

Paul Ricoeur
Existence
and hermeneutics

(translated by Kathleen McLaughlin)

My purpose here is to explore the paths opened to contemporary philosophy by what could be called the graft of the *hermeneutic problem* onto the *phenomenological method*. I shall limit myself to a brief historical reminder before undertaking the investigation as such, an investigation which should, at least at its close, give an acceptable sense to the notion of *existence* – a sense which would express the renewal of phenomenology through hermeneutics.

I. The origin of hermeneutics

The hermeneutic problem arose long before Husserl's phenomenology; this is why I speak of grafting and, properly, must even say a late grafting.

It is useful to recall that the hermeneutic problem was first raised within the limits of *exegesis*, that is, within the framework of a discipline which proposes to understand a text – to understand it beginning with its intention, on the basis of what it attempts to say. If exegesis raised a hermeneutic problem, that is, a problem of interpretation, it is because every reading of a text always takes place within a community, a tradition, or a living current of thought, all of which display presuppositions and exigencies – regardless of how closely a reading may be tied to the *quid*, to 'that in view of which' the text was written. Thus, based on philosophical principles in physics and in ethics, the reading of Greek myths in the Stoic school implies a hermeneutics very different from the rabbinical interpretation of the Torah in the Halakah or the Haggadah. In its turn, the apostolic generation's interpretation of the Old Testament in the light of the Christic event gives quite another reading of the events, institutions, and personages of the Bible than the rabbinical interpretation.

In what way do these exegetic debates concern philosophy? In this way: that exegesis implies an entire theory of signs and significations, as we see, for example, in Saint Augustine's *de doctrina christiana*. More precisely, if a text can have several meanings, for example a historical meaning and a spiritual meaning, we must appeal to a notion of signification that is much more complex than the system of so-called univocal signs required by the logic of argumentation. And finally, the very work of interpretation reveals a profound intention, that of overcoming distance and cultural differences and of matching the reader to a text which has become foreign, thereby incorporating its meaning into the present comprehension a man is able to have of himself.

Consequently, hermeneutics cannot remain a technique for specialists – the *technē hermēneutikē* of those who interpret oracles and marvels; rather, hermeneutics involves the general problem of comprehension. And, moreover, no noteworthy interpretation has been formulated which does not borrow from the modes of comprehension available to a given epoch: myth, allegory, metaphor, analogy, etc. This connection between interpretation and comprehension, the former taken in the sense of textual exegesis and the latter in the broad sense of the clear understanding of signs, is manifested in one of the traditional sense of the word 'hermeneutics' – the one given in Aristotle's *Peri hermēneias*. It is indeed remarkable that, in Aristotle, *hermēneia* is not limited to allegory but concerns every meaningful discourse. In fact, meaningful discourse is *hermēneia*, 'interprets' reality, precisely to the degree that it says 'something *of* something.' Moreover, discourse is *hermēneia* because a discursive statement is a grasp of the real by meaningful expressions, not a selection of so-called impressions coming from the things themselves.

Such is the first and most primordial relation between the concept of interpretation and that of comprehension; it relates the technical problems of textual exegesis to the more general problems of meaning and language.

But exegesis could lead to a general hermeneutics only by means of a second development, the development of classical philology and the *historical sciences* that took place at the end of the eighteenth century and the start of the nineteenth century. It is with Schleiermacher and Dilthey that the hermeneutic problem becomes a philosophic problem. The title of the present section, 'The Origin of Hermeneutics,' is an explicit allusion to the title of Dilthey's famous essay of 1900. Dilthey's problem, in the age of positivistic philosophy, was to give to the *Geisteswissenschaften* a validity comparable to that of the natural sciences. Posed in these terms, the problem was epistemological; it was a question of elaborating a critique of historical knowledge as solid as the Kantian critique of the knowledge of nature and of subordinating to this critique the diverse procedures of classical hermeneutics: the laws of internal textual connection, of context, of geographic, ethnic, and social environments, etc. But the resolution of the problem exceeded the resources of mere epistemology. An interpretation, like Dilthey's, bound to information fixed by writing is only a province of the much vaster domain of understanding, extending from one psychic life to another psychic life. The hermeneutic problem is thus seen from the perspective of psychology: to understand, for a finite being, is to be transported into another life. Historical understanding thus involves all the paradoxes of historicity: how can a historical being understand history historically? These paradoxes, in turn, lead back to a much more fundamental question: in expressing itself, how can life objectify itself, and, in objectifying itself, how does it bring to light meanings capable of being taken up and understood by another historical being, who overcomes his own historical situation? A major problem, which we will find again at the close of our investigation, is thus raised: the problem of the relationship between force and meaning, between life as the bearer of meaning and the mind as capable of linking meanings into a coherent series. If life is not originally meaningful, understanding is forever impossible; but, in order for this understanding to be fixed, is it not necessary to carry back to life itself the logic of immanent development which Hegel called the *concept*? Do we not then surreptitiously provide ourselves with all the resources of a philosophy of the spirit[1] just when we are formulating a philosophy of life? Such is the major difficulty which justifies our search for a favorable structure within the domain of *phenomenology* or, to return to our initial image, for the young plant onto which we can graft the hermeneutic slip.

II. Grafting hermeneutics onto phenomenology

There are two ways to ground hermeneutics in phenomenology. There is the short route, which I shall consider first, and the long route, the one I propose to travel. The short route is the one taken by an *ontology of understanding*, after the manner of

Heidegger. I call such an ontology of understanding the 'short route' because, breaking with any discussion of *method*, it carries itself directly to the level of an ontology of finite being in order there to recover *understanding*, no longer as a mode of knowledge, but rather as a mode of being. One does not enter this ontology of understanding little by little; one does not reach it by degrees, deepening the methodological requirements of exegesis, history, or psychoanalysis: one is transported there by a sudden reversal of the question. Instead of asking: On what condition can a knowing subject understand a text or history? one asks: What kind of being is it whose being consists of understanding? The hermeneutic problem thus becomes a problem of the Analytic of this being, Dasein, which exists through understanding.

Before saying why I propose to follow a more roundabout, more arduous path, starting with linguistic and semantic considerations, I wish to give full credit to this ontology of understanding. If I begin by giving due consideration to Heidegger's philosophy, it is because I do not hold it to be a contrary solution; that is to say, his Analytic of Dasein is not an alternative which would force us to choose between an ontology of understanding and an epistemology of interpretation. The long route which I propose also aspires to carry reflection to the level of an ontology, but it will do so by degrees, following successive investigations into semantics (in part III of this essay) and reflection (part IV). The doubt I express toward the end of this section is concerned only with the possibility of the making of a direct ontology, free at the outset from any methodological requirements and consequently outside the circle of interpretation whose theory this ontology formulates. But it is the *desire* for this ontology which animates our enterprise and which keeps it from sinking into either a linguistic philosophy like Wittgenstein's or a reflective philosophy of the neo-Kantian sort. My problem will be exactly this: what happens to an epistemology of interpretation, born of a reflection on exegesis, on the method of history, on psychoanalysis, on the phenomenology of religion, etc., when it is touched, animated, and, as we might say, inspired by an ontology of understanding?

Let us then take a look at the requirements of this ontology of understanding.

In order to thoroughly understand the sense of the revolution in thought that this ontology proposes, we must in one leap arrive at the end of the development running from Husserl's *Logical Investigations* to Heidegger's *Being and Time*, prepared to ask ourselves later what in Husserl's phenomenology seems significant in relation to this revolution in thought. What must thus be considered in its full radicalness is the reversal of the question itself, a reversal which, in place of an epistemology of interpretation, sets up an ontology of understanding.

It is a question of avoiding every way of formulating the problem *erkenntnistheoretisch* and, consequently, of giving up the idea that hermeneutics is a *method* able to compete on an equal basis with the method of the natural sciences. To assign a method to understanding is to remain entangled in the presuppositions of objective knowledge and the prejudices of the Kantian theory of knowledge. One must deliberately move outside the enchanted circle of the problematic of subject and object and question oneself about being. But, in order to question oneself about being in general, it is first necessary to question oneself about that being which is the 'there' of all being, about Dasein, that is, about that being which exists in the mode of understanding being. Understanding is thus no longer a mode of knowledge but a mode of being, the mode of that being which exists through understanding.

I fully accept the movement toward this complete reversal of the relationship between understanding and being; moreover, it fulfills the deepest wish of Dilthey's philosophy, because for him life was the prime concept. In his own work, historical understanding was not exactly the counterpart of the theory of nature; the relationship between life and its expressions was rather the common root of the double relationship of man to nature and of man to history. If we follow this suggestion, the problem is not to strengthen historical knowledge in the face of physical knowledge but to burrow under scientific knowledge, taken in all its generality, in order to reach a relation between historical being and the whole of being that is more primordial than the subject–object relation in the theory of knowledge.

If the problem of hermeneutics is posed in these ontological terms, of what help is Husserl's phenomenology? The question invites us to move from Heidegger back to Husserl and to reinterpret the latter in Heideggerian terms. What we first encounter on the way back is, if course, the later Husserl, the Husserl of the *Crisis*; it is in him first of all that we must seek the phenomenological foundation of this ontology. His contribution to hermeneutics is twofold. On the one hand, it is in the last phase of phenomenology that the critique of 'objectivism' is carried to its final consequences. This critique of objectivism concerns the hermeneutic problem, not only indirectly, because it contests the claim of the epistemology of the natural sciences to provide the only valid methodological model for the human sciences, but also directly, because it calls into question the Diltheyan attempt to provide for the *Geisteswissenschaften* a method as objective as that of the natural sciences. On the other hand, Husserl's final phenomenology joins its critique of objectivism to a positive problematic which clears the way for an ontology of understanding. This new problematic has as its theme the *Lebenswelt*, the 'life-world,' that is, a level of experience anterior to the subject–object relation, which provided the central theme for all the various kinds of neo-Kantianism.

If, then, the later Husserl is enlisted in this subversive undertaking, which aims at substituting an ontology of understanding for an epistemology of interpretation, the early Husserl, the Husserl who goes from the *Logical Investigations* to the *Cartesian Meditations*, is held in grave suspicion. It is he, of course, who cleared the way by designating the subject as an intentional pole, directed outward,[2] and by giving, as the correlate of this subject, not a nature but a field of meanings. Considered retrospectively from the point of view of the early Husserl and especially from the point of view of Heidegger, the early phenomenology can appear as the very first challenge to objectivism, since what it calls phenomena are precisely the correlates of intentional life. It remains, nevertheless, that the early Husserl only reconstructed a new idealism, close to the neo-Kantianism he fought: the reduction of the thesis of the world is actually a reduction of the question of being to the question of the sense of being; the sense of being, in turn, is reduced to a simple correlate of the subjective modes of intention [*visée*].

It is thus finally against the early Husserl, against the alternately Platonizing and idealizing tendencies of his theory of meaning and intentionality, that the theory of understanding has been erected. And if the later Husserl points to this ontology, it is because his effort to reduce being failed and because, consequently, the ultimate result of phenomenology escaped the initial project. It is in spite of itself that phenomenology discovers, in place of an idealist subject locked within its system of meanings, a living being which from all time has, as the horizon of all its intentions, a world, the world.

In this way, we find delimited a field of meanings anterior to the constitution of a mathematized nature, such as we have represented it since Galileo, a field of meanings anterior to objectivity for a knowing subject. Before objectivity, there is the horizon of the world; before the subject of the theory of knowledge, there is operative life, which Husserl sometimes calls anonymous, not because he is returning by this detour to an impersonal Kantian subject, but because the subject which has objects is itself derived from this operative life.

We see the degree of radicality to which the problem of understanding and that of truth are carried. The question of historicity is no longer the question of historical knowledge conceived as method. Now it designates the manner in which the existent 'is with' existents. Understanding is no longer the response of the human sciences to the naturalistic explanation; it involves a manner of being akin to being, prior to the encounter with particular beings. At the same time, life's ability to freely stand at a distance in respect to itself, to transcend itself, becomes a structure of finite being. If the historian can measure himself against the thing itself, if he can compare himself to the known, it is because both he and his object are historical. Making this historical character explicit is thus prior to any methodology. What was a limit to science – namely, the historicity of being – becomes a constituting element of being. What was a paradox – namely, the relation of the interpreter to his object – becomes an ontological trait.

Such is the revolution brought about by an ontology of understanding. Understanding becomes an aspect of Dasein's 'project' and of its 'openness to being.' The question of truth is no longer the question of method; it is the question of the manifestation of being for a being whose existence consists in understanding being.

However great may be the extraordinarily seductive power of this fundamental ontology, I nevertheless propose to explore another path, to join the hermeneutic problem to phenomenology in a different manner. Why this retreat before the Analytic of Dasein? For the following two reasons. With Heidegger's radical manner of questioning, the problems that initiated our investigation not only remain unresolved but are lost from sight. How, we asked, can an organon be given to exegesis, to the clear comprehension of texts? How can the historical sciences be founded in the face of the natural sciences? How can the conflict of rival interpretations be arbitrated? These problems are not properly considered in a fundamental hermeneutics, and this by design: this hermeneutics is intended not to resolve them but to dissolve them. Moreover, Heidegger has not wanted to consider any particular problem concerning the understanding of this or that being. He wanted to retrain our eye and redirect our gaze; he wanted us to subordinate historical knowledge to ontological understanding, as the derived form of a primordial form. But he gives us no way to show in what sense historical understanding, properly speaking, is derived from this primordial understanding. Is it not better, then, to begin with the derived forms of understanding and to show in them the signs of their derivation? This implies that the point of departure be taken on the same level on which understanding operates, that is, on the level of language.

The first observation leads to the second: if the reversal from epistemological understanding to the being who understands is to be possible, we must be able to describe directly – without prior epistemological concern – the privileged being of Dasein, such as it is constituted in itself, and thus be able to recover understanding as one of these modes of being. The difficulty in passing from understanding as a mode of knowledge to understanding as a mode of being consists in the following: the understanding which is the result of the Analytic of Dasein is precisely the understanding through which and in which this being understands itself as being. Is it not once again *within language* itself that we must seek the indication that understanding is a mode of being?

These two objections also contain a positive proposition: that of substituting, for the short route of the Analytic of Dasein, the long route which begins by analyses of language. In this way we will continue to keep in contact with the disciplines which seek to practice interpretation in a methodical manner, and we will resist the temptation to separate *truth*, characteristic of understanding, from the *method* put into operation by disciplines which have sprung from exegesis. If, then, a new problematic of existence is to be worked out, this must start from and be based on the semantic elucidation of the concept of interpretation common to all the hermeneutic disciplines. This semantics will be organized around the central theme of meanings with multiple or multivocal senses or what we might call symbolic senses (an equivalence we will justify in due time).

I will indicate immediately how I intend to reach the question of existence by the detour of this semantics. A purely semantic elucidation remains suspended until one shows that the understanding of multivocal or symbolic expressions is a moment of *self*-understanding; the *semantic* approach thus entails a *reflective* approach. But the subject that interprets himself while interpreting signs is no longer the *cogito*: rather, he is a being who discovers, by the exegesis of his own life, that he is placed in being before he places and possesses himself. In this way, hermeneutics would discover a manner of existing which would remain from start to finish a *being-interpreted*. Reflection alone, by suppressing itself as reflection, can reach the ontological roots of understanding. Yet this is what always happens in language, and it occurs through the movement of reflection. Such is the arduous route we are going to follow.

III. The level of semantics

It is first of all and always in language that all ontic or ontological understanding arrives at its expression. It is thus not vain to look to semantics for an *axis* of references for the whole of the hermeneutic *field*. Exegesis has already accustomed us to the idea that a text has several meanings, that these meanings overlap, that the spiritual meaning is 'transferred' (Saint Augustine's *translata signa*) from the historical or literal meaning because of the latter's surplus of meaning. Schleiermacher and Dilthey have also taught us to consider texts, documents, and manuscripts as expressions of life which have become fixed through writing. The exegete follows the reverse movement of this objectification of the life-forces in psychical connections first and then in historical series. This objectification and this fixation constitute another form of meaning transfer. In Nietzsche, values must be interpreted because they are expressions of the strength and the weakness of the will to power. Moreover, in Nietzsche, life itself is interpretation: in this way, philosophy itself becomes the interpretation of interpretations. Finally, Freud, under the heading of 'dream work,' examined a series of procedures which are notable in that they 'transpose' (*Entstellung*) a hidden meaning, submitting it to a distortion which both shows and conceals the latent sense in the manifest meaning. He followed the ramifications of this distortion in the cultural expressions of art, morality, and religion and in this way constructed an exegesis of culture very similar to Nietzsche's. It is thus not senseless to try to zero in on what could be called the *semantic node* of every hermeneutics, whether general or individual, fundamental or particular. It appears that their common element, which is found everywhere, from exegesis to psychoanalysis, is a certain architecture of meaning, which can be termed 'double meaning' or 'multiple meaning,' whose role in every instance, although in a different manner, is to show while concealing. It is thus within the semantics of the shown-yet-concealed, within the semantics of multivocal expressions, that this analysis of language seems to me to be confined.

Having for my part explored a well-defined area of this semantics, the language of avowal, which constitutes the *symbolism of evil*, I propose to call these multivocal expressions 'symbolic.' Thus, I give a narrower sense to the word 'symbol' than authors who, like Cassirer, call symbolic any apprehension of reality by means of signs, from perception, myth, and art to science; but I give it a broader sense than those authors who, starting from Latin rhetoric or the neo-Platonic tradition, reduce the symbol to analogy. *I define 'symbol' as any structure of signification in which a direct, primary, literal meaning designates, in addition, another meaning which is indirect, secondary, and figurative and which can be apprehended only through the first.* This circumscription of expressions with a double meaning properly constitutes the hermeneutic field.

In its turn, the concept of interpretation also receives a distinct meaning. I propose to give it the same extension I gave to the symbol. *Interpretation, we will say, is the work of thought which consists in deciphering the hidden meaning in the apparent meaning, in unfolding the levels of meaning implied in the literal meaning.* In this way I retain the initial reference to exegesis, that is, to the interpretation of hidden meanings. Symbol and interpretation thus become correlative concepts; there is interpretation wherever there is multiple meaning, and it is in interpretation that the plurality of meanings is made manifest.

From this double delimitation of the semantic field – in regard to symbols and in regard to interpretation – there results a certain number of tasks, which I shall only briefly inventory.

In regard to symbolic expressions, the task of linguistic analysis seems to me to be twofold. On the one hand, there is the matter of beginning an enumeration of symbolic forms which will be as full and as complete as possible. This inductive path is the only one accessible at the start of the investigation, since the question is precisely to determine the structure common to these diverse modalities of symbolic expression. Putting aside any concern for a hasty reduction to unity, this enumeration should include the cosmic symbols brought to light by a phenomenology of religion – like those of Van der Leeuw,. Maurice Leenhardt, and Mircea Eliade; the dream symbolism revealed by psychoanalysis – with all its equivalents in folklore, legends, proverbs, and myths; the verbal creations of the poet, following the guideline of sensory, visual, acoustic, or other images or following the symbolism of space and time. In spite of their being grounded in different ways – in the physiognomical qualities of the cosmos, in sexual symbolism, in sensory imagery – all these symbolisms find their expression in the element of language. There is no symbolism before man speaks, even if the power of the symbol is grounded much deeper. It is in language that the cosmos, desire, and the imaginary reach expression; speech is always necessary if the world is to be recovered and made hierophany. Likewise, dreams remain closed to us until they have been carried to the level of language through narration.

This enumeration of the modalities of symbolic expression calls for a criteriology as its complement, a criteriology which would have the task of determining the semantic constitution of related forms, such as metaphor, allegory, and simile. What is the function of analogy in 'transfer of meaning'? Are there ways other than analogy of relating one meaning to another meaning? How can the dream mechanisms discovered by Freud be integrated into this symbolic meaning? Can they be superimposed on known rhetorical forms like metaphor and metonymy? Do the mechanisms of distortion, set in motion by what Freud terms 'dream work,' cover the same semantic field as the symbolic operations attested to by the phenomenology of religion? Such are the structural questions a criteriology would have to resolve.

This criteriology is, in turn, inseparable from a study of the operations of interpretation. The field of symbolic expressions and the field of operations of interpretation have in fact been defined here in terms of each other. The problems posed by the symbol are consequently reflected in the methodology of interpretation. It is indeed notable that interpretation gives rise to very different, even opposing, methods. I have alluded to the phenomenology of religion and to psychoanalysis. They are as radically opposed as possible. There is nothing surprising in this: interpretation begins with the multiple determination of symbols – with their overdetermination, as one says in psychoanalysis; but each interpretation, by definition, reduces this richness, this multivocity, and 'translates' the symbol according to its own frame of reference. It is the task of this criteriology to show that the form of interpretation is relative to the theoretical structure of the hermeneutic system being considered. Thus, the phenomenology of religion deciphers the religious object in rites, in myth, and in faith, but it does so on the basis of a problematic of the sacred which defines its theoretical structure. Psychoanalysis, on the contrary, sees only one dimension of the symbol: the dimension in which symbols are seen as derivatives of repressed desires. Consequently, it considers only the network of meanings constituted in the unconscious, beginning with the initial repression and elaborated by subsequent secondary repressions. Psychoanalysis cannot be reproached for this narrowness; it is its *raison d'être*. Psychoanalytic theory, what Freud called his metapsychology, confines the rules of decipherment to what could be called a semantics of desire. Psychoanalysis can find only what it seeks; what it seeks is the 'economic' meaning of representations and affects operating in dreams, neuroses, art, morality, and religion. Psychoanalysis will thus be unable to find anything other than the disguised expressions of representations and affects belonging to the most archaic of man's desires. This example well shows, on the single level of semantics, the fullness of a philosophical hermeneutics. It begins by an expanding investigation into symbolic forms and by a comprehensive analysis of symbolic structures. It proceeds by the confrontation of hermeneutic styles and by the critique of systems of interpretation, carrying the diversity of hermeneutic methods back to the structure of the corresponding theories. In this way it prepares itself to perform its highest task, which would be a true arbitration among the absolutist claims of each of the interpretations. By showing in what way each method expresses the form of a theory, philosophical hermeneutics justifies each method within the limits of its own theoretical circumscription. Such is the critical function of this hermeneutics taken at its purely semantic level.

Its multiple advantages are apparent. First of all, the semantic approach keeps hermeneutics in contact with methodologies as they are actually practiced and so does not run the risk of separating its concept of truth from the concept of method. Moreover, it assures the implantation of hermeneutics in phenomenology at the level at which the latter is most sure of itself, that is, at the level of the theory of meaning developed in the *Logical Investigations*. Of course, Husserl would not have accepted the idea of meaning as irreducibly nonunivocal. He explicitly excludes this possibility in the First Investigation, and this is indeed why the phenomenology of the *Logical Investigations* cannot be hermeneutic. But, if we part from Husserl, we do so within the framework of his theory of signifying expressions; it is here that the divergence begins and not at the uncertain level of the phenomenology of the *Lebenswelt*. Finally, by carrying the debate to the level of language, I have the feeling of encountering other currently viable philosophies on a common terrain. Of course, the semantics of multivocal expressions opposes the theories of metalanguage which would hope to remake existing languages according to ideal models. The opposition is as sharp here as in regard to Husserl's ideal of univocity. On the other hand, this semantics enters into a fruitful dialogue with the doctrines arising from Wittgenstein's *Philosophical Investigations* and from the analysis of ordinary language in the Anglo-Saxon countries. It is likewise at this level tht a general hermeneutics rejoins the preoccupations of modern biblical exegesis descending from Bultmann and his school. I see this general hermeneutics as a contribution to the grand philosophy of language which we lack today. We have at our disposal today a symbolic logic, a science of exegesis, an anthropology, and a psychoanalysis; and, for the first time perhaps, we are capable of encompassing as a single question the reintegration of human discourse. The progress of these dissimilar disciplines has at once made manifest and worsened the dislocation of this discourse. The unity of human speech is the problem today.

IV. The level of reflection

The preceding analysis, dealing with the semantic structure of expressions with double or multiple meanings, is the narrow gate through which hermeneutic philosophy must pass if it does not want to cut itself off from those disciplines which, in their method, turn to interpretation: exegesis, history, and psychoanalysis. But a semantics of expressions with multiple meanings is not enough to qualify hermeneutics as philosophy. A linguistic analysis which would treat these significations as a whole closed in on itself would ineluctably set up language as an absolute. This hypostasis of language, however, repudiates the basic intention of a sign, which is to hold 'for,' thus transcending itself and suppressing itself in what it intends. Language itself, as a signifying milieu, must be referred to existence.

By making this admission, we join Heidegger once again: what animates the movement of surpassing the linguistic level is the desire for an ontology; it is the demand this ontology makes on an analysis which would remain a prisoner of language.

Yet how can semantics be integrated with ontology without becoming vulnerable to the objections we raised earlier against an Analytic of Dasein? The intermediary step, in the direction of existence, is reflection, that is, the link between the understanding of signs and self-understanding. It is in the self that we have the opportunity to discover an existent.

In proposing to relate symbolic language to self-understanding, I think I fulfill the deepest wish of hermeneutics. The purpose of all interpretation is to conquer a remoteness, a distance between the past cultural epoch to which the text belongs and the interpreter himself. By overcoming this distance, by making himself contemporary with the text, the exegete can appropriate its meaning to himself: foreign, he makes it familiar, that is, he makes it his own. It is thus the growth of his own understanding of himself that he pursues through his understanding of the other. Every hermeneutics is thus, explicitly or implicitly, self-understanding by means of understanding others.

So I do not hesitate to say that hermeneutics must be grafted onto phenomenology, not only at the level of the theory of meaning expressed in the *Logical Investigations*, but also at the level of the problematic of the *cogito* as it unfolds from *Ideen I* to the *Cartesian Meditations*. But neither do I hesitate to add that the graft changes the wild stock! We have already seen how the introduction of ambiguous meanings into the semantic field forces us to abandon the ideal of univocity extolled in the *Logical Investigations*. It must now be understood that by joining these multivocal meanings to self-knowledge we profoundly transform the problematic of the *cogito*. Let us say straight off that it is this internal reform of reflective philosophy which will later justify our discovering there a new dimension of existence. But, before saying how the *cogito* is exploded, let us say how it is enriched and deepened by this recourse to hermeneutics.

Let us in fact reflect upon what the self of self-understanding signifies, whether we appropriate the sense of a psychoanalytic interpretation or that of a textual exegesis. In truth, we do not know beforehand, but only afterward, although our desire to understand ourselves has alone guided this appropriation. Why is this so? Why is the self that guides the interpretation able to recover itself only as a result of the interpretation?

There are two reasons for this: it must be stated, first, that the celebrated Cartesian *cogito*, which grasps itself directly in the experience of doubt, is a truth as vain as it is invincible. I do not deny that it is a truth; it is a truth which posits itself, and as such it can be neither verified nor deduced. It posits at once a being and an act, an existence and an operation of thought: I am, I think; to exist, for me, is to think; I exist *insofar as* I think. But this truth is a vain truth; it is like a first step which cannot be followed by any other, so long as the *ego* of the *ego cogito* has not been recaptured in the mirror of its objects, of its works, and, finally, of its acts. Reflection is blind intuition if it is not mediated by what Dilthey called the expressions in which life objectifies itself. Or, to use the language of Jean Nabert, reflection is nothing other than the appropriation of our act of existing by means of a critique applied to the works and the acts which are the signs of this act of existing. Thus, reflection is a critique, not in the Kantian sense of a justification of science and duty, but in the sense that the *cogito* can be recovered only by the detour of a decipherment of the documents of its life. Reflection is the appropriation of our effort to exist and of our desire to be by means of the works which testify to this effort and this desire.

The *cogito* is not only a truth as vain as it is invincible; we must add, as well, that it is like an empty place which has, from all time, been occupied by a false *cogito*. We have indeed learned, from all the exegetic disciplines and from psycho-analysis in particular, that so-called immediate consciousness is first of all 'false consciousness.' Marx, Nietzsche, and Freud have taught us to unmask its tricks. Henceforth it becomes necessary to join a critique of false consciousness to any re-discovery of the subject of the *cogito* in the documents of its life; a philosophy of reflection must be just the opposite of a philosophy of consciousness.

A second reason can be added to the preceding one: not only is the 'I' able to recapture itself only in the expressions of life that objectify it, but the textual exegesis of consciousness collides with the initial 'misinterpretation' of false consciousness. More-over, since Schleiermacher, we know that hermeneutics is found wherever there was first misinterpretation.

Thus, reflection must be doubly indirect: first, because existence is evinced only in the documents of life, but also because consciousness is first of all false consciousness, and it is always necessary to rise by means of a corrective critique from misunderstanding to understanding.

At the end of this second stage, which we have termed the reflective stage, I should like to show how the results of the first stage, which we termed the semantic stage, are consolidated.

During the first stage, we took as a fact the existence of a language irreducible to univocal meanings. It is a fact that the avowal of guilty consciousness passes through a symbolism of the stain, of sin, or of guilt; it is a fact that repressed desire is expressed in a symbolism which confirms its stability through dreams, proverbs, legends, and myths; it is a fact that the sacred is expressed in a symbolism of cosmic elements: sky, earth, water, fire. The philosophical use of this language, however, remains open to the logician's objection that equivocal language can provide only fallacious arguments. The justification of hermeneutics can be radical only if one seeks in the very nature of reflective thought the principle of a logic of double meaning. This logic is then no longer a formal logic but a transcendental logic. It is established at the level of conditions of possibility: not the conditions of the objectivity of a nature, but the conditions of the appropriation of our desire to be. It is in this sense that the logic of the double meaning proper to hermeneutics can be called transcendental. If the debate is not carried to this level, one will quickly be driven into an untenable situation; in vain will one attempt to maintain the debate at a purely semantic level and to make room for equivocal meanings alongside univocal meanings, for the theoretical distinction between two kinds of equivocalness – equivocalness through a surplus of meaning, found in the exegetic sciences, and equivocalness through the confusion of meanings, which logic chases away – cannot be justified at the level of semantics alone. Two logics cannot exist at the same level. Only a problematic of reflection justifies the semantics of double meaning.

V. The existential level

At the end of this itinerary, which has led us from a problematic of language to a problematic of reflection, I should like to show how we can, by retracing our steps, join a problematic of existence. The ontology of understanding which Heidegger sets up directly by a sudden reversal of the problem, substituting the consideration of a mode of being for that of a mode of knowing, can be, for us who proceed indirectly and by degrees, only a horizon, an aim rather than a given fact. A separate ontology is beyond our grasp: it is only within the movement of interpretation that we apperceive the being we interpret. The ontology of understanding is implied in the methodology of interpretation, following the ineluctable 'hermeneutic circle' which Heidegger himself taught us to delineate. Moreover, it is only in a conflict of rival hermeneutics that we perceive something of the being to be interpreted: a unified ontology is as inaccessible to our method as a separate ontology. Rather, in every instance, each hermeneutics discovers the aspect of existence which founds it as method.

This double warning nevertheless must not deter us from clearing the ontological foundations of the semantic and reflective analysis which precedes it. An implied ontology, and even more so a truncated ontology, is still, is already, an ontology.

We will follow a track open to us, the one offered by a philosophical reflection on psychoanalysis. What can we expect from the latter in the way of a fundamental ontology? Two things: first, a true dismissal of the classical problematic of the subject as consciousness; then, a restoration of the problematic of existence as desire.

It is indeed through a critique of consciousness that psychoanalysis points to ontology. The interpretation it proposes to us of dreams, fantasies, myths, and symbols always contests to some extent the pretension of consciousness in setting itself up as the origin of meaning. The struggle against narcissism – the Freudian equivalent of the false *cogito* – leads to the discovery that language is deeply rooted in desire, in the instinctual impulses of life. The philosopher who surrenders himself to this strict schooling is led to practice a true ascesis of subjectivity, allowing himself to be dispossessed of the origin of meaning. This abandonment is of course yet another turn of reflection, but it must become the real loss of the most archaic of all objects: the self. It must then be said of the subject of reflection what the Gospel says of the soul: to be saved, it must be lost. All of psychoanalysis speaks to me of lost objects to be found again symbolically. Reflective philosophy must integrate this discovery with its own task; the self [*le moi*] must be lost in order to find the 'I' [*le je*]. This is why psychoanalysis is, if not a philosophical discipline, at least a discipline for the philosopher: the unconscious forces the philosopher to deal with the arrangement of significations on a level which is set apart in relation to the immediate subject. This is what Freudian topography teaches: the most archaic significations are organized in a 'place' of meaning that is separate from the place where immediate consciousness reigns. The realism of the unconscious, the topographic and economic treatment of representations, fantasies, symptoms, and symbols, appears finally as the condition of a hermeneutics free from the prejudices of the ego.

Freud invites us, then, to ask anew the question of the relationship between signification and desire, between meaning and energy, that is, finally, between language and life. This was already Leibniz' problem in the *Monadology*: how is representation joined to appetite? It was equally Spinoza's problem in the *Ethics*, Book III: how do the degrees of the adequation of ideas express the degrees of the *conatus*, of the effort which constitutes us? In its own way, psychoanalysis leads us back to the same question: how is the order of significations included within the order of life? This regression from meaning to desire is the indication of a possible transcendence of reflection in the direction of existence. Now an expression we used above, but whose meaning was only anticipated, is justified: by understanding ourselves, we said, we appropriate to ourselves the meaning of our desire to be or of our effort to exist. Existence, we can now say, is desire and effort. We term it effort in order to stress its positive energy and its dynamism; we term it desire in order to designate its lack and its poverty: Eros is the son of Poros and Penia. Thus the *cogito* is no longer the pretentious act it was initially – I mean its pretension of positing itself; it appears as *already* posited in being.

But if the problematic of reflection can and must surpass itself in a problematic of existence, as a philosophical meditation on psychoanalysis suggests, it is always in and through interpretation that this surpassing occurs: it is in deciphering the tricks of desire that the desire at the root of meaning and reflection is discovered. I cannot hypostasize this desire outside the process of interpretation; it always remains a being-interpreted. I have hints of it behind the enigmas of consciousness, but I cannot grasp it in itself without the danger of creating a mythology of instinctual forces, as sometimes happens in coarse conceptions of psychoanalysis. It is behind itself that the *cogito* discovers, through the work of interpretation, something like an *archaeology of the subject*. Existence is glimpsed in this archaeology, but it remains entangled in the movement of deciphering to which it gives rise.

This decipherment, which psychoanalysis, understood as hermeneutics, compels us to perform, other hermeneutic methods force us to perform as well, although in different ways. The existence that psychoanalysis discovers is that of desire; it is existence as desire, and this existence is revealed principally in an archaeology of the subject. Another hermeneutics – that of the philosophy of the spirit, for example – suggests another manner of shifting the origin of sense, so that it is no longer behind the subject but in front of it. I would be willing to say that there is a hermeneutics of God's coming, of the approach of his Kingdom, a hermeneutics representing the prophecy of consciousness. In the final analysis, this is what animates

Hegel's *Phenomenology of the Spirit*. I mention it here because its mode of interpretation is diametrically opposed to Freud's. Psychoanalysis offered us a regression toward the archaic; the phenomenology of the spirit offers us a movement in which each figure finds its meaning, not in what precedes but in what follows. Consciousness is thus drawn outside itself, in front of itself, toward a meaning in motion, where each stage is suppressed and retained in the following stage. In this way, a teleology of the subject opposes an archaeology of the subject. But what is important for our intention is that this teleology, just like Freudian archaeology, is constituted only in the movement of interpretation, which understands one figure through another figure. The spirit is realized only in this crossing from one figure to another; the spirit is the very dialectic of these figures by means of which the subject is drawn out of his infancy, torn from his archaeology. This is why philosophy remains a hermeneutics, that is, a reading of the hidden meaning inside the text of the apparent meaning. It is the task of this hermeneutics to show that existence arrives at expression, at meaning, and at reflection only through the continual exegesis of all the significations that come to light in the world of culture. Existence becomes a self – human and adult – only by appropriating this meaning, which first resides 'outside,' in works, institutions, and cultural monuments in which the life of the spirit is objectified.

It is within the same ontological horizon that the phenomenology of religion – both Van der Leeuw's and Mircea Eliade's – would have to be interrogated. As phenomenology it is simply a description of rite, of myth, of belief, that is, of the forms of behavior, language, and feeling by which man directs himself towards something 'sacred.' But if phenomenology can remain at this descriptive level, the reflective resumption of the work of interpretation goes much further: by understanding himself in and through the signs of the sacred, man performs the most radical abandonment of himself that it is possible to imagine. This dispossession exceeds that occasioned by psychoanalysis and Hegelian phenomenology, whether they are considered individually or whether their effects are combined. An archaeology and a teleology still unveil an *archē* and a *telos* which the subject, while understanding them, can command. It is not the same in the case of the sacred, which manifests itself in a phenomenology of religion. The latter symbolically designates the alpha of all archaeology, the omega of all teleology; this alpha and this omega the subject would be unable to command.

The sacred calls upon man and in this call manifests itself as that which commands his existence because it posits this existence absolutely, as effort and as desire to be.

Thus, the most opposite hermeneutics point, each in its own way, to the ontological roots of comprehension. Each in its own way affirms the dependence of the self upon existence. Psychoanalysis shows this dependence in the archaeology of the subject, the phenomenology of the spirit in the teleology of figures, the phenomenology of religion in the signs of the sacred. Such are the ontological implications of interpretation.

The ontology proposed here is in no way separable from interpretation; it is caught inside the circle formed by the conjunction of the work of interpretation and the interpreted being. It is thus not a triumphant ontology at all; it is not even a science, since it is unable to avoid the *risk* of interpretation; it cannot even entirely escape the internal warfare that the various hermeneutics indulge in among themselves.

Nevertheless, in spite of its precariousness, this militant and truncated ontology is qualified to affirm that rival hermeneutics are not mere 'language games,' as would be the case if their absolutist pretensions continued to oppose one another on the sole level of language. For a linguistic philosophy, all interpretations are equally valid within the limits of the theory which founds the given rules of reading. These equally valid interpretations remain language games until it is shown that each interpretation is grounded in a particular existential function. Thus, psychoanalysis has its foundation in an archaeology of the subject, the phenomenology of the spirit in a teleology, and the phenomenology of religion in an eschatology.

Can one proceed any further? Can these different existential functions be joined in a unitary figure, as Heidegger tried to do in the second part of *Being and Time*? This is the question the present study leaves unresolved. But, if it remains unresolved, it is not hopeless. In the dialectic of archaeology, teleology, and eschatology an ontological structure is manifested, one capable of reassembling the discordant interpretations on the linguistic level. But this coherent figure of the being which we ourselves are, in which rival interpretations are implanted, is given nowhere but in this dialectic of interpretations. In this respect, hermeneutics is unsurpassable. Only a hermeneutics instructed by symbolic figures can show that these different modalities of existence belong to a single problematic, for it is finally through the richest symbols that the unity of these multiple interpretations is assured. These symbols alone carry all the vectors, both regressive and progressive, that the various hermeneutics dissociate. True symbols contain all hermeneutics, those which are directed toward the emergence of new meanings and those which are directed toward the resurgence of archaic fantasies. It is in this sense, beginning with our introduction, that we have insisted that existence as it relates to a hermeneutic philosophy always remains an interpreted existence. It is in the work of interpretation that this philosophy discovers the multiple modalities of the dependence of the self – its dependence on desire glimpsed in an archaeology of the subject, its dependence on the spirit glimpsed in its teleology, its dependence on the sacred glimpsed in its eschatology. It is by developing an archaeology, a teleology, and an eschatology that reflection suppresses itself as reflection.

In this way, ontology is indeed the promised land for a philosophy that begins with language and with reflection; but, like Moses, the speaking and reflecting subject can only glimpse this land before dying.

Notes

1 [Throughout this book we have translated Ricoeur's '*esprit*' (Hegel's '*Gesit*') as 'spirit' rather than 'mind,' and in harmony with this the title of Hegel's work will appear in the text as *The Phenomenology of the Spirit*. – EDITOR.]

2 [The French term used here to describe the subject is *porteur de visée*, which in turn renders the German *die Meinung*, employed frequently by Husserl. The French substantive (*visèe*) and verb (*viser*) are often translated in English as 'intention' and 'to intend,' respectively. When asked about his use of the term, Ricoeur himself stressed the outward directedness of intention, the fact that the subject points toward or aims at its object. Indeed, in expressions such as *visée intentionnelle* he makes it impossible to view *visée* and *intention* as completely equivalent terms. In the present essay (and elsewhere in the book, as well – ED.) *visée* and *viser* have been rendered variously by 'directed outward,' 'aim,' and 'intention,' according to the context in which they appear. – TRANSLATOR.]

Conclusion

In concluding this introduction to contemporary hermeneutics I shall draw out the main ideas of each strand.

Interpretative sociology owes hermeneutics the clarification of the concept of 'meaning' as the intentional, teleological character of action and of the situational determination of its interpretation; 'data' are seen in a historical context that refers to the self-understanding of social groups which itself is determined by tradition. The hermeneutical sciences help the preservation and extension of communication about the meaning of life, goals of socio-political development, public and private styles of life, etc., through making accessible the meaning of texts and actions and by themselves anticipating or projecting possible ways of – better – living.

Hermeneutic philosophy alerted us to the danger of objectivism underneath the methodical, objectifying approach to the interpretation of human expressions. By developing our awareness of the 'fore-structure' of understanding it furthermore precluded the naive assumption of the possibility of completely objective or neutral knowledge, given the fact that we have interpreted an object 'as' something even before we come to investigate it.

The conception of the universality of the hermeneutic problem connected with this insight also seemed to exclude the claims made by critical hermeneutics as 'hermeneutical understanding expanded into criticism' (Habermas), which serves the emancipatory intention through the critique of 'tradition' and 'authority'. 'Interpretation' means here largely the reconstruction of historically suppressed possibilities of existence and the projection of new ones.

It follows that the object of hermeneutics can be rejected *in toto* only at a price: the blindness towards the moment of transcendence inherent in cultural manifestations. Bloch's concepts of 'hope', 'day-dream' and *Vorschein* and the 'exact phantasy' employed by Adorno and Benjamin point at the unrealized or unintended truth apparent in superstructural phenomena.

The consideration of a reality projected or displayed by, say, a text links critical hermeneutics with hermeneutic philosophy which emphasized the role of a work of art in opening a 'world' before us rather than any concern with the psychology of the author. The latter approach translated this insight, however, into the superiority of the text or of tradition as such. In its idealist reliance on language as the unquestionable absolute lies the failure to perceive the tendency towards a 'universal history' (Habermas) apparent in Gadamer's theory.

The critique of ideology recurs to such an objective context in order to explicate the subjective and objective meaning of social actions; in it, tradition is considered in relation to other moments of the totality of life which, too, affect the constitution of a context of action within which the rules for the comprehension of existence and for the formation of action-orienting motives takes place.

The difference between the three strands of hermeneutics can now be expressed by reference to the varying conceptions of the relationship between whole and part which lies at the heart of the interpretation of meaning.

Hermeneutical theory uses the methodological device of the hermeneutical circle in which a text is brought to the understanding through the reciprocal interpretation of a whole and its constituent elements. The 'hermeneutic circle' hermeneutic philosophy has evidenced envelops the subject of interpretation as well and thereby destroys the objectivist self-conception of the hermeneutical sciences by pointing to the role of the subject's historicality. Whereas here the 'whole' still appears as the 'horizon' which guides the 'anticipation of perfection', critical hermeneutics recasts it as a totality as such from where the anticipation of the goal of history, as the process of the formation of humanity and the critique of the past and present in its light, becomes possible in addition to the interpretation of the meaning of historical events.

To Gadamer and positivists alike, this critical–anticipatory moment in understanding must appear as unfounded and unjustifiable in objective terms. Ultimately, the possibility of critical hermeneutics depends on the framework that Habermas is attempting to construct out of a materialist theory of society and of social evolution in conjunction with a theory of ordinary language.

In a sense, this state of uncertainty is not a bad one to be in, and it is certainly not inappropriate for ending a book on hermeneutics. I myself can only hope that my own prejudices have been productive ones in the course of writing it.

Notes

Introduction

1 I owe this distinction to J. Robinson and J. Cobb, who used it in their discussion of theological hermeneutics; see *The New Hermeneutic* (1964), Introduction.

2 The course of this dispute can be retraced as: Betti (1954) – Gadamer (1960) – Betti (1962) – Gadamer, *Hermeneutik und Historismus (Philos. Rundschau*, vol. 9, 1962); also in the fourth edition (1975) of *Wahrheit und Methode*, and in the English translation. (Gadamer here merely had to reiterate the points he had already made in 1960, and especially in a letter to Betti quoted by the latter as a note in 1962.)

3 The steps within this debate are: Gadamer (1960) – Habermas (1970 – appeared already in 1967 in *Philosophische Rundschau*) – Gadamer (1971a – appeared already in Gadamer (1967)) – Habermas (1971b) (translated as Reading IV in this book) – Gadamer (1971b) – Habermas, New Introduction to *Theorie und Praxis* (1971); see also recent comments by Gadamer (1975).

4 The inverted commas were placed by Lorenzer.

Part I

1 *Die Entstehung der Hermeneutik*, in *Gesammelte Schriften*, vol. V, pp. 317–38.

2 Wolf defines hermeneutics as the 'science of the rules through which the meaning of signs is known'; quoted in Wach (1929), vol. II.

3 Quoted in Wach (1926), vol. I, p. 129.

4 The unconscious had been considered by romanticists as feeling that could never err – in contrast to reflection, i.e. judgment, which at times inadequately portrays the content of the intuition or feeling.

5 Gadamer, *Wahrheit und Methode*, p. 188.

6 Droysen, quoted in Wach (1933), vol. III, p. 145, note 4.

7 Ibid., p. 152.

8 Ibid., p. 155.

9 Ibid., p. 135.
10 The relevant passages for this aspect are in vols. I, V, VII of the *Gesammelte Schriften*; useful here are also the introductions to these volumes.
11 This self-conception throws doubt on Gadamer's contention that the influence of the epistemology of the natural sciences ran counter to Dilthey's true intentions.
12 See *Einleitung in die Geisteswissenschaften*, vol. I.
13 I use the German word in order to indicate the use of 'understanding' as a method.
14 'Meaning-full' is my rendering of '*sinnhaltig*' (literally, 'containing').
15 The German word '*schöpfen*' both means 'to create' and 'to draw from (a well, etc.)'.
16 Dilthey's conception of the superiority of *verstehen* over explanation seems characteristic of traditional hermeneutics; it is based on the recognition that in *verstehen* 'life meets life', whereas explanation is concerned with external objects which have no affinity with the observer.
17 E.g. Jaspers, K., 'Each limit to understanding represents a new challenge for causal questioning' ('Jede Grenze des Verstehens ist ein neuer Anstoss zu kausaler Fragestellung'); Jaspers, *Allgemeine Psychopathologie*, 2nd edn, (1920) p. 175; quoted in Apel (1955, p. 177).
18 See Hegel, *Phänomenologie des Geistes*, Gesammelte Werke, III, Suhrkamp, Frankfurt, 1972, p. 119.

Part II

1 In his phenomenological analysis of Dasein as the Being of mankind.
2 References to this book will be from the translation by J. Macquirre and E. Robinson. Since they indicate the pagination of the original in their translation it is to the original that my page numbers refer too.
3 Gadamer was a student of Bultmann's and Heidegger's.
4 Whether Bultmann followed Heidegger far enough, or whether his utilization of Heidegger's existentiales presented a short-cut that avoided the painstaking questioning of Being – with the result of deriving mere abstractions of living experience: existential insights reduced to mere form – is a problem Ricoeur has hinted at. (Cf. Ricoeur, *Préface à Rudolf Bultmann*, in Ricoeur, 1969b, pp. 197.)
5 This leads to the use of non-mythological concepts such as the 'future of God', 'Word of God', etc.
6 Both Betti and Ricoeur are concerned about the effect of this 'translation' upon the original message.

7 Fuchs, quoted in Robinson and Cobb (1964), p. 60; it is this book which this outline of the work of Fuchs and Ebeling relies on.

8 References are to Gadamer, *Wahrheit und Methode*, 1975, and to the translation, *Truth and Method*, where two numbers appear; reference to the German text only indicates own translation.

9 Gadamer, 1975, p. xxiv, states that when he came across Wittgenstein's concept it 'seemed to me quite natural'.

10 Cf. *Gesammelte Aufsätze zur Wissenschaftslehre*, pp. 536, 541–6.

Part III

1 The strand not mentioned – neo-positivism – is criticized extensively in Apel (1967).

2 Gadamer followed Dilthey in asserting the historicity of knowledge which all interpretations are subject to in the face of Hegel's postulation of 'absolute knowledge'. But, as Apel argues, it does not follow from the insight that a text may teach us something that we should revert to a pre-Enlightenment position.

3 For an interesting development of this concept within the context of sociology, see Bauman (1976).

4 Sartre (1976) uses this term to describe the transformation of the reign of necessity into the reign of freedom in the course of the emergence of the 'group-in-fusion' out of impassive 'seriality'.

5 Bauman (1976, p. 3) states that 'Science, as we know it, can be defined as knowledge of unfreedom.'

6 This concept derives from Ch. S. Peirce's *Logical Socialism*, in which the interpretative community formed by all scientists represents the necessary horizon for the determination of the rules and goals of the scientific process. The communication scientists are engaged in can be extrapolated on to all human communication which requires for its success the existence of conditions conducive to the formation of a well-informed consensus (e.g. the socialization of the means of intellectual production).

7 In *Method and Measurement in Sociology*, Free Press, New York, 1964.

8 Husserl's *Lebenswelt* and *Welt der Wissenschaften*.

9 The concept of 'metalanguage' arose with Carnap's attempt to construct a formal language, cleansed of all subjective elements. The rules of the construction of such a language would, however, have to be formulated in another, overarching language, i.e. a metalanguage, for which the same requirements would be apparent so that eventually a hierarchy of meta-, meta-, meta-languages would be constructed. Carnap could not escape the fact that, ultimately, it is everyday language with all its 'impurity' –

i.e. subjective connotations, fields of meaning, etc. – that has to be used for the introduction of new formal languages.

10 Wellmer's differentiation between Reason as abstractly counter-posed to authority and Reason as the principle of communication free from force, as intention towards the realization of freedom, seems to dispose of Gadamer's reservations against this element of Enlightenment thought at the centre of critical hermeneutics. (Cf. A. Wellmer, *Kritische Gesellschaftstheorie und Positivismus*, Frankfurt, 1969, pp. 46–8.)

11 Habermas reproduces here arguments which have already been formulated in a systematic context in *Knowledge and Human Interests*, especially chapter 11.

12 'On Systematically Distorted Communication' and 'Towards a Theory of Communicative Competence' in *Inquiry*, vol. 13 (1970), parts 3 (pp. 205–18) and 4 (pp. 360–75); J. Habermas and N. Luhmann, *Theorie der Gesellschaft oder Sozialtechnologie*, Suhrkamp, Frankfurt, 1971; 'Postscript to Knowledge and Human Interests', in *Phil. of Social Science*, vol. 3 (1973), pp. 157–89; 'Wahrheitstheorien', in *Festschrift für Walter Schulz*, Neske, Pfullingen, 1973; 'Some Distinctions in Universal Pragmatics', in *Theory and Society*, vol. 3 (1976), pp. 155–67.

13 Lenin, *Gesammelte Schriften*, vol. 14, pp. 150–1; quoted in Sandkühler (1972, p. 984).

14 Lucien Sève, *Marxisme et theorie de la personalité*, Paris, 1969 (now in print in English; a synopsis of this book has appeared as *Marxism and the Theory of Human Personality*, Lawrence & Wishart, London, 1975, which represents a translation of an essay originally published in 1968 in *Les Cahiers de L'université nouvelle*, Paris).

15 L. Sève (1969, p. 291) quoted in Sandkühler (1972, p. 1001); for a further debate between Sève and Althusser-inspired structuralist 'anti-humanism' see the debate between Sève and Godelier in *International Journal of Sociology*, vol. 2 (1972), pp. 2–3.

16 These idealizations refer to the consistency and intelligibility, the potentiality and the underlying consensus of communication.

17 *Weltanschauung* literally means 'a way of looking at the world'.

18 Heidegger's appreciation of Marx is pertinent here: 'Marx, discovering this alienation, reaches into an essential dimension of history, the Marxist view of history excels all other history' (Heidegger, 1967, p. 186).

19 The two central developments Habermas pinpoints as underlying the need to reconsider the analyses of Marx's political economy concern, one, the still-increasing intervention of the state in the economy, and, two, the demise of labour as the first productive force through the advent of science and technology in their closely related progress; see especially the essay entitled 'Science and technology as "ideology"', in *Towards A Rational Society*, Heinemann, London, 1971.

Part IV

1 Even though they are based on some misconceptions, especially concerning the role of the fore-structure of understanding, they nevertheless contain a number of justifiable elements.

2 See D. Rasmussen (1971, p. 229) for this account.

3 1965c; a translation of this essay appears in this book as Reading IV.

4 J. Culler (1973) has provided an outline of the relationship between structuralism and Merleau-Ponty's phenomenology of the *Lebenswelt*.

5 R. Boudon (1969) includes among the latter category people like Foucault whom he regards as presenting an 'arbitrary radicalization' or even 'caricature' of the sound methodological work of people such as Chomsky.

6 In Ricoeur (1973); it appeared originally as 'Structure et Herméneutique', in *Esprit*, November 1963, pp. 596–627.

7 Or, rather, monologue, since the response from the other side has, so far, to my knowledge been one of deafening silence.

8 Which Bultmann had called the 'upon-which'.

9 'Qu'est-ce qu'une texte?' (Ricoeur, 1971b), p. 197.

10 Ricoeur (1973, p. 53) quotes from the beginning of Hegel's *Phenomenology of Mind* to support this view: 'le dire s'évanouit, mais le dit subsiste'.

11 'L'ecriture ne représente aucune révolution radicale dans la constitution de discours, mais accomplit son voeu le plus profond' (1973, p. 53).

12 C. S. Pierce, *Collected Papers*, vol. I (1931, p. 564); quoted in Betti (1954, p. 81, note 5).

Glossary

Act meaning
meaning of the act to the actor – in contrast to action meaning, i.e.
its meaning to the social scientist (A. Kaplan).

Application, *Applikation*
'the task of mediating past and present, You and I' (Gadamer).

A priori knowledge
knowledge absolutely independent of all experience.

Being, *Dasein*
as the ontological essence of ontic Beings or entities (*Seiendes*)
differentiated from the latter through the 'ontological difference'
(Heidegger).

Belonging, *Zugehörigkeit, appartenance*
the process of cognition seen as part of the object and not
primarily an activity of the subject.

Category
a priori concept of the understanding which constitutes the
phenomenal object (Kant); general mode of the Being of Beings
(Heidegger), as opposed to 'existentiale'.

Communicative action
'symbolically mediated interaction on the basis of reciprocal
expectations of behaviour' (Habermas).

Communicative competence, theory of
required for explanatory understanding; as a meta-hermeneutic it
contains two parts: a theory of the acquisition of the basic
qualifications for role-guided behaviour, and a theory of the
psychological development of personality structures; assists in the
depth-hermeneutical decoding of specifically inadequate expressions (Habermas).

Constituted in subjectivity
what is real and true is defined by the actor (Husserl).

Critical hermeneutics
'hermeneutics expanded into criticism' takes the form of a critique
of systematically distorted communication (Habermas).

Dasein
ontic Being characterized by its concern with its own ontological
Being (Heidegger).

Demythologization
turning away, or at least relativization, of the theology of
revelation as the basis for biblical exegesis.

Dialogue
'follows the hermeneutic logic of questioning in which the
questioner himself is being questioned' (Gadamer); develops on
the basis of the reciprocal recognition of subjects, and thereby
includes a dialectical relation between general and individual
(Habermas).

Discourse, *Rede, parole*
as a language-event (written or spoken) in contrast to language as a
system (*langue*, code, sign, etc.)

Effective-history, *Wirkungsgeschichte*
on-going mediation of past and present which encompasses subject
and object and in which tradition asserts itself as a continuing
impulse and influence (Gadamer).

Effective-history, awareness of, *wirkungsgeschichtliches Bewusstsein*
recognition of the past as the determinant of our consciousness,
that is, that 'Being is more than consciousness'.

Effective-structure, *Wirkungszusammenhang*
'Structure contained in its lasting products' (Dilthey); 'organic
interrelationship, mutual dependency, coherence and conclusiveness' (Betti).

Existence
'Dasein always understands itself in terms of its existence – in
terms of a possibility of itself: to be itself or not itself'
(Heidegger); 'the mode of being Man' (Sartre).

Existential, *existenzial*
'the analysis of what constitutes existence has the character of an
understanding which is not existentiell, but rather' (Heidegger).

Existentiale, *Existenzial*
'Because Dasein's characters of Being are defined in terms of
existentiality, we call them "existentiales". These are to be sharply
distinguished from what we call "categories".'

Existentiell, *existenziell*
an understanding of oneself through existing (Heidegger).

Fore-structure of understanding
basis of the 'hermeneutic circle' given in *Vor-habe* (fore-having)
Vor-sicht (fore-sight) and *Vor-griff* (fore-conception).

Fusion of horizon, *Horizontverschmelzung*
'it is part of real understanding that the concepts of a historical
past are regained in such a way that they include, at the same time,
our own' (Gadamer).

Geisteswissenschaften, human sciences
attempt 'to bring human life to objective understanding' (Dilthey);
('*Geist*' should here be understood in the sense of Hegel's 'objective spirit' or Montesquieu's 'l'esprit des lois').

Hermeneutical circle
methodological device in interpretation which considers a whole
in relation to its parts, and vice versa.

Hermeneutical theory
the methodology and epistemology of interpretative understanding
practised as a science.

Hermeneutic arch, *arc hermeneutique*
replaces explanation and interpretation by a global conception
which integrates both explanation and understanding in the
reading of a text as the recovery of its sense and meaning.

Hermeneutic circle
ontological condition of understanding; proceeds from a com-
munality that binds us to tradition in general and that of our object
of interpretation in particular; provides the link between finality
and universality, and between theory and praxis.

Hermeneutic consciousness
reflexive knowledge about the structure of natural language and
the subject's dependence on, and use of, it (Habermas).

Hermeneutic experience
based on the character of language as an event; refers to the
dialogue between tradition and interpretation; 'is the corrective
through which thinking reason escapes the power of the linguistic

even while it is itself linguistically constituted; finds its completion in the awareness of effective-history.

Hermeneutic philosophy
the philosophical enquiry into the – ontological – preconditions of understanding.

Hermeneutic principle or hermeneutic problem
resides in the fact that no understanding can proceed without a pre-understanding of its 'object'.

Hermeneutic situation
where to find ourselves in relation to the tradition we have to understand on the basis of our prejudices.

Hermeneutics
generally the theory of the interpretation of meaning.

Historical consciousness
awareness of the relativity of all historical reality and phenomena (Dilthey); leads to the interpreter becoming critical of himself (his situatedness) and striving for objective knowledge.

Historicality, *Geschichtlichkeit*
the ontological reference to human existence as a life in responsibility for the future; understanding as the knowledge one gains about self and existence on the basis of 'prejudice' and within a changing 'horizon'.

Historicism, *Historizismus*, historicistic
outlook that arises from the recognition of the process of change and becoming underlying historical reality – and with it our knowledge of it (Dilthey, Mannheim).

Historicity, *Historizität*
as an epistemological category refers to the situational (historical, cultural, social) determinateness of thought which prevents the immediate access to human expressions and leads to the relativization of knowledge.

Historism, *Historismus*, historistic
the attempt of acquiring objective (value-free) knowledge of historical phenomena by disregarding the role of the knowing subject in order to let the 'object' 'speak for itself'; the approach of the 'historical school' (especially von Ranke).

History
(a) something that has happened;

(b) the discipline giving an account of (a);
(c) 'call to historicality' (Bultmann), 'finalization of a projection of the future', 'dialogue with the tradition that influences and carries us' (Gadamer).

Hypostatization
mistaking an abstract entity for a physical one.

Intentional action
'guided by norms on which the actor orients himself' (Habermas).

Intentionality
'the turning towards objectivity is the intentionality of the theoretical attitude as the understanding and consciousness of something' (Husserl).

Interpretation
Weber distinguishes three levels: philological, evaluative, rational (or causal, or explanatory); Betti differentiates between *Sinngebung* or *Deutung* (subjective or speculative interpretation) and *Auslegung* (exegesis – objective – interpretation; explication) which aims at 'a relative objectivity of understanding' through the use of hermeneutical canons.

Kunstlehre
system of formal procedures for ascertaining the meaning of, especially, texts.

Language
as *langue*, *Sprache*, the objective system of linguistic signs that imposes itself on every speaker' as speech (*parole*, *Rede*) it is the actual physical utterance.

Leben
as counterposed to abstract thought and overarching it, the productive capacity as such (Dilthey).

Lived experience, *Erlebnis*
counterposed to the abstractions of the understanding and the mere conceptual ordering of sensations in 'experiences', it refers to the totality and infinitude of human existence.

To mean, *meinen*
refers to the author's intention or the meaning of a text and indicates the relationship of word or sentence to a larger whole; as an internal relationship (*bedeuten*) it is distinguished from the external relationship of an arbitrarily chosen sign to an object: to denote, *hinweisen*.

Meaning
  (1) Husserl's distinctions are important here:
    (a) as an act which confers meaning on words: sense;
    (b) the object meant, or referred to, the meaning of which we
        know 'if we know under what conditions we are to apply it in
        a concrete case' (Carnap); designatum, signification;
    (c) in the sense of an ideal content; the result of (a): *noema*,
        eidos.
  (2) as a general term covering both 'sense' and 'significance'.

Meaning-context, meaningful coherence, complex of meanings,
Sinnzusammenhang
  the relations of meaning sought in interpretative understanding –
  in opposition to their causal analysis.

Meaning-full forms, *sinnhaltige Formen*
  'forms through which an other mind addresses us' (Betti).

Mind, *Geist, esprit, pneuma*
  in Dilthey, the physical, social and historical existence of man.

Mündigkeit, l'age adulte, 'being-of-age'
  term used by Habermas to refer to one's ability as a competent,
  self-determining speaker and participant in social interaction;
  linked to Enlightenment tenets, such as *'sapere aude'*.

Objectification, *Versachlichung*
  the expression of an idea in concrete form; the process of ordering
  the world into objects; the presentation of something 'internal'
  (e.g. intentions, meaning) as an object of sense for the purpose of
  scientific investigation.

Objectivation, *Vergegenständlichung*
  the process whereby a subject externalizes himself (through labour
  or the use of language) and thereby becomes an object which, as a
  part of his environment, may react back on him; the actualization
  of a subject in cultural objects.

Objectivism
  'programme that denies the systematic significance of the meaningful structuring of society' (Habermas); 'to treat everything as an
  object in the world, or as relations between such objects,
  exclusively . . . what is lost to view is mind as correlate of the
  world of objects, as that for which there is a world constituted'
  (Skjervheim).

Pre-understanding, *Vorverständnis*
  a living relationship with the subject-matter of a text as the pre-

condition of any interpretation; all observations constitute themselves through the prior organization of our experience (in natural science experiences are channelled by existing theories; in the human sciences by the knowledge of things we bring with us from our everyday life); 'the constituting intentionality of the horizon' (Husserl).

Quaestio facti
question of what does occur in the process of cognition.

Quaestio iuris
question concerning the justifiability of knowledge-claims and the ways for arriving at true knowledge; (the problem Kant raised against the psychologism of British epistemology which failed to inquire into the validity of knowledge).

Sense, *Sinn, Bedeutung*
the content of a word, sentence, sign, work of art, etc., in relation to a larger context (of actions, of life, of a style, of tradition); the pattern of a whole which contains 'meaning'; distinguished by Frege from reference (nominatum) (e.g. 'morning star' and 'evening star' refer to the same star (Venus) but have a different sense).

Significance, *Bedeutsamkeit*
   (a) the part of an element within the pattern of a whole: 'internal' significance;
   (b) the 'meaning-for-us' (Betti): 'external' significance.

Temporality, *Zeitlichkeit*
concretely lived time, as distinguished from time as a pure dimension or measurable relation, is characterized by the finality of human existence as well as by the unity of identity and difference and of past and present in a life-history; its categorical moments are past, present, future (i.e. the 'ecstases of temporality' which, in Heidegger, "is" the meaning of care').

Transcendental
providing the conditions for the possibility of knowledge.

Verstehen
objective–idealist form of understanding guided by hermeneutical canons, is directed at subjectively intended meaning or at meaning-contexts (Dilthey, Betti, Weber).

Bibliography

Ia Authors discussed

Apel, K.-O. (1955), *Das Verstehen*, Archiv für Begriffsgeschichte, Bonn.

Apel, K.-O. (1967), *Analytic Philosophy of Language and the Geisteswissenschaften*, D. Reidel, Holland.

Apel, K.-O. (1972), 'Communication and the Foundation of the Humanities', *Acta Sociologica*, vol. 15.

Apel, K.-O. (1973), *Transformation der Philosophie* (2 vols), Suhrkamp, Frankfurt.

Apel, K.-O. (1977), 'Types of Social Science in the Light of Human Interests of Knowledge', *Social Research*, vol. 44, no. 3, pp. 425–70.

Apel, K.-O. *et al.* (1971), *Hermeneutik und Ideologiekritik*, Suhrkamp, Frankfurt.

Betti, E. (1949), *Posizioni dello Spirito rispetto all'Oggetività*, Giuffrè, Milan.

Betti, E. (1954), 'Zur Grundlegung einer allgemeinen Auslegungslehre', in *Festschrift für E. Rabel*, J. C. B. Mohr, Tübingen, vol. II.

Betti, E. (1955), *Teoria Generale della Interpretazione* (2 vols), Dott. A. Giuffrè, ed. Istituto di Teoria della Interpretazione, Milan. Translated (1967) as *Allgemeine Auslegungslehre als Methodik der Geisteswissenschaften* (abridged to one volume), J. C. B. Mohr, Tübingen.

Betti, E. (1962), *Die Hermeneutik als allgemeine Methode der Geisteswissenschaften*, J. C. B. Mohr, Tübingen. Translated in this book as 'Hermeneutics as the General Methodology of the Geisteswissenschaften'.

Boeckh, A. (1966), *Enzyklopädie und Methodenlehre der philologischen Wissenschaften* (ed. Bratuscheck, 1877); unveränderter Nachdruck, Wissenschaftliche Verlagsanstalt, Darmstadt.

Bultmann, R. (1950), 'Das Problem der Hermeneutik', *Zeitschrift für Philosophie und Kirche*, vol. 47, 19.

Bultmann, R. (1969), *Faith and Understanding* (translated by L. Pettibone Smith), CSM Press, London.

Dilthey, W. (1958), *Gesammelte Schriften* (18 vols), 2nd edn, Verlag
B. G. Teubner, Leipzig and Berlin; vol. VII: *Der Aufbau der
geschichtlichen Welt in den Geisteswissenschaften* (ed. B.
Groethuysen) (first published 1927).
Droysen, Johann Gustav (1960), *Historik. Vorlesungen über
Enzyklopädie und Methodologie der Geschichte*, Munich.
Ebeling, Gerhard (1968), *The Word of God and Tradition*, Collins,
London.
Fuchs, Ernst (1958), *Hermeneutik*, Müllerschön, Bad Cannstatt.
Fuchs, Ernst (1971), *Jesus: Wort und Tat*, J. C. B. Mohr, Tübingen.
Gadamer, Hans-Georg (1960), *Wahrheit und Methode, Grundzüge
einer philosophischen Hermeneutik* (4th edn, 1975), Mohr,
Tübingen.
Gadamer, Hans-Georg (1967), *Kleine Schriften* (3 vols), J. C. B.
Mohr, Tübingen; partly translated by David Linge, *Philosophical
Hermeneutics*, California University Press, Berkeley, 1976.
Gadamer, Hans-Georg (1969), 'Hermeneutik', in Klibansky, 1969.
Gadamer, Hans-Georg (1971a), 'Rhetorik, Hermeneutik und
Ideologiekritik. Metakritische Erörterungen zu "Wahrheit und
Methode"'; in Apel *et al.*, 1971, pp. 57–82.
Gadamer, Hans-Georg (1971b), 'Replik', in Apel *et al.*, 1971, pp.
283–317.
Gadamer, Hans-Georg (1973), 'Jusqu'à quel point la langue préforme-
t-elle la pensée?', in Castelli, 1973.
Gadamer, Hans-Georg (1975), 'Hermeneutics and Social Science',
Cultural Hermeneutics, vol. 2, no. 4.
Habermas, Jürgen (1967), *Theorie und Praxis* (4th revised edn, 1971),
Suhrkamp, Frankfurt; translated as *Theory and Practice*,
Heinemann, London, 1974.
Habermas, Jürgen (1968a), *Erkenntnis und Interesse*, Suhrkamp,
Frankfurt; translated as *Knowledge and Human Interests*,
Heinemann, London, 1968.
Habermas, Jürgen (1968b), *Technik und Wissenschaft als 'Ideologie'*,
Suhrkamp, Frankfurt; partly translated in *Towards a Rational
Society*, Heinemann, London, 1971.
Habermas, Jürgen (1969), *Protestbewegung und Hochschulreform*,
Suhrkamp, Frankfurt; partly translated in *Towards a Rational
Society*, Heinemann, London, 1971.
Habermas, Jürgen (1970), *Zur Logik der Sozialwissenschaften*
(originally, 1967), Suhrkamp, Frankfurt.
Habermas, Jürgen (1971), 'Der Universalitätsanspruch der Hermen-
eutik, in Apel *et al.* (1971), pp. 120–159; first published in Bubner
et al. (1970), vol. I; translated in this book as 'The Hermeneutic
Claim to Universality'.
Habermas, Jürgen (1973), *Legitimationsprobleme im Spätkapitalis-
mus*, Suhrkamp, Frankfurt; translated as *Legitimation Crisis*,
Heinemann, London, 1976.
Heidegger, Martin (1949), *Sein und Zeit* (6th edn), Neomarius,

Tübingen; translated as *Being and Time*, Harper & Row, New York, 1962.

Heidegger, Martin (1950), 'Hegels Begriff der Erfahrung', in *Holzwege*, V. Klostermann, Frankfurt; translated as *Hegel's Concept of Experience*, Harper & Row, New York.

Heidegger, Martin (1959), *Unterwegs zur Sprache* (3rd edn, 1965), Pfullingen.

Heidegger, Martin (1966), *Discourse on Thinking* (translation of *Gelassenheit*), Harper & Row, New York.

Heidegger, Martin (1967), 'Brief über den "Humanismus"', in *Wegmarken*, V. Klostermann, Frankfurt, pp. 145–94.

Hirsch, Eric D., Jr (1965), 'Truth and Method in Interpretation', *Review of Metaphysics*, pp. 489–507.

Hirsch, Eric D., Jr (1967), *Validity in Interpretation*, Yale University Press, New Haven.

Hirsch, Eric D., Jr (1972), 'Three Dimensions of Hermeneutics', *New Literary History*, vol. 3, no. 2.

Lorenzer, Alfred (1972), *Zur Begründung einer materialistischen Sozialisationstheorie*, Suhrkamp, Frankfurt.

Lorenzer, Alfred (1973), *Über den Gegenstand der Psychoanalyse, oder: Sprache und Interaktion*, Suhrkamp, Frankfurt.

Ricoeur, Paul (1965a), *De l'interpretation. Essai sur Freud*, Editions du Seuil, Paris; translated as *Freud and Philosophy: An Essay on Interpretation*, Yale University Press, New Haven, 1970.

Ricoeur, Paul (1965b), *History and Truth*, North-Western University Press, Evanston.

Ricoeur, Paul (1965c), 'Existence et Herméneutique', in *Festschrift für Romano Guardini*, Echtor Verlag, Würzburg; translated in this book as 'Existence and Hermeneutics'.

Ricoeur, Paul (1969a), 'Philosophie et Langage', in Klibansky, 1969, pp. 272–95.

Ricoeur, Paul (1969b), *Le Conflit des Interpretations. Essais d'herméneutique*, du Seuil, Paris; translated as *The Conflict of Interpretations. Essays in Hermeneutics*, North-Western University Press, Evanston, 1974; also translated as *Hermeneutik und Strukturalismus. Der Konflikt der Interpretationen I, Hermeneutik und Psychoanalyse. Der Konflikt der Interpretationen II*, Kösel Verlag, Munich, 1973 and 1974.

Ricoeur, Paul (1971a), 'The Model of the Text: Meaningful Action Considered as a Text', *Social Research*, vol. 38, no. 3.

Ricouer, Paul (1971b), 'Qu'est-ce qu'une texte?'; in Bubner *et al.*, 1970.

Ricoeur, Paul (1973), 'Herméneutique et Critique des idéologies'; in Castelli, 1973.

Ricoeur, Paul (1975a), *'Le Métaphore vivre. L'ordre philosophique*, Editions du Seuil, Paris.

Ricoeur, Paul (1975b), 'Phenomenology and Hermeneutics', *Noûs*, vol. II, no. 1.

Sandkühler, Hans Jörg (1972), 'Zur Begründung einer materialistischen Hermeneutik', *Das Argument*, vol. 14.

Sandkühler, Hans Jörg (1973), *Praxis und Geschichtsbewusstsein, Fragen einer dialektischen und historisch-materialistischen Hermeneutik*, Suhrkamp, Frankfurt.

Schleiermacher, Friedrich Daniel Ernst (1959), *Hermeneutik* (nach den Handschriften neu herausgegeben und eingeleitet von Heinz Kimmerle), Carl Winter Universitätsverlag, Heidelberg.

Ib Authors referred to

Abel, Theodore (1974), 'The Operation Called Verstehen' (reprint from *A.J.S.*, 54 (1948), pp. 211–18), in Truzzi, 1974.

Abel, Theodore (1975), 'Verstehen I and Verstehen II', *Theory and Decision*, vol. 6, 1.

Antoni, C. (1962), *From History to Sociology: the Transition in German Historical Thinking*, Merlin Press, London.

Austin, J. L. (1970/1962), *How to do Things with Words*, Oxford University Press, London.

Austin, J. L. (1970), *Philosophical Papers*, Oxford University Press, London.

Bauman, Z. (1976), *Towards a Critical Sociology*, Routledge & Kegan Paul, London.

Berlin, Isaiah (1976), *Vico and Herder*, Hogarth Press, London.

Bloch, Ernst (1976), *Das Prinzip Hoffnung*, 3 vols, Suhrkamp, Frankfurt.

Boudon, R. (1969), 'Le Structuralisme', in Klibansky, 1969.

Collingwood, R. G. (1967/1946), *The Idea of History*, Oxford University Press, London.

Culler, Jonathan (1973), 'Phenomenology and Structuralism', *The Human Context*, vol. 5, 1.

Gauthier, Yvon (1968), 'Die Sprache und der andere Schauplatz. Über die Sprachtheorie Lacans', in *Akten des XIV Internationalen Kongresses für Philosophie*, Vienna, vol. III, p. 412.

Herder, Johann Gottfried (1960), *Schriften* (ed. and introduction by Walter Fleming), Goldmann, Munich.

Horkheimer, Max (1968), 'Psychologie und Soziologie im Werk Wilhelm Diltheys', in *Kritische Theorie* (ed. A. Schmidt), vol. II, Suhrkamp, Frankfurt.

Husserl (1970), *Logical Investigations* (translated by N. Finlay from 2nd German edition (1913) of *Logische Untersuchungen*, Bd I, u. II), Routledge & Kegan Paul, London.

Jaspers, Karl (1913), *Allgemeine Psychopathologie*, Berlin (7th edn, 1959).

Jaspers, Karl (1971), *Philosophy of Existence*, Blackwell, Oxford.

Krüger, Gerhard (1967), *Philosophie und Moral in der Kantschen Kritik* (2nd edn), J. C. B. Mohr, Tübingen.

Krüger, Gerhard (1965/1957), *Grundfragen der Philosophie. Geschichte. Wahrheit. Wissenschaft*, Klostermann, Frankfurt.

Lévi-Strauss, Claude (1963), *Structural Anthropology*, Basic Books, New York.

Lévi-Strauss, Claude (1974/1972), *The Savage Mind*, Weidenfeld & Nicolson, London.

Mill, John Stuart (1970), *A System of Logic*, Longman, London.

Misch, Georg (1947), *Vom Lebens und Gedankenkreis Wilhelm Diltheys*, Verlag G. Schulte-Bulmke, Frankfurt.

Misch, Georg (1967), *Lebensphilosophie und Phänomenologie* (Eine Auseinandersetung der Diltheyschen Richtung mit Heidegger und Husserl), B. G. Teubner, Stuttgart.

Peirce, Charles S. (1960), *Collected Papers*, vols 5 and 6 (ed. C. Hartshorne and P. Weiss), Harvard University Press, Cambridge (reprinted 1967).

Rasmussen, David M. (1971), *Mythic–Symbolic Language and Philosophical Anthropology: A Constructive Interpretation of the Thought of Paul Ricoeur*, Martinus Nijhoff, The Hague.

Rickert, Heinrich (1902), *Die Grenzen der Naturwissenschaftlichen Begriffsbildung*, Tübingen–Leipzig.

Rickert, Heinrich (1929), *Wilhelm Windelband*, J. C. B. Mohr, Tübingen.

Robinson, James H., and Cobb, John B., Jr (1964), *The New Hermeneutic*, Harper & Row, New York.

Sartre, J.-P. (1963), *The Problem of Method*, Methuen, London.

Searle, J. R. (1970/1969), *Speech Acts: An Essay in the Philosophy of Language*, Cambridge University Press.

Simmel, Georg (1892), *Probleme der Geschichtsphilosophie*, Leipzig (2nd edn, 1905).

Wach, Joachim (1926–33), *Das Verstehen*, 3 vols, J. C. B. Mohr, Tübingen.

Weber, Max (1922), *Gesammelte Aufsätze zur Wissenschaftslehre*, J. C. B. Mohr, Tübingen.

Weber, Max (1925), *Wirtschaft und Gesellschaft*, J. C. B. Mohr, Tübingen.

Winch, Peter (1969), *Studies in the Philosophy of Wittgenstein*, Routledge & Kegan Paul, London.

Winch, Peter (1970/1958), *The Idea of a Social Science and its Relation to Philosophy*, Routledge & Kegan Paul, London.

Wittgenstein, Ludwig (1968), *Philosophical Investigations* (translated by G. E. M. Anscombe), Blackwell, Oxford.

York von Wartenburg, P. (1956), *Bewusstseinsstellung und Geschichte* (introduction and edited by I. Fetcher), J. C. B. Mohr, Tübingen.

II Further sources

a Collections
Akten des XIV Internationalen Kongresses für Philosophie (1968), Vienna.

Bubner, R., Cramer, K., Wiehl, R. (eds) (1970), *Hermeneutik und Dialektik*, vols I and II, J. C. B. Mohr, Tübingen.
Castelli, Enrico (ed.) (1973), *Ideologie et Demythisation*, Aubier, Paris.
Festschrift für Romano Guardini (1965); *Interpretation der Welt*, Echtor Verlag, Würzburg.
Festschrift für Ernst Rabel (1954), 2 vols, J. C. B. Mohr, Tübingen.
Hermeneutik und Ideologiekritik (1971) (mit Beiträgen von Apel, Bormann, Bubner, Gadamer, Giegel, Habermas), Suhrkamp, Frankfurt.
Klibansky, Raymond (ed.) (1969), *Contemporary Philosophy. A Survey*, vol. III, La Nuova Italia Editrice, Florence.
Lawrence, A., and O'Connor (eds) (1968), *Existential Phenomenology*, Prentice-Hall, Englewood Cliffs.
Oppholzer, Siegfried (ed.) (1966), *Hermeneutik, Phänomenologie, Dialektik, Methodenkritik*, Ehrenwirth, Munich.
Rickman, H. P. (ed.) (1962), *Pattern and Meaning in History. Thoughts on History and Society*, Harper & Row, New York.
Truzzi, Marcello (ed.) (1974), *Subjective Understanding in the Social Sciences*, Addison-Wesley, Reading, Massachusetts.
Verhandlungen des Sechsten Deutschen Soziologentages 1928 (1929), Tübingen.
Warnach, Viktor (ed.) (1971), *Hermeneutik als Weg Heutiger Wissenschaft*, Anton Pustet, Salzburg.

b Other books and articles
Albert, Hans (1970), 'Verstehen und Geschichte', *Zeitschrift für Allgemeine Wissenschaftstheorie*, vol. I.
Albert, Hans (1971), *Plädoyer für Kritischen Rationalismus*, Piper, Munich.
Axelos, Kostas (1966), *Einführung in ein künftiges Denken. Über Marx und Heidegger*, Max Niemayer, Tübingen.
Bauman, Zygmunt (1978), *Hermeneutics and Social Science*, Hutchinson, London.
Biemel, Walter (1968), 'Briefwechsel Dilthey–Husserl', *Man and World*, vol. 1, 3.
Bollnow, Otto Friedrich (1944), 'Über das Kritische Verstehen', *Deutsche Vierteljahresschrift für Literaturwissenschaft*, vol. 22, pp. 1–29.
Bubner, Rüdiger (1975), 'Theory and Practice in the Light of the Hermeneutic-Criticist Controversy', *Cultural Hermeneutics*, vol. 2, 4.
Cahnman, Werner, J., and Boskoff, Alvin (1964), *Sociology and History*, Free Press, Chicago and London.
Dahmer, Helmut (1975), 'Psychoanalyse als Gesellschaftstheorie', *Psyche*, vol. II, pp. 991–1010.
Fialkowski, Aline (1967), 'Paul Ricoeur et l'Herméneutique des Mythes', *Esprit*, vol. 35, 7/8.

Funke, Gerhard (1960), 'Problem und Theorie der Hermeneutik',
Zeitschrift für Philosophische Forschung, vol. 14, 2.

Giddens, Anthony (1976), *New Rules of Sociological Method*,
Hutchinson, London.

Giddens, Anthony (1977), *Studies in Social and Political Theory*,
Hutchinson, London.

Gründer, K. F. (1967), 'Hermeneutik und Wissenschaftstheorie',
Philosophisches Jahrbuch der Görres-Gesellschaft, vol. 75, pp.
152–65.

Henrichs, Norbert (1968), *Bibliographie der Hermeneutik und ihre
Anwendungsbereiche seit Schleiermacher*, Philosophia Verlag,
Düsseldorf.

Hodges, H. A. (1944), *Wilhelm Dilthey. An Introduction*, Routledge,
London.

Holborn, Hajo (1950), 'Wilhelm Dilthey and the Critique of
Historical Reason', *Journal of the History of Ideas*, vol. II.

Hülzmann, Heinz (1967), 'Hermeneutik und Gesellschaft', *Soziale
Welt*, vol. 18.

Jacoby, Russell (1972), 'Negative Psychoanalysis and Marxism:
Towards an Objective Theory of Subjectivity', *Telos*, vol. 14,
pp. 1–22.

Jähnig, Dieter (1970), 'Nietzsches Kritik der Historischen Wissenschaften', *Praxis*, parts 1–2.

Jameson, Frederic (1972), 'The Rise of Hermeneutics', *New Literary
History*, vol. 3, 2.

Johach, Helmut (1974), *Handelnder Mensch und Objektiver Geist.
Zur Theorie der Geistes-und Sozialwissenschaften bei W. Dilthey*,
Verlag Anton Hain, Meisenheim am Glen.

Kamper, Dieter (1974), 'Hermeneutik – Theorie einer Praxis?',
Zeitschrift für allgemeine Wissenschaftstheorie, vol. 5, 1.

Kemp, Peter (1970), 'Phänomenologie und Hermeneutik in der
Philosophie Paul Ricoeurs', *Zeitschrift für Theologie und Kirche*,
vol. 67, pp. 335–47.

Kimmerle, Heinz (1974), 'Die Funktion der Hermeneutik',
Zeitschrift für allgemeine Wissenschaftstheorie, vol. 5, 1.

Kimmerle, Heinz (1964), 'Metahermeneutik. Applikation, Hermen-
eutische Sprachbildung', *Zeitschrift für Theologie und Kirche*,
vol. 61, pp. 221–75.

Lieber, Hans-Joachim (1965), 'Geschichte und Gesellschaft im
Denken Diltheys', *Kölner Zeitschrift für Soziologie*, vol. 17.

Linge, David E. (1973), 'Dilthey and Gadamer. Two Theories of
Historical Understanding', *Journal of the American Academy of
Religion*, vol. XLI, pp. 536–53.

MacQuarrie, John (1955), *An Existentialist Theology: A Comparison
of Heidegger and Bultmann*, Library of Philosophy and Theology,
Harper & Row, New York.

Makkreel, Rudolf A. (1969), 'W. Dilthey and the Neo-Kantians',
Journal of the History of Ideas, vol. 7, 4.

Makkreel, Rudolf A. (1975), *Dilthey. Philosopher of the Human Studies*, Princeton University Press.

Marković, Mihailo (1970), 'Critical Social Theory in Marx', *Praxis*, nos. 3–4, pp. 27–38.

Marković, Mihailo (1972), 'The Problem of Reification and the Verstehen–Erklären Controversy', *Acta Sociologica*, 1972–3.

Mitscherlich, Alexander *et al.* (1970), 'Uber Psychoanalyse und Soziologie', *Psyche*, vol. 24, 3.

Oedingen, Karlo (1958), 'Review of E. Betti' (1955), *Kantstudien*, vol. 50.

Ott, Heinrich (1973), 'L'Expérience de "l'ouvert" comme expérience fondamentale d'une anthropologie Chrétiene', in Castelli, 1973.

Otto, Eckart (1974), 'Die Applikation als Problem der Politischen Hermeneutik', *Zeitschrift für Theologie und Kirche*, vol. 71, 2.

Pannenberg, Wolfhart (1976), *Theology and the Philosophy of Science*, Darton, Longman & Todd, London.

Presas, Mario A. (1974), 'Von der Phänomenologie zum Denken des Seins', *Zeitschrift für philosophische Forschung*, vol. 28, 2.

Radnitzky, Gerard (1970/1968), *Contemporary Schools of Metascience*, Akademiförlaget, Göteborg.

Richardson, William T. (1963), *Heidegger. Through Phenomenology to Thought*, Martinus Nijhoff, The Hague.

Rickman, H. P. (1961), *Meaning in History. W. Dilthey's Thoughts on History and Society*, Allen & Unwin, London.

Riedel, Manfred (1970), 'Das Erkenntniskritische Motiv in Diltheys Theorie der Geisteswissenschaften', in Bubner *et al.*, 1970.

Rothacker, Erich (1948), *Logik und Systematik der Geisteswissenschaften*, Bouvier, Bonn.

Sartre, Jean-Paul (1974), *Between Existentialism and Marxism* (translated by J. Matthews), Gollancz, London.

Sartre, Jean-Paul (1976), *Critique of Dialectical Reason* (translated by Sh. Smith), Gollancz, London.

Schneider, Gerhard (1972), 'Der Ursprung des Positivisms in der Gestalt des Historisms', *Archiv fur Rechts und Sozialphilosophie*, vol. 58, 2.

Schulz, Walter (1970), 'Anmerkungen zur Hermeneutik Gadamers', in Bubner *et al.*, 1970.

Skjervheim, Hans (1974), 'Objectivism and the Study of Man', *Inquiry*, vol. 17, pp. 213–39, and vol. 18, pp. 265–302.

Strasser, Stephan (1963), *Phenomenology and the Human Sciences. A Contribution to a New Scientific Ideal*, Duquesne University Press, Pittsburg.

Taylor, Charles (1971), 'Interpretation and the Sciences of Man', *Review of Metaphysics*, vol. 25, September.

Tort, Michel (1966), 'De l'Interpretation ou la machine herméneutique', *Les Temps Modernes*, vol. 21.

Truchon, P. (1966), 'Compréhension et vérité dans les sciences de l'esprit', *Archives de Philosophie*, vol. 29, pp. 281–302.

Wolff, Janet (1975), *Hermeneutic Philosophy and the Sociology of Art*, Routledge & Kegan Paul, London.

Wolff, Janet (ed.) (1977), *The Sociology of Literature. Theoretical Approaches, Sociological Review* Monograph 25.

Name index

Subject index